INVOCATION AND ASSENT

INVOCATION AND ASSENT

*The Making and Remaking
of Trinitarian Theology*

Jason E. Vickers

WILLIAM B. EERDMANS PUBLISHING COMPANY

GRAND RAPIDS, MICHIGAN / CAMBRIDGE, U.K.

Published 2008 by
Wm. B. Eerdmans Publishing Co.
2140 Oak Industrial Drive N.E., Grand Rapids, Michigan 49505 /
P.O. Box 163, Cambridge CB3 9PU U.K.

Printed in the United States of America

13 12 11 10 09 08   7 6 5 4 3 2 1

Library of Congress Cataloging-in-Publication Data

Vickers, Jason E.
Invocation and assent : the making and remaking of Trinitarian theology /
Jason E. Vickers.
p.   cm.
Includes bibliographical references.
ISBN 978-0-8028-6269-3 (pbk.: alk. paper)
1. Trinity — History of doctrines.   I. Title.

BT111.3.V53   2008
231′.04409 — dc22

2008015511

www.eerdmans.com

To Garrett

Contents

Acknowledgments		viii
Introduction		x
1.	Invocation: The Trinity and Salvation	1
2.	Assent: Scripture and Salvation	29
3.	The Protestant Dilemma	69
4.	Boethius's Ghost	103
5.	Locke's Legacy	135
6.	Wesley's Hymns and Prayers	169
7.	The Work of Trinitarian Theology Today	191
Bibliography		199
Index		211

Acknowledgments

It is with great joy that I thank those who have contributed so generously to the conception and production of this volume. At the outset, I thank William S. Babcock for alerting me to the gap in the literature that this volume seeks to fill and for his invaluable assistance in the identification and exploration of primary sources in the earliest stages of the work. Above all else, I thank William J. Abraham for countless hours of assistance in the conceptualization and development of the first draft of this work (especially the long hours spent at Kuby's and La Madeleine's), and for his help in making the transition from dissertation to book. I also thank Bruce D. Marshall and Nicholas Wolterstorff for their probing questions and assistance at a crucial juncture in the life of this project. In addition, I thank my colleagues at Southern Methodist University, Hood Theological Seminary, and United Theological Seminary for their support along the way, including Reggie Broadnax, Andrea Dickens, Tom Dozeman, Wendy Edwards, Dick Eslinger, Lisa Hess, Chris Hutson, Emma Justes, Doug Koskela, Vivian Johnson, Mark Powell, Kendall McCabe, Horace Six-Means, Andrew Sung Park, Natalie Van Kirk, David Watson, and David Whitford. I also thank Sam Powell for his critical comments and suggestions on numerous chapters, and I thank Randy Maddox, Dan Spross, and Andy Wood for their scholarly friendship over the years. Moreover, I especially thank all those who have assisted with proofreading and editing and with the preparation of the index and bibliography, including Reinder Van Til and Jenny Hoffman at Eerdmans and Evan and Julia Abla here at United Theological Seminary. Needless to say, all of the mistakes and deficiencies are mine. Finally, I thank my wonderful family, including my parents for their loving support and encouragement from the beginning, my beautiful wife, Lacey, for her steadfast love and companionship (and for putting up with all of my quirks), and most especially Garrett, to whom this volume is dedicated, for making me laugh more times than I can remember and for being my best friend.

Introduction

It is commonplace in Christian theology today to note the wide-spread resurgence of interest in the Trinity that began in the mid-twentieth century with the work of Karl Barth and Karl Rahner respectively. That resurgence has continued in the work of a host of other Christian theologians in the late twentieth and early twenty-first centuries, including Hans Urs von Balthasar, Leonardo Boff, Ellen Charry, Sarah Coakley, Colin Gunton, Robert Jenson, Elizabeth Johnson, Catherine LaCugna, Bruce Marshall, Jürgen Moltmann, Wolfhart Pannenberg, Thomas F. Torrance, Miroslav Volf, and John Zizioulas.[1] And there are no signs that the level of interest is likely to diminish any time soon. New books on the Trinity continue to appear with mind-numbing frequency.

What is rarely discussed is how the Trinity came to need such a massive retrieval effort on the part of contemporary Christian theologians in the first place. To be sure, there are stock references to Schleiermacher's Appendix, which are endlessly repeated as though Schleiermacher could have single-handedly removed the Trinity from the center of Christian theology. Suffice it to say, it is time to give poor Schleiermacher a break. Theologians and historians need to investigate more fully the reasons for the demise of the Trinity in Christian theology in the modern West.

---

1. Several introductions to recent Trinitarian theology are now available. For example, see Stanley J. Grenz, *Rediscovering the Triune God: The Trinity in Contemporary Theology* (Minneapolis: Fortress Press, 2004).

To date, the work of Catherine LaCugna constitutes the most important and influential account of the demise of the Trinity in Christian theology in the West.[2] The core of her thesis is that, beginning with Augustine and continuing through medieval Catholic theology, the Trinity became increasingly disconnected from the Christian life. According to LaCugna, the disconnection of the Trinity from the Christian life occurred when Christian theological reflection on the immanent Trinity (the eternal being of God) lost its moorings in the economic Trinity (what we know and learn of God through God's saving activities on our behalf).

In this book I intend to complement LaCugna's overall thesis in a very specific way. Whereas LaCugna's work focused on the loss of the connection between the Trinity and the Christian life in Catholic theology, my own concern has to do with a similar loss in English Protestant theology. My core proposal is that the working out of a distinctively English Protestant version of *sola Scriptura* led to the separation of the immanent Trinity from the economic Trinity in that stream of theology and thus to the perception in English Protestant Christianity that the Trinity has little, if anything, to do with the Christian life. In my judgment, the devastating effects of the English Protestant experiment with *sola Scriptura* for Trinitarian theology are still very much with us today.

Even here it is easy to claim too much. The extent of the disappearance of the Trinity in English Protestant theology in the modern period (or in any other tradition and period, for that matter) will depend to no small degree on what counts as theology and on what one regards as the proper locus or home of theology. For example, if the production of hymns and sermons and other liturgical materials such as prayers and blessings counts as theology, then those who have eyes to see may perceive that the Trinity flourished in the life of the church even as it languished in the work of her theologians.[3] In this respect,

2. Catherine Mowry LaCugna, *God for Us: The Trinity and Christian Life* (San Francisco: HarperSanFrancisco, 2001).

3. Historical theologians have recently been paying attention to the theology embedded in sermons, hymns, and other liturgical materials in the modern period, much of which is Trinitarian in nature and content. For examples of this development, see Teresa Berger, *Theology in Hymns? A Study of the Relationship of Doxology and Theology According to A Collection of Hymns for the People Called Methodists* (Nashville: Kingswood

obituary notices for the Trinity at any given point in the tradition may prove to be premature.

In order to argue for a diminution of Trinitarian theology at any place and at any time, one must first identify what kind of thing the Trinity is. More precisely, one must first identify the originating nature and function of Trinitarian discourse. Therefore, in Chapter 1, I spell out what I take the Trinity to be by paying close attention to the originating nature and function of Trinitarian language. I make the case that, in early Christianity, the Trinity was first and foremost the *proper personal name* for God. As the proper personal name for God, "Father, Son, and Holy Spirit" functioned originally in catechetical and liturgical settings, including baptism, prayer, praise, blessings, worship, proclamation, demon exorcism, and the like.

In order for that name to function as a proper personal name in these settings, the Christian community found it both necessary and natural to develop corresponding *identifying descriptions*. Identifying descriptions accompany proper personal names to indicate who it is that proper personal names pick out. Thus Trinitarian discourse includes both the proper personal name "Father, Son, and Holy Spirit" and the accompanying identifying descriptions that emerged in the early protocreedal and creedal materials. Early Christian theologians regarded these protocreedal and creedal materials as *the rule of faith*, and they used them extensively in catechesis and initiation. These materials identified the saving activities of Father, Son, and Holy Spirit, that is, the economic Trinity.

The deep issue at stake here has to do with the purpose or function of Trinitarian discourse in early Christianity. As the proper personal name for the Christian God, the Trinity — or "Father, Son, and Holy Spirit" — was intimately related to the entire range of ecclesial materials and practices through which Christians responded in worship and in thanksgiving for the saving activities of their God. Thus the Trinity was indispensable for Christian initiation, formation, worship, prayer, blessings, reading Scripture profitably, and so on. By enabling humans to address God and, by extension, to be addressed by God, the Trinity

---

Books, 1995); Dawn DeVries, *Jesus Christ in the Preaching of Calvin and Schleiermacher* (Louisville: Westminster John Knox Press, 2002); and Amy Plantinga Pauw, *The Supreme Harmony of All: The Trinitarian Theology of Jonathan Edwards* (Grand Rapids: Eerdmans, 2002).

was the indispensable means by which humans were initiated into the fullness of Christian ontology.

To put the matter pointedly, if people are to encounter God, to have communion with God, or to know and love God, they need to know the name by which they can address, worship, invoke, and call upon the Christian God. On this analysis, Trinitarian discourse is a fundamentally ontological discourse. As the name for God, the Trinity enables Christians to invite God to be present in the Eucharist, to worship God through hymns, to seek God's will for their lives, to welcome God into their hearts, and to present God with praises and petitions in prayer. Thus Trinitarian language is fundamentally performative in its originating nature and function.[4] To paraphrase Evagrius, a Trinitarian theologian is one who prays to the Father, Son, and Holy Spirit, and one who prays to God the Father, Son, and Holy Spirit is a Trinitarian theologian.

In this analysis, the primary function of Trinitarian discourse in early Christianity had to do with initiating Christians into and enabling them actively to participate in the fullness of Christian ontology.[5] It is precisely this primary function of Trinitarian discourse that is lost from view in English Protestant theology beginning in the late seventeenth century. The burden of the ensuing chapters is to show how and why English Protestant theologians lost sight of the Trinity as the proper personal name for God by which the church responds in thanksgiving and praise for her salvation.

4. I came to this conclusion about the originating nature and function of Trinitarian discourse through the application of crucial insights about the nature and uses of language in contemporary philosophy of language. Within the philosophy of language, I benefited from the work of J. L. Austin, Saul Kripke, and Ludwig Wittgenstein. Indeed, when I speak here of "performative utterances," it is Austin's concept that I have in mind. I am specifically indebted to Kripke for insights pertaining to the logic of proper names and naming. I am indebted to Wittgenstein for crucial insights into the relationship between meaning and usage. Within theology itself, I have benefited from two works by Robert Jenson: *The Triune Identity: God According to the Gospel* (Philadelphia: Fortress Press, 1982) and *Systematic Theology, Volume I: The Triune God* (Oxford: Oxford University Press, 1997). Anyone familiar with Jenson's account will notice that, while we both emphasize the Trinity as the proper name for God, we develop this basic fundamental insight in different yet complementary ways.

5. For more on theology and participation in the fullness of Christian ontology, see William J. Abraham, Jason E. Vickers, and Natalie B. Van Kirk, eds., *Canonical Theism: A Proposal for Theology and the Church* (Grand Rapids: Eerdmans, 2008).

Before I introduce the content of these chapters, a word of warning is in order. It would be a mistake to assume that what follows is a mere exercise in historical investigation. To be sure, the central narrative of this text is historical in nature, describing several episodes that combine to make up the Trinitarian controversy in late seventeenth-century England. Yet the assumptions about the primary goal of theological discourse in general and Trinitarian discourse in particular, assumptions that underlie each of these episodes, are very much with us today. To the extent that these assumptions remain unnoticed and unchallenged, theology in general and Trinitarian theology in particular will continue to have little, if any, significant impact on the ongoing life of the church. But the ability to notice and to challenge these assumptions does not come easy. On the contrary, it requires a careful and prolonged reading of theological discourse that is founded on and guided by these assumptions.

In Chapter 2, I identify three crucial commitments that underlie English Protestant theological discourse in the seventeenth century and beyond. These commitments that do not emerge spontaneously. Rather, they emerge gradually in response to two crucial events in English church and society: the Reformation and the Baconian revolution in natural philosophy. The first commitment has to do with the identity and content of the rule of faith. As I note in Chapter 1, the term "rule of faith" designated protocreedal and creedal materials in early Christianity. After the Reformation, "rule of faith" refers exclusively to Scripture in late seventeenth-century English Protestant theology. Like the rule of faith in the early church, the rule of faith in English Protestant theology was intimately related to faith and salvation. Yet the change in the identity of the rule of faith was accompanied by a deep shift in the understanding of what counts as faith and therefore as salvation.

The second commitment has to do with the nature of faith and salvation. From early Christianity to the Continental Reformation, faith had primarily to do with personal trust (*fiducia*) in God and with appropriate response to God for God's saving activities in Jesus Christ and in the Holy Spirit. In the coming of Christ and of the Holy Spirit, the earliest Christians had come face to face with the living God. Moreover, subsequent generations of Christians were convinced that they continued to know and enjoy the presence of Christ and of the Holy

Spirit in the worshiping life of the church. Thus salvation itself had fundamentally to do with coming to know, to trust, and to love God in and through the liturgical and sacramental practices of the church. In this understanding, the triune God was present to humans in the church through an entire range of *charisms,* or means of grace. The church viewed the Holy Spirit as dwelling in humans through their active participation in the means of grace, straightening out the crookedness of the human soul through the formation of the divine virtues.[6]

By contrast, many late seventeenth-century English Protestant theologians understood faith as having primarily to do with assent *(assensus)* to clear and intelligible propositions contained in Scripture. In turn, salvation had more to do with holding right beliefs about God than with the transforming presence and work of God in the means of grace and ultimately in the human soul itself.[7] Whereas knowing, trusting, and loving God had long been regarded as dependent on the presence and work of the Holy Spirit, human beings could now obtain saving knowledge simply by doing their epistemic best.

The third commitment is more subtle but no less crucial. If anything, it is more crucial for its subtlety, because in a profound way it informed how many late seventeenth-century English Protestant theologians understood both Scripture as the rule of faith and faith itself. This third commitment had to do with the nature and purpose of language and therefore with what was understood by "clear and intelligible" propositions. In late seventeenth-century England, Baconian sensibilities concerning the nature and purpose of language were widespread, emphasizing the need for language to describe the world in empirically accurate and thus useful ways. Success in natural philosophy, after all, depended on it.

The upshot for Trinitarian discourse of these three commitments was that English Protestant theologians increasingly saw the doctrine of the Trinity as a proposition or network of propositions that clearly and intelligibly described the divine nature, that is, the immanent Trinity. To be sure, no one considered God to be subject to empirical obser-

6. For a helpful discussion of this understanding of salvation, see Ellen T. Charry, "Augustine of Hippo: Father of Christian Psychology," *Anglican Theological Review* 88, no. 4 (2006): 575-90.

7. This criticism of English Protestant Christianity would be shared in the coming centuries by figures as diverse as John Wesley, Mark Pattison, and John Henry Newman.

vation. The problem lay elsewhere, that is, with the use of a term whose meaning was tied to empirically observable analogues, namely, the term "person" or "persons." According to Baconian sensibilities about language, the term "person" or "persons" had to be used in a way that cohered with empirical observations about actual persons. If this could not be done, then the use of the term "persons" to describe God would be unintelligible; if unintelligible, it would not be among the propositions necessary to be believed for salvation.

Most English Protestant theologians did not immediately see the implications of these commitments for the Trinity. On the contrary, most assumed that the doctrine of the Trinity was in fact comprised of a network of clear and intelligible propositions contained in Scripture. However, a growing number of English Unitarians who shared the three commitments identified above were keen to challenge this assumption. From their perspective, there was no way to understand the term "person" or "persons" in which the use of these terms in Trinitarian doctrine was either clear or intelligible but did not result in tritheism.

In Chapter 3, I show how English Protestant theologians committed to the Trinity could not ignore the Unitarian challenge. With increasing frequency, astute Catholic theologians and pamphleteers were incorporating the Unitarian challenge into their Counter Reformation polemics. How, they asked, could English Protestant theologians maintain their basic commitments in the rule of faith, the nature of faith and salvation, and the nature and purpose of language, and avoid drawing Unitarian conclusions? The safe course, they urged, was to return to the Catholic Church: there the Trinity was secured by methodological and material commitments to the revelatory force of tradition.

One of the burdens of telling the story of the demise of the Trinity in late seventeenth-century English Protestant theology is getting across the extent to which leading Protestant theologians were caught between these two alternatives. Nor was this merely an intellectual problem: it was also an ecclesiastical problem. English Protestant theologians were concerned that a growing number of people were converting to Unitarianism on the one hand or returning to Catholicism on the other. Therefore, late seventeenth-century English Protestant theologians attempted to identify a *via media* between Unitarianism and Catholicism. This task occupied the time and energies of some of the best minds in late seventeenth-century English Protestantism, including

Edward Stillingfleet, John Tillotson, William Sherlock, Robert South, and John Locke.

English Protestant theologians were confident that they could chart a middle way between Unitarianism and Catholicism. They would need only to provide a conception of personhood that would render the doctrine of the Trinity among the clear and intelligible propositions necessary to be believed for salvation. Those who set out to meet this challenge took it for an easy task, and they presented their accounts of personhood with great confidence and flair. They could not have been more wrong, and the results could not have been more devastating for the Trinity in English Protestant theology. With every attempt to give a clear and intelligible account of the relationships among the three divine persons, theological reflection came to focus sharply on the immanent Trinity quite apart from the saving activities of the economic Trinity.

Chapters 4 and 5 narrate three attempts to render the doctrine of the Trinity intelligible on the basis of the concept of personhood. In Chapter 4, I review the efforts of William Sherlock and John Wallis to provide an account of the term "person" according to which the doctrine of the Trinity might appear clear and intelligible. Sherlock, for his part, attempted to salvage the immanent Trinity by adopting Descartes's concept of personhood. As Robert South showed, however, the Cartesian concept of personhood compromised the Trinity in the direction of tritheism. Wallis, by contrast, sought to render the immanent Trinity intelligible by retrieving the pre-Boethian Latin concept of person. In response, Stephen Nye observed that Wallis's Latin solution compromised the Trinity in the opposite direction, namely, Unitarianism. The result of these efforts was truly problematic: if Sherlock's Cartesian solution endangered the essential unity of the Godhead, then Wallis's so-called Ciceronian solution put at risk the real distinctions within the Godhead.

Chapter 5 summarizes Edward Stillingfleet's attempt to provide an intelligible account of the immanent Trinity by using categories derived from John Locke's epistemology and theory of language. Much to Locke's dismay, Stillingfleet sought to salvage the Trinity by modifying Locke's philosophy to allow for the notion of substance. The result was, as Locke himself pointed out, a return to just the kind of confusion Locke had tried to eliminate from philosophy. In the end, Stillingfleet's solution, like Sherlock's and Wallis's before him, fell short of demonstrating that the Trinity was contained in clear and intelligible propositions necessary to be believed for salvation.

The repeated attempts to secure the Trinity on English Protestant methodological grounds made the Trinity appear increasingly dubious to many. The issue here was a simple one: on English Protestant theological grounds, doctrines necessary to be believed for salvation were to be contained in clear and intelligible propositions. The mere fact that English Protestant theologians had to write lengthy treatises in their efforts to demonstrate the intelligibility of the Trinity suggested that the Trinity was not so contained. Clear and intelligible propositions were, after all, the kinds of things that could be understood by the common plowman; they should not require lengthy explanations. This was precisely the conclusion John Locke reached in his book *The Reasonableness of Christianity* (1695). More than any other work, this book embodied the three commitments now so deeply embedded in English Protestant theology. As Mark Pattison would later observe, the cumulative effect of these commitments was that "Christianity appeared made for nothing else but to be 'proved'; what use to make of it when it was proved was not much thought about."[8]

The upshot of the above narrative is that, by the turn of the eighteenth century, a major shift had occurred in English Protestant theology in general and in Trinitarian theology in particular. Late seventeenth-century English Protestant theologians understood the theological task as having primarily to do with demonstrating the clarity and intelligibility of Christian beliefs. On this understanding, theology was first and foremost a matter of logical consistency or rationality and only secondarily, if at all, a matter of the re-formation of the human soul through incorporation into the praying and worshiping community of the faithful. To put it another way, second-order theological reflection lost its moorings in the first-order liturgical tasks of baptism, prayer, and worship. The aim of theology was not so much to assist humans to come to know and love God as it was to identify and assent to clear and intelligible propositions about God. Salvation was more a matter of holding right beliefs than of personal encounter with the God who answers to the name "Father, Son, and Holy Spirit."

8. See Mark Pattison, "Tendencies of Religious Thought in England, 1688-1750," in *Essays*, vol. 2 (Oxford: Clarendon Press, 1889), p. 48.

In Chapter 6, I suggest that the loss of interest in the Trinity on the part of English Protestant theologians during the seventeenth and eighteenth centuries was both predictable and understandable. Given the assumptions about the task of theology and the nature of salvation that had taken deep hold in English Protestant theology — assumptions that linger on in many quarters today — one would hardly expect any prolonged interest in the Trinity. Yet I also maintain that, while the Trinity became increasingly marginalized in English Protestant theology, it continued to maintain a prominent place in English Protestant Christianity. As the name for God, the Trinity went right on enabling people to come to know and love God through baptism, prayer, and worship. In short, the Trinitarian name for God continued to enable people to respond in prayer and praise for the saving activities of Father, Son, and Holy Spirit on their behalf. Hence I show that the Trinity resurfaced in the eighteenth century in the sermons, hymns, and prayers of Charles Wesley. It is true that Charles Wesley did not write a major work on Trinitarian theology. However, he did produce an entire collection of hymns and prayers to the Trinity, and they reminded people of the rightful home for Trinitarian discourse, namely, the worshiping life of the church, and the rightful end of Trinitarian discourse, namely, praise and thanksgiving to God for their salvation.

In the concluding chapter, I have resisted the temptation of merely summarizing what I have said throughout the work. Instead, I offer a series of suggestions and questions concerning the nature and function of Trinitarian theology. These suggestions and questions are largely an attempt to learn from the mistakes of the past.

Finally, by way of introduction, I am keenly aware that the marginalization of the Trinity in Christian theology in the modern West is more complicated and far-reaching than the events that transpired in English Protestant Christianity in the late seventeenth and eighteenth centuries. Therefore, I agree with what Nicholas Lash says about the demise of the Trinity in early modern theology: "There are vast puzzles here, puzzles whose roots lie deep in the history of modern Western culture; puzzles whose adequate elucidation would demand the resources of erudition and intelligence beyond the reach of any individual inquirer."[9]

---

9. Nicholas Lash, "Considering the Trinity," *Modern Theology* 2 (1986): 183.

The good news is that the vastness of these puzzles has not deterred historians and theologians from beginning what is bound to be a long journey of discovery and disentanglement. I have intended this volume to be a contribution to that process. I have no illusions that the following story approaches anything like a full explanation of the travails of the Trinity from late medieval to late modern Christian theology. On the contrary, I am convinced that the story of the marginalization of the Trinity in modern Christian theology will vary in accordance with location and time. The story that follows has to do with the demise of the Trinity in early modern English Protestant theology. Other stories concerning the Trinity will have to be told at other times and in other places.

Chapter 1

Invocation: The Trinity and Salvation

If you are a theologian you truly pray, if you truly pray you are a theologian.

Evagrius of Pontus

What the Trinity is and why it matters or fails to matter depends entirely on what one is *doing* when one engages in Trinitarian discourse. Similarly, how one understands salvation and how the Trinity relates to salvation (if at all) has at least as much to do with the kind of *activity* one takes to be fundamentally constitutive of salvation as it does with the resulting cognitive contents of any particular doctrine of salvation. Likewise, whether or not the Trinity is significant for theology depends to no small degree on the kind of activities one takes to be most constitutive of theology.

In the following chapters, I will show that the demise of the Trinity in English Protestant theology in the modern West is the result of a deep shift in the kind of activity taken to be most constitutive of both salvation and theology. At times I will describe this shift in activity as a shift from *invocation*, or prayer, to intellectual *assent*. At other times I will refer to a shift from *doxological* to *epistemological* activity.[1] To put the

---

1. For an analysis of the wider dimensions of this shift in the history of theology in the West, see William J. Abraham, *Canon and Criterion in Christian Theology: From the Fathers to Feminism* (Oxford: Oxford University Press, 1998); see also William J. Abraham, Jason E. Vickers, and Natalie B. Van Kirk, eds., *Canonical Theism: A Proposal for Theology and the Church* (Grand Rapids: Eerdmans, 2008).

matter succinctly, what the Trinity is and whether or not it matters depends entirely on what kind of activity one takes to be most constitutive of salvation and theology: praying or giving intellectual assent,
doxological or epistemological activity.[2]

In order to demonstrate the consequences for the Trinity of the
shift in emphasis from invocation to assent or from doxological to
epistemological activity, I need to begin with the relationships among
the Trinity, the rule of faith, and salvation in early Christianity. The
crucial thing to notice with regard to this nexus of themes in early
Christianity is that the Trinity, the rule of faith, and salvation were related in a fundamental way to the church's work of worship, evangelism, initiation, and catechesis. In these contexts, the Trinity was the
divine personal name used in prayer and praise, thanksgiving and sup-
plication, baptism and benediction. The rule of faith was a set of identifying descriptions related directly to the Trinity as the personal name
for God used in these same catechetical and liturgical activities. Salvation was a matter of dynamic interaction between Father, Son, and
Holy Spirit and humans in the context of the worshiping life of the
people of God.

The Trinity, the Rule of Faith, and Salvation
in Early Christianity

In early Christianity, salvation was intimately and inextricably related
to the Trinity. The reason for this is straightforward: "Father, Son, and
Holy Spirit" was the personal name that Christians used to invoke
their God in prayer, baptism, the Eucharist, demon exorcism, hymn-
singing, preaching, confession, absolution, and benediction.[3] As the

---

2. The contrast between invocation and assent is a heuristic device intended to pro-
voke critical thinking about a range of issues related to the doctrine of the Trinity. I am
well aware of the heuristic nature and thus limitations of this distinction. If the distinction evokes debate over the nature of the relationship between invocation and assent
with regard to the Trinity, then it will have served its purpose. As will become evident in
what follows, the assent that accompanied invocation of the Trinity in the early church
was primarily, if not exclusively, an assent to propositions concerning the saving activities of the Christian God, that is, to propositions about the economic Trinity.

3. Other divine names preceded the widespread use of "Father, Son, and Holy

practice of invocation suggests, salvation in the early church had fundamentally to do with a complex scheme of interaction and encounter between the triune God and human beings. As the name for the Christian God, the Trinity was indispensable for coming to know and love God and thus indispensable for human salvation. Human salvation, in turn, was a matter of thanksgiving and petition, call and response, submission and obedience, initiation and formation.

As Robert Jenson observes, the first appearances in the surviving literature of the Trinitarian formula "are all glimpses of the church's liturgical life." He continues:

> In the immediately postapostolic literature there is no use of a trinitarian formula as a piece of theology or in such fashion as to depend upon antecedent development in theology, yet the formula is there. Its home is in the liturgy, in baptism and the Eucharist, and there its use was regularly seen as the heart of the matter.[4]

Robert Louis Wilken makes the same point more succinctly: "Before there was a 'doctrine' of the Trinity, Christian prayers invoked the Holy Trinity."[5]

Within the framework of the church's worship, evangelism, catechesis, and initiation, the early Christian understanding of salvation was from beginning to end a matter of divine-human encounter for which the triune name was utterly indispensable. Jenson observes: "The function of naming God in initiation, in baptism as elsewhere, is to address the initiate to new reality, to grant new access to God."[6] The Christian God was neither deaf nor dumb. On the contrary, Christians believed that their God was present and responsive when they called on the Trin-

---

Spirit" in the early church. For a summary overview of the use of divine names in ancient Israel and the early church, see Robert W. Jenson, *Systematic Theology: The Triune God* (Oxford: Oxford University Press, 2001), ch. 1. See also Jenson's earlier but still helpful work *The Triune Identity: God According to the Gospel* (Philadelphia: Fortress Press, 2001), ch. 1. With regard to the relationship between the name of Jesus and the Trinitarian formula, Jenson is surely right when he says that "the causal connections are probably no longer recoverable" (Jenson, *The Triune Identity*, p. 9).

4. Jenson, *The Triune Identity*, p. 11. Jenson provides numerous examples.

5. Robert Louis Wilken, *The Spirit of Early Christian Thought* (New Haven: Yale University Press, 2003), p. 31.

6. Jenson, *The Triune Identity*, p. 16.

ity in prayer and when they invoked Father, Son, and Holy Spirit in proclamation, baptism, the Eucharist, demon exorcism, and the like. The triune God of early Christianity was a God who spoke and who could be spoken to, a God who called and who could be called upon.

To be sure, various ways of understanding the objective and subjective consequences of this encounter for humans have emerged over time in the form of the church's teaching about salvation. These take the form of doctrines of justification and sanctification. Regardless of the metaphors and analogies one may use, the conceptual nerve center of the church's teaching about salvation has to do with the divine-human encounter and exchange that occurs when Christians invoke their God by name. Salvation is fundamentally a matter of being addressed by God in the coming of Jesus Christ and the Holy Spirit, both historically in the incarnation and Pentecost and continually in the worshiping life of the church. By extension, salvation involves the giving of thanksgiving and praise for the saving activities and presence of God. It is, like theology itself, a matter of prayer.

Within the framework of catechism, baptism, and the liturgy of the early church, the rule of faith was second in importance only to the divine name itself. This was a perfectly natural development. After all, inquirers into the Christian faith were likely to have questions concerning the identity of the Christian God. It is not difficult to imagine the kinds of questions that inquirers into the faith might have asked. Who is this God? What, if anything, differentiates the Christian God from other gods? What can one expect from this God? What has the Christian God done to be worthy of prayer and praise in the first place? How can one be sure that the Christian God can be trusted for salvation?

In the early church the rule of faith provided inquirers into the Christian faith with summary identifying descriptions of the God whom Christians invoked in prayer, in baptism, and in worship. It indicated what the God who answers to the name "Father, Son, and Holy Spirit" was like by highlighting the presence and work of the triune God in creation, in the incarnation, and in the coming of the Holy Spirit. Most importantly, the rule of faith made clear that the triune God was a God favorably disposed toward humans, a God who desired ongoing communion with all of creation, a God who was willing to go to any length necessary to obtain and to sustain it. In short, it identified the saving activities of the triune God.

In the earliest forms of the rule of faith, God was routinely depicted as present and providentially active in creation, in the affairs of ancient Israel, and in the incarnation, crucifixion, and resurrection of Jesus Christ. Furthermore, God was said to be present in the coming of the Holy Spirit at Pentecost and in the ongoing work of the Holy Spirit in the life of the church. Thus Irenaeus identified the rule of faith as follows:

> The Church . . . [believes] in one God, the Father Almighty, the Creator of heaven and earth and the seas and all things that are in them; and in one Jesus Christ, the Son of God, who was enfleshed for our salvation; and in the Holy Spirit, who through the prophets preached the economies, the coming, the birth from a virgin, the passion, the resurrection from the dead, and the bodily ascension into heaven of the beloved Son, Christ Jesus our Lord, and his coming from heaven in the glory of the Father to recapitulate all things, and to raise up all flesh of the whole human race.[7]

Similarly, Tertullian says:

> It is the rule of faith, moreover, that we now profess what we henceforth defend; that rule by which it is believed that there is only one God and no other beside him, Creator of the world, who brought forth everything from nothing through his Word, which was sent out before everything; and that this Word, called his Son, appeared in various visions in the name of God to the patriarchs, was heard always in the prophets, and finally was brought down by the Spirit and power of God the Father into the Virgin Mary, made flesh in her womb and was born from her as Jesus Christ. Thereafter, he proclaimed a new law and a new promise of the kingdom of heaven, performed great deeds, was nailed to the cross, rose again on the third day, was taken up to heaven and sat at the right hand of the Father, and sent in his place the power of the Holy Spirit who guides believers, and he will come again in glory to summon saints into eternal life and to the enjoyment of celestial promises, and to condemn the

---

7. Irenaeus, *Adversus haereses*, 1.10.1, in *Creeds and Confessions of Faith in the Christian Tradition*, 3 vols., ed. Jaroslav Pelikan and Valerie Hotchkiss (New Haven: Yale University Press, 2003), 1:49; see also Irenaeus, *Adversus haerseses*, 3.4.1-2; 4.33.7.

impious to perpetual fire, both parties being raised from the dead and having their flesh restored. This rule is from Christ.[8]

The first thing to notice about these third-century examples of the rule of faith is that they are Trinitarian in structure.[9] The rule of faith was organized around the triune name for God. The second thing is that these early versions of the rule of faith preceded the Niceno-Constantinopolitan Creed.[10] Indeed, the earliest versions of the rule of faith contain in nascent form most of the content that would later be enshrined in the creed at Nicea in 325 and Constantinople in 381.[11]

It is worth noting an objection at this point. Some Protestant theologians argue that the identity of the rule of faith in the early church is not early confessional statements and creeds, but Scripture. The standard argument here is that the rule of faith is really just a summary of Scripture. In other words, the rule of faith (whether the third-century formulations or the creed) is derived from Scripture; therefore, Scripture is the true rule of faith. Typically, proponents of this argument point to Cyril of Jerusalem's observation that the Creed is for people who either did not have access to Scripture or who could not read, concluding that Scripture is the true rule of faith for the literate.[12]

---

8. Tertullian, *De praescriptione haereticorum*, 13.1-6, in Pelikan and and Hotchkiss, *Creeds and Confessions of Faith,* 1:56.

9. The same can be said, of course, for the Apostles' Creed. For a discussion of the origins and content of the Apostles' Creed, see Frances Young, *The Making of the Creeds* (Harrisburg, PA: Trinity Press International, 1991), pp. 2-5.

10. Jaroslav Pelikan, *Credo: Historical and Theological Guide to Creeds and Confessions of Faith in the Christian Tradition* (New Haven: Yale University Press, 2003), pp. 10-11.

11. It is worth noting that no two expressions of the rule of faith are exactly the same. This is true even when they occur in the same author or in the same text, e.g., Irenaeus's *Adversus haereses* (see above, n. 7). Thus the reader who observes the definite article in *"the* rule of faith" should not assume that there was one rule of faith prior to Nicea and Constantinople. However, the similarities among the various rules of faith in the third century, both to one another and to earlier confessions of faith, or to protocreeds, are striking. Most striking is the Trinitarian structure and content common to almost all of them. It is true, of course, that some of the earliest confessions of faith were binitarian. For a comparative analysis of three early confessions of faith, including the Nicene Creed of 381, the Apostles' Creed, and the Jerusalem Creed, see Young, *The Making of the Creeds,* p. 4. For an in-depth analysis of the journey from binitarian to Trinitarian confessions of faith, see J. N. D. Kelly, *Early Christian Creeds* (New York: HarperCollins, 1978).

12. Cyril says: "For since all cannot read the Scriptures, some being hindered as to

As Frances Young observes in *The Making of the Creeds,* there are at least two problems with the argument that the rule of faith is merely a summary of Scripture. First, says Young, "[i]f the creeds were intended as summaries of scripture, they have an unexpected shape: there is no summary of Israel's history as God's chosen people, no summary of the life and teaching of Jesus, etc." (p. 5). Second, Young points out that not all of the "catch phrases" enshrined in the early confessions of faith and creeds are drawn from Scripture (p. 7). While the confessions of faith and the creed clearly draw on and perhaps reflect Scripture, it is difficult to sustain an argument that they are *mere* summaries of Scripture or that they are *derived entirely* from Scripture, much less that Scripture itself was the rule of faith.

Young's observations raise a twofold question. If the rule of faith was not merely a summary of Scripture, then where did it come from and why were its contents chosen? Suppose that Scripture is the primary source for the rule of faith. One still needs to know why the early church fathers selected these contents and not some other contents as the rule of faith. As Young points out, the early fathers could easily have selected any number of other things in Scripture to include in the rule of faith, including the history of Israel, the Ten Commandments, or selections from Jesus' sermons and moral teachings. Why, then, did the various formulations of the rule of faith always have a Trinitarian structure and content?

In answering this question, we will find it helpful to recall J. N. D. Kelly's important work on the history of Christian creeds and confessions, *Early Christian Creeds.* When Kelly set out to inquire about the origin and development of early Christian creeds, there was something approaching a consensus among historians and theologians that creeds were a relatively late development in the life of the early church (pp. 6, 11).[13] Protestant theologians, in particular, had for

---

the knowledge of them by want of learning, and others by a want of leisure, in order that the soul may not perish from ignorance, we comprise the whole doctrine of the Faith in a few lines." Cyril of Jerusalem, "The Catechetical Lectures," in *Nicene and Post-Nicene Fathers,* 2nd ser., ed. Philip Schaff (New York: Christian Publishing, 1893), 7:32, para. 12 ("Lecture on Faith").

13. Kelly identifies two important exceptions, namely, A. Seeberg and Paul Feine. See A. Seeberg, *Der Katechismus der Urchristenheit* (Leipzig, 1903), and Paul Feine, *Die Gestalt des apostolischen Glaubensbekenntnisses in der Zeit des N.T.* (Leipzig, 1925).

years subscribed to a two-stage view of the history of the early church, beginning with an early and pure "scriptural" stage that eventually gave way to a later, institutionalized, and corrupted "creedal" stage. The creedal stage, it was said, came about largely as a result of theological controversies, representing a "hellenization of Christianity," which was to be contrasted with a pure, scriptural or apostolic stage (pp. 5-11, 119-26).[14]

In this view, the origin of the creeds was generally identified with the development of the rule of faith, a development that took place amid polemical disputes and theological controversy. It is during the disputes and controversies of the third and fourth centuries that the pure theology of the scriptural stage was purportedly corrupted when it incorporated Greek philosophical categories and concepts. Moreover, there was supposedly no evidence that the early church possessed any "official, textually determined confession of faith" during the so-called pure, scriptural stage (Kelly, pp. 5-7).[15]

In the context of scholarly consensus about the late development of the creeds, Kelly broke new ground by calling into question the two-stage theory concerning the history of the early church. The crucial move Kelly made, however, was not to challenge the thesis that the earliest churches did not have a fixed, textually determined creed, or rule of faith; he agreed with that conclusion. Instead, Kelly opposed the two-stage view by challenging the working definition of a creed as something fixed, official, and textually determined.

After arguing that "the choice of alternatives" offered was neither fair nor reasonable, Kelly hypothesized that "creeds of a looser sort, lacking the fixity and the official character of the later formularies but none the less foreshadowing them, were in use comparatively early" (p. 7). Kelly went so far as to argue that creeds were as old as Christianity itself, originating as part of the evangelistic agenda of the earliest Christian churches (pp. 7-8).[16] Indeed, Kelly devoted the first five chap-

---

14. The major figure behind this was Adolf von Harnack. See also Robert Louis Wilken, *The Spirit of Early Christian Thought: Seeking the Face of God* (New Haven: Yale University Press, 2003), pp. xvi, 118.

15. For an extended critique of Harnack's hypothesis, see Paul Gavrilyuk, *The Suffering of the Impassable God: The Dialectics of Patristic Thought* (Oxford: Oxford University Press, 2005).

16. "Like other groups with a saving message," says Kelly, the early Christians were

ters of *Early Christian Creeds* to the testing of this hypothesis by identifying protocreedal and protoconfessional materials in the New Testament and various other documents from the first three centuries of the church's life.

By loosening the working definition of "creed" or "confession of faith," Kelly saw that the originating *Sitz im Leben* of the Trinitarian content enshrined in the rule of faith and the Nicene Creed was not the theological controversies of the third and fourth centuries after all. This was by far the most important consequence of Kelly's argument. If this aspect of Kelly's thesis was correct, then the two-stage view had to be rethought. If there were protocreedal and protoconfessional materials in the New Testament and other early writings that were Trinitarian in content, then one had to inquire about the settings in which these materials first emerged and functioned. Kelly had opened the way for historians to reconsider the originating settings and function of the Trinitarian confessional materials that would eventually be enshrined in the Nicene Creed. In doing so, he also provided an important clue about the early church fathers' rationale for selecting a Trinitarian content and structure (and not some other content and structure) as the rule of faith.

Kelly immediately noticed the implications of his new working definition, pointing out that the protocreedal and protoconfessional materials in the early period had been "provoked by particular situations in the Church's life." No longer bound by the two-stage view, Kelly was free to look for situations and settings other than the polemical disputes and theological controversies of the third and fourth centuries. In a lengthy but very important passage, Kelly observes:

> Particular occasions lent themselves to the exposition of or declaration of Christian doctrine: they called for something like a creed. . . . Some kind of assurance of faith, and thus some sort of avowal of belief, was required of candidates seeking admission to the Church. But it would be a mistake to concentrate exclusively on baptism. . . . The Catechetical instruction preceding baptism was also a moment sympathetic to the shaping of creedal summaries. So was preaching: the method and style of preachers doubtless varied, but the content and

---

"driven by an inward impulse to embody it in their liturgy, their institutions, and their propaganda, and to seize every opportunity of harping on it."

wording of their message must have tended to run along certain accepted lines. The day-to-day polemic of the Church, whether against
heretics within or pagan foes without, provided another situation
propitious to the production of creeds. Yet another was supplied by
the liturgy: solemn expressions of faith, in the form of hymns, prayers
and devotional cries, had a natural place there. An interesting special
case is the rite of exorcism. The exorcism of devils was widely prac-
tised in the early Church, and the codification of suitable formulae of
proved potency seems to have set in relatively soon. Nor should we
overlook the formal correspondence of Church leaders with their
flocks. In the ancient as in the modern world, letters, especially official ones (and it must be remembered that Christian letters were often intended to be read aloud at Church meetings), abounded in ste-
reotyped turns of phrase, and sometimes these had something of the
character of brief formal confessions. (pp. 13-14)

It is difficult to exaggerate the importance of Kelly's work at this
point. By challenging the two-stage theory, Kelly was able not only to
identify protocreedal and protoconfessional materials; he was also able
to call attention to the various settings in which those materials had
emerged and functioned. As the foregoing list suggests, the polemical
setting was only one of the settings in which creedal and confessional
materials were formed and functioned. Baptism, catechesis, preaching,
the liturgy, and exorcisms were all settings in which early Trinitarian
confessions of faith emerged and functioned.

These settings not only created "the occasion for tentative creeds,"
they also "determined their style, substance and structure." In other
words, the settings and *function* of these materials determined their *contents*. Kelly comments:

Sometimes diffusiveness was appropriate, sometimes terseness and
aridity. If a dry enumeration of Christ's redemptive deeds was suitable in a catechetical instruction, a more enthusiastic, fulsome utterance might be expected in an act of worship. In certain circumstances what seemed fitting was a Trinitarian or a binitarian
ground-plan, the former emphasizing belief in the three Divine Persons, the latter belief in the Father and the Son. More often than
not, a single-clause Christological statement was sufficient for the
purpose in hand. (p. 14)

Unfortunately, historians of creeds and confessions have only recently begun to follow up on the illuminating character and significance of Kelly's judgment on this point. Thus Jaroslav Pelikan rightly laments that not nearly enough work has been done in this area.[17] However, despite the lack of a further development of Kelly's argument, Pelikan also notes that there is substantial "scholarly agreement" concerning Kelly's most important insight, namely, that baptism and catechesis were the primary original settings in which Trinitarian confessional materials emerged and functioned.[18] To take a recent example, Frances Young says in *The Making of the Creed*, "The creeds took the form they did in response to the situation in which they arose, namely the context of catechesis and baptism" (p. 6). Young goes on to say that the creeds "did not originate . . . as tests of orthodoxy, but as summaries of faith taught to new Christians by their local bishop, summaries that were traditional to each local church and which in detail varied from place to place" (p. 3). To be sure, Young acknowledges that in special circumstances, the creeds functioned as "tests of orthodoxy"; but she immediately adds that, if we are "to understand their fundamental character," then we must realize that "creeds belonged originally to a different context" (p. 12).

At this point I should repeat that I am not arguing that the rule of faith did not function as a criterion of identity or "test of orthodoxy" in the midst of the controversies with the Gnostics, the Arians, and the like.[19] Rather, the Trinitarian confessional materials enshrined in the rule of faith and the creed did not *originally* function that way, nor were they intended *primarily* to function that way. Trinitarian confessional materials were not made first and foremost for resolving doctrinal disputes; they were intended for use in catechesis, baptism, and the liturgy, that is, in the making of Christians and in the worship of God. Thus Irenaeus is careful to note that he received "the rule of truth . . . through baptism."[20] Moreover, during and after the theological controversies of the third and fourth centuries, the rule of faith (in the

---

17. Pelikan, *Credo*, p. 178.

18. Pelikan, *Credo*, pp. 179, 377-83.

19. For the function of confessional materials in early Christian apologetics, see Pelikan, *Credo*, pp. 383-88.

20. Ireneaus, *Adv. Haer.*, 1.9.4.

form of either the Apostles' Creed or the Nicene Creed) continued to function *primarily* in catechetical, baptismal, and liturgical contexts.[21]

But what precisely was the fundamental character of Trinitarian confessional materials in these settings? How exactly did they function in catechesis, baptism, and the liturgy? Most importantly, what was it about catechesis, baptism, and liturgy that led the early church to formulate Trinitarian confessions of faith in the first place?

While Kelly's argument concerning the originating and primary settings of Trinitarian confessional materials in the early church has been widely embraced by historians of doctrine, there has been very little discussion of how these settings affect our view of the fundamental character of those materials. Despite the scholarly consensus among historians of doctrine concerning the basic features of Kelly's argument, there is still a tendency among theologians to begin discussions of the Trinity with the "emergence" of Trinitarian confessional materials in the polemical and apologetic contexts of the third and fourth centuries.[22] Indeed, one rarely finds serious reflection on how Trinitarian confessions of faith were *functioning* in the contexts of baptism, catechesis, liturgy, preaching, exorcism, and the like.

Given that most scholars now agree with Kelly that it is primarily in the baptismal, catechetical, and liturgical contexts that Trinitarian confessional materials emerged, it is puzzling that so few have ventured to think about how the function of Trinitarian confessional materials in those original settings may have influenced the third-century fathers' decision to designate variously worded Trinitarian confessions as the rule of faith. Scholars who have attempted to build on Kelly's argument have done so primarily by focusing on one crucial question: What is the relationship between the so-called interrogatory creeds associated with early baptismal rites and the so-called declaratory creeds that emerged somewhat later?[23] The overriding concern here is ultimately to establish and trace the emergence and development of writ-

---

21. See Pelikan, *Credo,* pp. 369-96.

22. In *Credo,* Pelikan has taken an initial step toward addressing this problem. For a good example of how scholars still tend to begin discussions of the Trinity with the "emergence" of Trinitarian confessions of faith in the polemical and apologetic contexts of the third and fourth centuries, see Roger E. Olson and Christopher A. Hall, *The Trinity* (Grand Rapids: Eerdmans, 2002), pp. 1-2.

23. Young, *Making of the Creeds,* pp. 6-12; Pelikan, *Credo,* pp. 380-83.

ten creeds from the earliest interrogatory baptismal creeds to the Nicene Creed. This is certainly an important scholarly endeavor; however, this project does little to elucidate further the most significant and illuminating part of Kelly's argument, namely, that Trinitarian confessional materials *functioned* originally and primarily in baptismal, catechetical, and liturgical settings.

What is needed at this juncture is an answer to another question: What were Trinitarian confessional materials doing in catechesis, baptism, preaching, liturgy, and exorcism? That is, how did Trinitarian confessions of faith function in the contexts in which they originated and in which they continued primarily to be used during and after the great theological controversies of the third and fourth centuries?

A good way to answer these questions is to pay close attention to what baptism was for and how it was done. According to Chrysostom, baptism was for the forgiveness of sins and the subsequent renewing of human nature,[24] and it was done in the name of the Father, the Son, and the Holy Spirit (Matt. 28:19).[25] Christians invoked the Trinity because the triune God was precisely the God who was capable of forgiving sins and restoring human nature. Here one can see an intimate connection between the Trinitarian confessions of faith instantiated in the early interrogatory creeds that preceded baptism and the performative utterance ("I baptize you *in the name of. . .*") that followed.[26] The Trinitarian content and structure of the interrogatory and declaratory creeds mirrors and anticipates the baptismal formula that follows.

Some scholars have argued that the interrogatory and declaratory creeds ultimately derive from the baptismal formula itself. The crucial point is that while these earliest creeds anticipate and mirror the baptismal formula (in both catechetical instruction and in the baptismal rite itself), they also "fill out" each of the names that are given in the baptismal formula with identifying descriptions. Thus, whereas the baptismal formula simply gives the names "Father," "Son," and "Holy

---

24. See John Chrysostom, *St. John Chrysostom: Baptismal Instructions,* trans. Paul W. Harkins (New York: Paulist Press, 1963), 9:21-26.

25. See Chrysostom, *Baptismal Instructions,* 2:27; 11:13.

26. For a philosophical analysis of performative utterances, see J. L. Austin, *How to Do Things with Words* (Cambridge, MA: Harvard University Press, 1962). As a performative utterance, "I baptize you in the name of" is analogous to "I now pronounce you husband and wife."

Spirit," an interrogatory creed like the one in Hippolytus's *Apostolic Tradition* adds a numenc of identifying descriptions. To "Father" it adds "almighty." To "Son" it adds "of God, who was born of the Holy Ghost of the Virgin Mary, and was crucified under Pontius Pilate, and was dead, and ascended into heaven, and sat at the right hand of the Father, and will come to judge the quick and the dead." And while it does not add identifying descriptions per se to the "Holy Spirit," it does associate the Holy Spirit with "the holy church, and the resurrection of the flesh."[27]

Why did the early church deem it important to "fill out" the name for God given in the baptismal formula? Why not, for example, simply ask baptismal candidates if they believe in the Father, Son, and Holy Spirit and leave it at that? Why did the early church develop and use interrogatory and declaratory creeds in catechesis or as part of the baptismal rite itself?

We can imagine at least two reasons for "filling out" the name given in the baptismal formula with the identifying descriptions that invariably show up in the interrogatory and declaratory creeds. The first reason has to do with the basic function of identifying descriptions in the logic of proper personal names.[28] The second reason has to do with a special additional function that identifying descriptions take on when they are used to help designate God in the context of initiating persons into the life of the church.

As amplifications of the baptismal formula, the identifying descriptions contained in the various confessions of faith of local early churches are best viewed in terms of the logic of proper personal names. In the baptismal context, Trinitarian confessions of faith are inextricably linked to the proper personal name for God invoked in the

---

27. Quoted in Young, *Making of the Creeds,* p. 6. As we have seen, Irenaeus and Tertullian provide a more elaborate set of identifying descriptions for the Holy Spirit.

28. For a rich and perceptive discussion of the nature and function of proper names, see Janet Martin Soskice, *Metaphor and Religious Language* (Oxford: Oxford University Press, 1985), pp. 127-29. Soskice relies on the classic essay by Saul Kripke, "Naming and Necessity," in *Semantics of Natural Language,* ed. Donald Davidson and Gilbert Harman (Dordrecht: D. Reidel Publishing Company, 1972), pp. 253-355. My reflections on names and naming here were inspired by Soskice and Kripke, but they move the discussion in a significantly different direction. Indeed, I am raising a set of issues that, to my knowledge, neither Soskice nor Kripke has addressed.

baptismal formula. Thus it will help to consider carefully the use and function of proper personal names. Clearly, one can use proper personal names when making assertions. For example, I might say, "George Washington was the first president of the United States." Yet, while one can use proper personal names when making assertions, that is arguably not their most basic or primitive function.

To get at the most basic function of personal names, I want to consider what, following Wittgenstein, one might call the many language games that make use of proper personal names. I can use proper personal names to designate individuals, for example, someone whom I am about to introduce to a third party. Or I might use a proper personal name to designate an individual to the hit man I have just hired to bump off said person in the middle of the night. However, designating individuals with proper personal names, whether for introduction or assassination, is simply one of the many things I can do with proper personal names. For that matter, designating individuals can rightly be seen as belonging to the language game of making assertions.

For which language games are proper personal names most indispensable? If I switch from a setting of description or identification to a setting of direct address, an entire range of language games immediately comes to mind. To be sure, there is a sense in which I am, when I identify or designate someone, in a setting of direct address. Thus I am usually speaking *to* someone when I designate an individual, say, for assassination. However, as I use the term here, a setting of "direct address" is one in which I use a proper personal name in order to address the person to whom the name belongs. In such settings, I use proper personal names to make a request, to issue an invitation, to say "thank you," to make inquiries about beliefs and preferences, to offer congratulations, and so on. Moreover, by using proper personal names in these ways, I can come to know, to love, to appreciate, to admire or detest, or to resent the person to whom the name belongs. I can use proper personal names for an entire range of language games through which I interact and ultimately come to know the desires, intentions, motivations, and purposes of other persons, and ultimately, one might say, the persons themselves.

Before returning to the relationship between Trinitarian confessional materials and the invocation of the Trinitarian name for God in the baptismal formula, we may find it helpful to consider one final language game in which I can use proper personal names, namely, the language game of invocation. In one sense, the language game of invocation is relatively straightforward. For example, I invoke someone when I use her name to call on her to answer the door, to pick up milk at the store, and so on. In this analysis, invocation seems to be simply another way of talking about the language game of making requests. However, the language game of invocation is unique insofar as it can, in a certain way, enable me to make someone present who is, prior to my invoking her name, absent. The language game of invocation enables proper personal names to *stand in for,* or represent, the persons to whom they belong. For instance, a commander in the king's army might order townspeople to leave the town by invoking the name of the king. In commanding the townspeople to evacuate the town *in the name of* the king, the commander makes the king present to the people in a certain sense.

Now let us return to the issue at hand, namely, the proper understanding of the relationship between Trinitarian confessional materials and the name for God in the baptismal formula. It is crucial, when we do so, to recall that baptism itself occurs in the wider context of catechesis, the liturgy, and ultimately the Eucharist. In other words, the invocation of the name of God in the baptismal formula occurs in contexts in which one can see the entire range of language games native to settings of direct address identified above. For example, Christians use the proper personal name for God to invite the Holy Spirit "to come" in the *epiclesis.* Similarly, they make requests of God when they ask the Lord "to have mercy" in the *kyrie,* when they ask the Father for forgiveness in the Lord's Prayer, and so on. Moreover, we know Christians regularly use the name for God in worship to offer salutations, praise, and thanksgiving to God. Thus, when asking about the function of early Trinitarian confessional materials, we must keep in mind that, more often than not, those materials were used in close connection with the many uses of the name for God in catechesis, baptism, exorcisms, the liturgy, prayer, and the Eucharist, that is, in those settings and activities through which Christians came to know and love their God.

In these settings and activities, it was only natural that identifying descriptions would be developed and used to fill out the Trinitarian name for God. Proper personal names often need to be extended in order successfully to designate individuals. For example, if I want to designate Jane either for introduction or assassination, I am likely to do so with identifying descriptions. I might say, "Jane is the one drinking a martini," or "Jane is the one who won the marathon." The use of identifying descriptions lessens the likelihood for mistaken identity. In the case of assassinations, this can be extremely important, because identifying descriptions will help to ensure that my assassin does not kill the wrong person — perhaps another person named Jane.

According to the foregoing analysis of proper personal names and naming, it is easy to understand why the early church might have seen fit to add to the name "Father, Son, and Holy Spirit" in the baptismal formula the identifying descriptions that begin to show up in the interrogatory and declaratory creeds. The identifying descriptions helped to ensure that the people being baptized understood which God was being designated by the name "Father, Son, and Holy Spirit." More specifically, the identifying descriptions helped to ensure that the person being baptized was not thinking of the wrong God. Therefore, one of the reasons Trinitarian confessions of faith emerge in the baptismal context is to pick out or designate the Christian God from among a variety of other gods whose names were known and no doubt used during various initiation rites in the first and second centuries.[29] Of course, the same can be said of the many other activities in which the early church used the name for God. For example, the identifying descriptions enabled Christians to address their praise, thanksgiving, and requests to the Christian God.

The second function of the Trinitarian confessions of faith in the baptismal context can be seen in terms of a special additional function that identifying descriptions take on when used to help designate God *in that context*. I have noted that identifying descriptions are normally used to help successfully "pick out" a person, for instance, in a room full of people. At their most basic and primitive level, identifying descriptions answer the question, which one is Jane? They are descriptive in nature. However, identifying descriptions can do more than that. After all, we rarely designate people for no reason other than simply to know that the woman "drinking a martini" is named "Jane." Indeed, in choosing identifying descriptions, we normally use what might be called a principle of *selective designation.*

Consider the above examples. I can designate a person in order to

---

29. See Keith Hopkins, *A World Full of Gods: The Strange Triumph of Christianity* (New York: Plume, 2001).

introduce her to another person for the purpose of having her killed. As things turn out, what I am up to when I designate a person is a crucial component in the logic of proper personal names and naming. Indeed, my purpose in designating a person will normally determine the *content* of the identifying descriptions to be given. Consequently, if I am designating "Jane" in a roomful of people so that the hit man I have hired can do his job, then I will only need to give identifying descriptions that will enable the hit man to identify Jane correctly. In this case, "drinking a martini" may be all I need to get the job done (if, e.g., every other woman in the room is drinking wine or coffee). However, if I am designating Jane for introduction to someone I am secretly trying to set up (on a date) with Jane, then I will probably provide a different set of identifying descriptions. For example, I might tell this person that Jane enjoys talking about her career.[30]

This second function is important because it is necessary to explain why the early fathers used the identifying descriptions that they did. After all, if they had wanted merely to designate successfully "Father, Son, and Holy Spirit" from among a list of gods, then any number of identifying descriptions would have done the job. For example, the early church could have successfully designated Jesus by using this identifying description: "the Son of Mary and Joseph and the brother of James." It seems safe to say that there was not more than one person named Jesus of whom "the son of Mary and Joseph and brother of James" could be truthfully predicated — and into whose name people were being baptized.

Similarly, the early church could have successfully designated Jesus by using this identifying description: "the Jewish rabbi who was a relative of John the Baptist, a good preacher, and a miracle worker." For that matter, it is easy to think of any number of identifying descriptions that could be truthfully predicated of Jesus and that would successfully designate or pick out Jesus as the one in whose name people were to be baptized. Among the various Trinitarian confessions of faith

---

30. Philosophical inquiry into the logic of proper names has traditionally been concerned with what is required for names and identifying descriptions successfully to designate a person. The point here is that we rarely designate merely for the sake of designating. Rather, we use proper names and identifying descriptions to designate for a reason or a purpose. I am suggesting that it is important to pay attention to the purpose for which we are using proper names to designate.

that emerged (whether interrogatory or declaratory), they all used roughly the same set of identifying descriptions. This is especially true of the identifying descriptions used to help designate Jesus: those used in Hippolytus's *Apostolic Tradition* are very similar to the ones selected by Irenaeus and Tertullian, as well as to the ones later enshrined in the Nicene-Constantinopolitan Creed.

Given the principle of selective designation, it is crucial to discern the purpose for which the identifying descriptions that make up the Trinitarian confessions of faith in the early church were selected and used. As things turned out, the early church selected and used identifying descriptions that highlighted the saving power and significance of Jesus and the Holy Spirit. What interested them most was what God had done in Jesus and through the Holy Spirit for the salvation of the world, that is, the saving activities of the economic Trinity.

Early Christian theologians were not interested chiefly in the internal relations among the three divine persons or the so-called immanent Trinity. On the contrary, they were primarily interested in the way the triune God had been and continued to be in relationship with humans. Thus, in his instructions to those preparing for baptism, Chrysostom says:

> Let me pass over that mysterious birth which has no human witnesses [i.e., the eternal generation of the Son from the Father]. Let me bring before you that birth which took place here below and was witnessed by many. Through this very explanation I shall secure your faith in things, because without faith, you would never be able to accept it.[31]

Chrysostom's comments manifest the crucial relationship between the creed and the practices that were necessary for salvation. So when Chrysostom says "without faith, you will never be able to accept" the way in which baptism affects salvation, he means "the confession of faith" contained in the creed and not faith as belief in the absence of conclusive evidence. The identifying descriptions in the confession of faith or creed designate God in such a way as to explain or make understandable how through baptism people's sins are forgiven and their na-

---

31. Chrysostom, *Baptismal Instructions,* 11:16.

ture restored. Thus Chrysostom uses an expanded version of one of the identifying descriptions in the creed:

> He who cannot be contained, He who contains all and rules all, came into a virgin's womb. How, tell me, and in what way? You cannot explain it. But if you come to believe, your faith will be able to satisfy you to the full. In matters that surpass the weakness of our reasoning we must turn to *the teaching of faith* [i.e., the Creed].[32]

Chrysostom's use of the creed illustrates how Trinitarian confessional materials functioned in the early church. It is true that Chrysostom was writing at a much later date; yet this can be seen as strengthening rather than weakening the case, because he was writing after the theological controversies of the third and fourth centuries. Even after the Trinitarian confession of faith had been used as a test of orthodoxy or criterion of identity, it clearly retained a different function for Chrysostom in the context of catechesis and baptism: to indicate what Father, Son, and Holy Spirit had done to make possible the forgiveness of sins and the renewal of human nature.

For Chrysostom, the creed functions first and foremost to answer the ontological question, "How can these things be?" (John 3:9, NASB). As identifying descriptions, Trinitarian confessions of faith functioned in the originating contexts of catechesis and baptism primarily to explain how it was possible that, by invoking the name "Father, Son and Holy Spirit" in baptism, people could be forgiven their sins and have their true nature restored. The confession of faith makes it clear that the God invoked in baptism was neither distant nor uninterested, but was actively seeking communion with humans. In short, the efficacy of baptism only makes sense in the context of divine action, and the confession of faith bears witness precisely to that action.

It is at this point that Catherine Mowry LaCugna's well-known distinction is helpful. The ontological question that Trinitarian confessional materials were put forth to answer had to do first and foremost with the "metaphysics of the economy of salvation" and not with the "metaphysics of 'theology.'"[33] Trinitarian confessional materials had to

---

32. Chrysostom, *Baptismal Instructions,* 11:17 (italics added).

33. Catherine Mowry LaCugna, *God for Us: The Trinity and Christian Life* (New York: HarperCollins, 1991), pp. 43-44.

do first and foremost with what God had done to save humans and
only secondarily, if at all, with the nature or being of God apart from
creation and salvation.

By now it should be clear why the early church chose the identifying descriptions that it did. Rather than designating God with identifying descriptions concerning, say, the classical attributes of the divine
being or with random data concerning Jesus' family, place of birth, occupation, and so on, the early church designates God by giving a series
of identifying descriptions of divine actions that bear directly on salvation. For example, Irenaeus identifies the Father as "Maker of heaven,
and earth, and the sea, and all things that are in them." Similarly, he
identifies Christ Jesus as "the Son of God, who became incarnate for
our salvation." And finally, he identifies the Holy Spirit as the one who

> . . . proclaimed through the prophets, the dispensations of God, and
> the advents, and the birth from a virgin, and the passion, and the
> resurrection from the dead, and the ascension into heaven in the
> flesh of the beloved Christ Jesus, our Lord, and His [future] manifes-
> tation from heaven in the glory of the Father "to gather all things in
> one," and to raise up anew all flesh of the whole human race.[34]

The rule of faith in the early church designates who God is by identifying what God has done "for us and for our salvation." In and
through Trinitarian confessional materials, the church designates God
in a way that helps catechumens understand how, through baptism in
the name of the Father, Son, and Holy Spirit, their sins could be forgiven and their natures restored. Catechumens were not being baptized
in the name of an uninterested or distant deity. Rather, they were invoking and putting their trust in a God who had acted repeatedly on
their behalf and who continued to do so through the presence and
work of the Holy Spirit in the waters of baptism.

This way of thinking about the function of Trinitarian confessional materials is dramatically confirmed by a common practice in the
early church that is rarely noticed or taken seriously by theologians and
historians of doctrine today.[35] The early church used Trinitarian con-

34. Irenaeus, *Adv. Haer.*, 1.10.1.
35. For a recent exception to this, see Graham H. Twelftree, *In the Name of Jesus: Exorcism among Early Christians* (Grand Rapids: Baker Academic, 2007).

fessions of faith to provide explanatory support for the practice of demon exorcism. Consider, for example, Justin Martyr's use of the rule of faith in conjunction with exorcism:

> *In the name of* this very Son of God and
> first-begotten of all creation,
> Who was born through the Virgin,
> and became a passible *[sic]* man,
> and was crucified under Pontius Pilate by your
> people,
> and died,
> and rose again from the dead,
> and ascended to heaven,
> every demon is exorcised, conquered, and subdued.[36]

Clearly, in the context of catechesis and baptism on the one hand and exorcism on the other, Trinitarian confessional materials are not functioning as a test of orthodoxy or a criterion of identity. Rather, they are functioning to explain how certain things are possible, namely, the forgiveness of sins and the restoration of human nature through baptism and the conquering and subduing of demons through exorcism. For such things to be possible, it was simply not enough to know that the name in which they are done designates "the son of Mary and Joseph and the brother of James." On the contrary, it was crucial for the church to identify Jesus as the one who was "the first-begotten of all creation," was "born through the Virgin," was "crucified under Pontius Pilate," who "rose again from the dead," and the like. Thus the confessional materials provided explanatory support for the use of the triune name in performative utterances in baptism and in demon exorcism. It was not just any name being used to baptize and to cast out demons. It was the name of the God who in the coming of Jesus Christ and of the Holy Spirit is "for us."

Whether in catechesis and baptism, demon exorcism, the liturgy, or preaching, Trinitarian confessional materials functioned first and foremost to identify "Father, Son, and Holy Spirit" in such a way as to make understandable the Christian vision of salvation. Thus, from the earliest protocreeds and protoconfessions to the creed hammered out

---

36. Justin Martyr, *Dialogue with Trypho*, 85:2, quoted in Pelikan, *Credo*, p. 392.

once and for all at Nicea and Constantinople, the church developed and used Trinitarian confessions of faith to designate who God is through a set of identifying descriptions that describe what God had done in Christ and through the Holy Spirit on our behalf. Because of the close connection with the use of "Father, Son, and Holy Spirit" as the name for God in worship, baptism, the Eucharist, and so on, the content of these identifying descriptions can be seen as informing Christians about not only the actions but also the motivations, purposes, and intentions of the God whom they were calling upon.

If the name for God helped to facilitate an ongoing personal encounter with God the "Father, Son, and Holy Spirit," then the identifying descriptions formed the Christian understanding concerning the nature and character of the Christian God. These identifying descriptions informed Christians not only about what their God had done in the past, but also, and equally important, about what they could expect from their God in the present and in the future. As Gregory of Nyssa so eloquently put it, the Christian God is the God who "[comes] to the aid of those in need."[37] Given the Christian God's ready willingness to respond to human need, it was no small thing to call the Christian God by name. To invoke the Trinity was to call upon none other than the God who had created the heavens and the earth, who had conquered sin and death, and who continued generously to give life to all who seek his face.

The Immanent Trinity in Early Christian Theology

I have so far been concerned primarily to offer a suggestion concerning the originating and primary function of Trinitarian confessions of faith in the early church given the baptismal and catechetical contexts in which they emerged. I have argued that Trinitarian confessions of faith should be understood as extensions of the proper personal name for God given in the baptismal formula. These materials are best understood as sets of identifying descriptions designed to help designate or pick out the God in whose name persons were to be baptized. The

---

37. Gregory of Nyssa, "Address on Religious Instruction," in *Christology of the Later Fathers,* ed. Edward Hardy (Philadelphia: Westminster, 1954), p. 306.

early church selected and used identifying descriptions highlighting the saving activities of Jesus Christ and the Holy Spirit, and it thereby helped catechumens understand how it was in and through baptism that their sins could be forgiven and their nature restored, as well as what they could expect from the Christian God.

A significant implication of this reading of the originating and primary function of Trinitarian confessions of faith in early Christianity should now be made clear. On the one hand, the Trinitarian structure of the name for God in the baptismal formula is reflected in the Trinitarian structure of the early confessions of faith. On the other hand, the content of the earliest Trinitarian confessional materials was focused on what we might anachronistically call the "economic" Trinity. Indeed, the earliest creedal formulations rarely go beyond the economic Trinity to speculate concerning the so-called immanent Trinity. Catherine Mowry LaCugna eloquently captures this aspect of the early history of Trinitarian doctrine:

> In the earliest centuries of Christian theology, the relationship of God, Christ, and the Spirit to each other was not pursued in its ontological dimensions, assisted by precise philosophical concepts. This would only come later. The focus of early theologians was the scriptural revelation of the one God (Father) in the incarnation of the Son and the sending of the Holy Spirit. The concern was with what was disclosed in *oikonomia,* not in contrast to *theologia,* nor with the Incarnation over against the Trinity, but simply the relationship of the one God (Father) to us as revealed in the drama of redemption.[38]

At this stage one can imagine someone objecting that an immanent doctrine of the Trinity is implicit in the early formulations of the rule of faith. Thus it is possible to maintain that the Trinitarian confession of faith presupposes a metaphysics of divine personhood. After all, proper personal names and identifying descriptions can and often

---

38. LaCugna, *God for Us,* p. 23. As LaCugna uses the terms, *oikonomia* refers to "the plan made known in the coming of Christ," while *theologia* refers to "the mystery of God's eternal nature" (p. 25). See also LaCugna, "The Trinitarian Mystery of God," in *Systematic Theology: Roman Catholic Perspectives,* ed. Francis Schussler Fiorenza and John P. Galvin (Minneapolis: Fortress, 1991).

do evoke metaphysical questions, especially when they are used to designate a divine person. This is a crucial point, especially as it pertains to
the final form the rule of faith eventually took at the Council of Constantinople in 381; but pursuing it will reinforce rather than undermine
my argument concerning the originating and primary function of
Trinitarian confessional materials in the early church.

Upon being taught a Trinitarian confession of faith, any intelligent
person who was baptized in the early church could have raised metaphysical questions concerning divine personhood. When early Christians began to raise such questions, the monarchian and modalist debates broke out in the third century. It is not difficult to see how this
happened. To the extent that Trinitarian confessions of faith were
functioning as sets of identifying descriptions that enabled people successfully to invoke the Christian God, the earliest of these confessions
do not make clear whether the proper personal name for God designates one God or three gods. Therefore, those who focused on the one
name of God embraced one or another version of modalism. Likewise,
those who emphasized the threefold name, "Father, Son, and Holy
Spirit," espoused subordinationism.[39]

During the fourth century, Arius, among others, began to raise a
series of questions concerning the nature of the God designated by the
baptismal formula and further identified by Trinitarian confessions of
faith (which were by this time instantiated in the various third-century
rules of faith).[40] Who is this God? What is the true nature of this God?
What kind of "person" is this? What kind of personal agent is this?

---

39. LaCugna is right when she argues that, prior to the fourth century, Christian
theologians advocated a "processional or economic subordinationism" and not "an ontological subordinationism." Eventually, however, "subordination at one level (the one
sent to the Sender) seemed to imply subordination at the other level (Son to Father)."
LaCugna, *God for Us,* p. 32.

40. There is a wealth of recent scholarship on Arius, the Arians, and the fourth-
century Arian controversy. Indeed, the work that has been done in this area was long
overdue, and the results have only just begun to make their way into general introduc-
tory textbooks on early Christian theology. Given the first-rate materials that are now
available on the topic, we can cut straight to the chase concerning the crucial questions
that the Arians were raising. For a full treatment of the Arian position, see Rowan Williams, *Arius: Heresy and Tradition* (London: Darton, Longman, and Todd, 1987). For an
analysis of the history of Arianism, see Maurice Wiles, *Archetypal Heresy: Arianism
Through the Centuries* (Oxford: Clarendon Press, 1996).

How are the Father, Son, and Holy Spirit related to one another? Are
they three separate persons? Are they one person? Are there three Gods,
or is there one God? In short, what is the true nature of this God?

In raising these questions, Arius was challenging the church to develop what theologians sometimes call a doctrine of the "immanent"
Trinity. LaCugna describes the situation eloquently as follows:

> For better or for worse, Arius pushed Christian theology and specu-
> lation away from *oikonomia,* with its undeniable subordination of
> Christ to God, to an ontology of *theologia.* . . . Arianism forces Chris-
> tian thinkers to spell out their convictions about the nature of ulti-
> mate reality in relation to the person of Christ. In effect, Arianism
> forced theologians to articulate what they believed to be the nature
> of *theologia* which, as was by then clear, was different in some impor-
> tant respects from what was revealed in *oikonomia.*[41]

The first thing to notice about the questions the Trinitarian rule
of faith evoked in the fourth century is that they are metaphysical and
not epistemological in nature. The very fact that the rule of faith
evoked metaphysical questions suggests that it was not functioning
first and foremost as a criterion in epistemology. On the contrary, it
was functioning to provide a realistic conception of God on which a
particular vision of redemption and the practices designed to initiate
persons into that vision could be explained and understood.

The next thing to notice is that, when Arius began to raise metaphysical questions with more force than such questions had ever been
raised before, it was not a foregone conclusion that the fourth-century
theologians would deem it necessary to respond. After all, apart from
the Arian controversy, early Christian theologians do not seem especially interested in speculation about the immanent Trinity. On the
contrary, they are quite content to leave such matters in the realm of
mystery. In fact, the evidence suggests that early Christian theologians
were deeply reluctant to say anything at all about the immanent Trinity. As William S. Babcock observes, even when they did say something,
the "key terms and concepts" that they used to mark "the distinctions
of person in God were systematically drained of content until they

---

41. LaCugna, *God for Us,* p. 37.

served only to register the point that the distinctions exist, that God is triune."[42] Babcock continues:

> Thus, Gregory of Nazianzus maintained that while begottenness is the distinguishing mark of the Son within the undivided being of God, not even the angels can conceive the manner of the Son's generation; and Augustine claimed that the word "person" is no more than the verbal counter we use in order to say something (rather than simply remaining silent) when we are asked about the three in God.[43]

While Babcock's point is an important one, it does not explain why the fourth-century theologians did not think it was acceptable simply to remain silent. In other words, Babcock's observation leaves unanswered the question of why the fourth-century church fathers deemed it necessary to take up the Arian challenge at all. Even a cursory analysis of the controversy reveals that fourth-century theologians took up the Arian challenge because they detected that the Christian vision of salvation was in jeopardy. They risked the introduction of immanent Trinitarian material into the rule of faith (e.g., the *homoousios*) strictly for the purposes of safeguarding the Christian vision of redemption. Thus Athanasius says:

> But this would not have come to pass, had the Word been a creature; for with a creature, the devil . . . would have ever continued the battle, and man, being between the two, had been ever in peril of death, having none in whom and through whom he might be joined to God and delivered from all fear. Whence the truth shews us that the Word is not of things originate, but rather Himself their Framer. For therefore did He assume the body originate and human, that having renewed it as its Framer, He might deify it in Himself, and thus might introduce us all into the kingdom of heaven after his likeness.[44]

The identifying descriptions incorporated into the rule of faith at Nicea and reaffirmed at Constantinople served the same purpose as

---

42. William S. Babcock, "A Changing of the Christian God," *Interpretation* 45, no. 2 (1991): 140.

43. Babcock, "Christian God," p. 140. Babcock cites Gregory of Nazianzus, *Orations*, 29:8, and Augustine, *On the Trinity*, 7.6.11.

44. Athanasius, *Against the Arians*, 2.21.70.

the identifying descriptions that were selected and used in the earliest Trinitarian confessions of faith. The identifying descriptions added at Nicea were added strictly to help designate God in such a way that catechumens could understand how, through participation in the activities constitutive of salvation in the early church, their sins could be forgiven and their nature restored. Far from undermining the preceding argument concerning the function of Trinitarian confessions of faith in the early church, the fourth-century church fathers' effort to "fill out" the name for God given in the rule of faith with identifying descriptions of the immanent relations between the three divine persons actually reinforces and strengthens it.

From the baptismal formula to the Nicene-Constantinopolitan Creed, Trinitarian confessions of faith in the early church functioned primarily to designate God in such a way as to explain, to make understandable, and ultimately to safeguard and to support a very rich conception of salvation — a conception of salvation on which the real transformation of humans was possible through participation in catechesis, prayer, baptism, the Eucharist, preaching, the liturgy, exorcism, and other practices around which the life of the church revolved. To be sure, assent was involved, but it was primarily assent to propositions about the saving activities of God, that is, propositions about the economic Trinity. Upon giving assent to these propositions, the Christian's natural response was to offer praise and thanksgiving to God, a task for which the triune name for God was indispensable.

Finally, as the name for God, the Trinity enabled early Christians to interact in a host of ways with the God who they believed was the very source of life and who was therefore capable of overcoming all that opposes life, including the demonic and even death itself. In their encounters with Jesus Christ and the Holy Spirit, early Christians had experienced physical, intellectual, and spiritual healing. They experienced the renewing of their minds, hearts, souls, and even their bodies. They were convinced that they had encountered none other than the high God of the universe. Their natural response to all of this was to use the name God had given them to invoke God in prayer and to give thanks in worship and praise. In early Christian theology, doxology took precedence over epistemology and metaphysical speculation.

CHAPTER 2

Assent: Scripture and Salvation

This assent is called faith.

William Laud

In the preceding chapter I maintained that the Trinity was first and foremost the proper personal name for God in the early church, and that the rule of faith was an accompanying set of identifying descriptions indicating the actions undertaken by the triune God on behalf of humans. The Trinitarian confessional statements enshrined in the rule of faith and the creed functioned primarily to inform people of the identity, character, and purposes of the God Christians were invoking in catechesis, demon exorcism, baptism, the Eucharist, and worship. The Christian God became incarnate in Jesus of Nazareth and dwelt continually among the Christians in the person of the Holy Spirit beginning at Pentecost. To invoke the triune God by name was to invoke a deity who was intimately involved in the world. Upon contemplating these things, it was only natural for Christians to invoke the Father, Son, and Holy Spirit in acts of repentance, in prayer, and in worship, thanksgiving, and praise.

In this chapter I fast-forward to the period of the Continental and English Reformations of the sixteenth and seventeenth centuries, where a gradual eroding of the Trinity as the rule of faith takes place. To be sure, the doctrine of the Trinity retains a prominent place in Protestant theology throughout most of this period. Over time, however, the content of the rule of faith shifts from the Trinity to Scripture, that is, from a set of identifying descriptions concerning divine identity and divine action supporting the use of the triune name for God in the catechetical and liturgical life of the church to a source containing clear and intelligible propositions to be consulted in a range of epistemological activities, most notably in intellectual assent.

To uncover what is at stake here, one must come to grips with three things. First, it is important to see how and why Scripture gradually displaces the Trinity as the official Protestant rule of faith. Thus I will argue that Scripture emerges initially as a second *unofficial* rule of faith alongside the Trinity and is only later officially and exclusively identified as such. Second, one needs to notice what happens when the shift is made from the Trinity to Scripture as the rule of faith, that is, from a set of identifying descriptions that aids invocation to an epistemic criterion that provides a reliable ground for intellectual assent. Of special importance here is what happens to the understanding of salvation as a result of this shift. Third, it is crucial to discern a subtle but powerful shift in the understanding of God that takes place when Scripture is made the rule of faith in English Protestant theology.

Resolving a Crisis of Assurance: Scripture as Unofficial Rule of Faith

It is difficult to identify when and how Scripture first began to displace the Trinity as the rule of faith in Protestant theology. Numerous background developments contribute to the transition, and I will not be able to provide a detailed history of the various issues involved. One of the most crucial issues in the process is a conceptual shift from canon to criterion in the understanding of Scripture itself. In the early church, Scripture was regarded as one among many ecclesial canons. As such, it functioned as a means of grace alongside baptism, the Eucharist, the liturgy, saints and images, and so on. By the time of the Reformation, however, Scripture was well on its way to functioning primarily as an epistemic criterion in theology and only secondarily, if at all, as a means of grace.[1]

---

1. For the conceptual shift in the understanding of Scripture from canon to criterion, see William J. Abraham, *Canon and Criterion in Christian Theology* (New York: Oxford

For my immediate purposes, I survey two closely related pastoral crises brought on by the Protestant Reformation. These crises set the stage for the gradual displacement of the creed by Scripture as the Protestant rule of faith and, with that displacement, the beginning of a deep and decisive shift in the Protestant understanding of God and salvation.

In the sixteenth-century Continental Reformation, it is only in an unofficial and subtle way that Scripture begins to displace the Trinity as the rule of faith. There can be no question, for example, that the Magisterial Reformers were deeply committed to the doctrine of the Trinity as expressed in the Nicene Creed.[2] I must emphasize that the Reformers, in breaking with Rome, at no point abandoned the Trinity. Thus the Augsburg Confession begins this way: "We unanimously hold and teach, in accordance with the decrees of the Council of Nicaea, that there is one divine essence, equal in power and alike eternal: God the Father, God the Son, God the Holy Spirit."[3] Indeed, all of the major Reformation confessions gave the doctrine of the Trinity a place of prominence.[4]

What is true of Protestant confessional statements with regard to the Trinity is equally true of the Magisterial Reformers themselves. For example, John Calvin acknowledged and stressed the importance of the Trinity: he argued that, unless we think of God as Trinity, "only the bare and empty name of God flits about in our brains, to the exclusion of the true God."[5] In the early stages of the Reformation, then, one should not imagine that the Trinity was not believed, taught, or confessed. On the contrary, through the writings of the Magisterial Re-

---

University Press, 1998); see also William J. Abraham, Jason E. Vickers, and Natalie B. Van Kirk, eds., *Canonical Theism: A Proposal for Theology and the Church* (Grand Rapids: Eerdmans, 2008).

2. In *The Small Catechism* of 1529, Martin Luther complained that people who were "supposed to be Christian" did not know "the Lord's Prayer, the Creed, or the Ten Commandments." Jaroslav Pelikan and Valerie Hotchkiss, eds., *Creeds and Confessions of Faith in the Christian Tradition,* 3 vols. (New Haven: Yale University Press, 2003), 2:31.

3. Pelikan and Hotchkiss, *Creeds and Confessions of Faith,* 2:58.

4. For an analysis of the place of the Trinity in Reformation confessions, see Jaroslav Pelikan, *Credo: Historical and Theological Guide to Creeds and Confessions of Faith in the Christian Tradition* (New Haven: Yale University Press, 2003), pp. 142-57, 472-80.

5. John Calvin, *Institutes of the Christian Religion,* ed. John T. McNeill, trans. Ford Lewis Battles (Philadelphia: Westminster, 1960), 1.13.2.

formers, the major Protestant confessional statements, and Protestant worship, the Trinity continued to function as the name for God and the rule of faith for Christian life and thought.[6]

However, if Scripture did not replace the Trinity as the rule of faith during the early years of the Reformation in an official way, there is good evidence that it began to do so in unofficial ways. For many people in the sixteenth and seventeenth centuries, the prospects of joining a Protestant church precipitated a crisis of assurance. It was no small thing to leave behind the Catholic Church into which they had been baptized and confirmed for an upstart, renegade church that had either eliminated or severely revised the various rituals and daily practices their family and friends had turned to for assurance.[7]

Among the practices the Reformers eliminated were the cult of the saints, the use of images, the sacrament of penance, and devotion to Mary. The practices associated with the Virgin that were designed to bring about consolation in believers' hearts were especially difficult to abandon: many had long found comfort and consolation in the daily cycle of prayers to the Virgin made available in the widely popular Books of Hours. Prayers entrusted to the Virgin were sure to be heard and answered, since the Son could not refuse the requests of his own mother. Similarly, absolution in penance and the real presence of Christ in the Eucharist had long provided a deep sense of assurance that the benefits of the atoning sacrifice of Christ, even Christ himself, were readily available in the Roman Catholic Church to all who truly repented of their sins. The entire late medieval penitential and sacramental system reflects a deep conviction among Catholic priests and laity alike that God had promised "to bestow grace on all those who did their best."[8]

6. It is worth noting that while the Magisterial Reformers retained the Trinity, the use of the term "rule of faith" is ambiguous at best, and rarely can it be shown to refer explicitly to the Trinity. For example, the Second Helvetic Confession of 1566 says that "Scripture is to be interpreted in no other way than out of itself and is to be explained by the rule of faith and love" (Helvetic Confession, 1:2, quoted in Pelikan, Credo, p. 152). Clearly, the rule of faith is not here equated with Scripture.

7. For the elimination of various rituals and practices, see John Calvin, "On the Necessity of Reforming the Church," in Calvin: Theological Treatises, trans. J. K. S. Reid (Philadelphia: Westminster Press, 1954), 22:184-216.

8. Madeleine Gray, The Protestant Reformation: Beliefs and Practices (Brighton, UK: Sussex Academic Press, 2003), pp. 18-19.

By contrast, questions abounded concerning the efficacy of baptism, the sacrament, ministers' orders, and the supposed salvation being offered in Protestant churches. It was thus incumbent on the Magisterial Reformers to identify the marks of a true church, and thus Luther argued that the true church was constituted by the word of God, the sacraments of baptism and Eucharist rightly administered, the office of the keys and of the ministry, public worship, and the bearing of the cross.

Despite the protestations of the Reformers, Catholic theologians and priests publicly denied the legitimacy of the salvation offered in Protestant communions. Thus the very existence of a rival church, with rival sacraments and a rival vision of salvation, triggered a crisis of assurance that was felt by many people in deep and profoundly personal ways. The dilemma posed by Protestantism was not simply a matter of people choosing from among an entire range of churches as long as they were sincere in their beliefs. What was at stake was nothing less than the truth about God and about where and how salvation was available to humans.[9]

Despite the insistence of Catholic priests that salvation was only available in the Catholic Church, it would have been difficult to ignore the fact that a rival church with a rival vision of salvation had emerged. In the Protestant vision, salvation was taken completely out of human

---

9. It is important to recall that the romantic idea that what matters most is not what one believes but how sincerely and passionately one believes it would have been entirely unintelligible to Catholics and Protestants alike. Thus Isaiah Berlin says: "Suppose you had a conversation in the sixteenth century with somebody fighting in the great religious wars which tore Europe apart at that period, and suppose you said to a Catholic of that period, engaged in hostilities, 'Of course these Protestants believe what is false; of course to believe what they believe is to court perdition; of course they are dangerous to the salvation of human souls, than which there is nothing more important; but they are so sincere, they die so readily for their cause, their integrity is so splendid, one must yield a certain need of admiration for the moral dignity and sublimity of people who are prepared to do that.' Such a sentiment would have been unintelligible. Anyone who really knew, supposed themselves to know, the truth, say, a Catholic who believed in the truths preached to him by the Church, would have known that persons able to put the whole of themselves into the theory and practice of falsehood were simply dangerous persons, and that the more sincere they were, the more dangerous, the more mad." Isaiah Berlin, *The Roots of Romanticism* (Princeton: Princeton University Press, 1999), p. 9.

hands and placed in the hands of God. Indeed, the whole Protestant outlook revolved around a conception of faith *(fiducia)* as radical trust in the grace and mercy of God for salvation. Because of the depths of human sin, the Reformers argued, individual humans could do nothing to merit God's forgiveness or pardon. A person's best and most sincere efforts were inescapably corrupt and self-serving. However, the good news was that salvation was from beginning to end a matter of divine grace and mercy, not human works.

The fracturing of the one, holy, catholic and apostolic church over the vision of salvation precipitated an epistemological crisis throughout much of Europe. Numerous questions surfaced quite naturally: How could a person know which church and which vision of salvation was the right one? Which vision of salvation was true? Were Protestant assertions of the falsehood of many Catholic beliefs warranted? On what basis could a person decide these matters?

By raising these questions, the Reformation triggered a crisis of assurance in and around the issue of ecclesial authority in an unprecedented way. To be sure, the Great Schism between East and West had raised the question of ecclesial authority with considerable force in the eleventh century. However, the epistemological crisis triggered by the Reformation was felt with even greater force and intensity than the crisis brought on by the Great Schism for the simple reason that Catholic and Reformation churches were in much closer proximity to each other than the Eastern and Western churches had been. In response to questions about the authority of the Protestant church and especially about the truthfulness or reliability of the Protestant vision of salvation, Luther took his well-known stand on Scripture over against the received tradition of the church.[10] Thus Luther developed the famous Protestant principle of *sola Scriptura* primarily with the vision of salvation or justification — *sola fidei* — in mind. The doctrine of the Trinity was simply not a matter of controversy at this time. The issue at hand had to do with what, if anything, humans were required to do in order to obtain salvation.

In time, Catholic theologians would press questions concerning how Protestants could secure the appeal to Scripture apart from the

---

10. Martin Luther, "On the Councils and the Churches," in *Selected Writings of Martin Luther, 1539-1546,* ed. Theodore G. Tappert (Philadelphia: Fortress, 1967), 4:325-42.

testimony of the church. They put the question this way: Apart from the witness of the church down through the ages, how can Protestants be certain that Scripture is the Word of God? Luther, in responding to this question, appealed to the conscience of the individual believer.[11] This move, as Catholic theologians never tired of pointing out, was arbitrary, if not question-begging.

Calvin took another route: he developed and used his famous doctrine of the inner witness of the Holy Spirit.[12] According to this doctrine, the Holy Spirit confirms in the mind and heart of each individual that Scripture is the Word of God. In addition to securing the appeal to Scripture, the doctrine of the inner witness could also function as a safeguard against any residual tendencies toward Pelagianism. According to this analysis, humans are completely reliant on the Holy Spirit to awaken them to the Word of God in Scripture.

It is crucial to recognize what was going on here. The problem of ecclesial authority was prompting Catholic and Protestant theologians to put forth warrants for their respective visions of salvation. Ironically, the efficacy of Catholic and Protestant visions of salvation and eucharistic and baptismal practices increasingly came to depend directly on epistemic proposals and only indirectly on divine identity and action. This had immediate effects in virtually every aspect of Christian life and practice. For example, whereas the Iconodules had once secured the use of images in worship and private devotion by appeal to divine identity and action in the incarnation, Reformation iconoclasts dismissed the use of images because it was prohibited in Scripture.[13]

---

11. For the appeal to conscience, see Luther's confession at the Diet of Worms of 1521 in *Documents of the Christian Church,* ed. Henry Bettenson (New York: Oxford University Press, 1947), p. 285.

12. For the argument from the inner witness of the Holy Spirit, see Calvin, *Institutes,* 1.7.4.

13. For the appeal to the incarnation, see St. John of Damascus, *On the Divine Images: Three Apologies Against Those Who Attack the Divine Images,* trans. David Anderson (Crestwood, NY: St. Vladimir's, 1997), 1:16. For an appeal to scriptural prohibitions, see Andreas von Karlstadt's "On the Abolition of Images," in *European Reformations Sourcebook,* ed. Carter Lindberg (Oxford: Blackwell Publishers, 2000), pp. 57-59. The elimination of images and the cult of the saints from the canonical heritage of the church during the English Reformation began with the Lorrardy movement in the mid-sixteenth century and is well documented. The best resources include John Phillips, *The Reformation of Images: Destruction of Art in England, 1535-1660* (Berkeley: University of Cali-

In unofficial ways, Scripture was fast emerging within Protestantism as a second rule of faith alongside the Trinity.[14] More precisely,
Scripture was emerging as a rule of faith designed to authorize the
Protestant vision of salvation and the sacraments. For a brief period
the term "rule of faith" could be used to refer to Scripture or the historic creeds.[15] Few, if any, noticed the equivocation in the use of the

---

fornia Press, 1973); Stanford E. Lehmberg, *The Reformation of Cathedrals: Cathedrals in English Society, 1485-1603* (Princeton: Princeton University Press, 1988), esp. chs. 3 and 4; Margaret Aston, *England's Iconoclasts: Laws Against Images* (Oxford: Clarendon Press, 1988); and
Eamon Duffy, *The Stripping of the Altars: Traditional Religion in England 1400-1580* (New Haven: Yale University Press, 1992).

14. A good place to see this is in the Augsburg Confession. While there is no article
on Scripture in the "Chief Articles of Faith," there are repeated appeals to Scripture as
the basis for corrections in the section entitled "Articles in which an Account is Given of
the Abuses Which have been Corrected" (Pelikan and Hotchkiss, *Creeds and Confessions of
Faith*, 2:77-118).

15. The appeal to Scripture as the rule of faith alongside the creeds emerges in the
Lutheran tradition in an official way for the first time in the Formula of Concord in
1577. The Formula presents itself at the outset as a "comprehensive summary, rule, and
norm according to which all doctrines should be judged and the errors which intruded
should be explained and decided in a Christian way." The first article then reads: "We
believe, teach, and confess that the prophetic and apostolic writings of the Old and New
Testaments are the only rule and norm according to which all doctrines and teachers
alike must be appraised and judged." Concerning the Apostles' Creed, the Nicene Creed,
and the Athanasian Creed, the third article says: "We pledge ourselves to these, and we
hereby reject all heresies and teachings which have been introduced into the church of
God contrary to them" (Pelikan and Hotchkiss, *Creeds and Confessions*, 2:168). The appeal
to Scripture as the rule of faith emerges in an official way much earlier in the Reformed
theological tradition. As early as 1528, for example, the second article of The Ten Theses
of Bern declares: "The church of Christ makes no laws or commandments without
God's word. Hence all human traditions, which are called ecclesiastical commandments, are binding upon us only in so far as they are based on and commanded by God's
word" (Pelikan and Hotchkiss, *Creeds and Confessions*, 2:217). Similarly, the Tetrapolitan
Confession of 1530 begins by exhorting Reformed ministers "to teach from the pulpit
nothing else than is either contained in the Holy Scriptures or hath sure ground
therein" (Pelikan and Hotchkiss, *Creeds and Confessions*, 2:221). Finally, the emergence of
the appeal to Scripture as the rule of faith is most clear in the First Helvetic Confession
(1536), whose first article reads: "The holy, divine, biblical Scripture, which is the word of
God inspired by the Holy Spirit and delivered to the world by the prophets and apostles,
is the most ancient, most perfect, and loftiest teaching and alone deals with everything
that serves the true knowledge, love, and honor of God, as well as true piety and the
making of a godly, honest, and blessed life" (Pelikan and Hotchkiss, *Creeds and Confes-*

term. However, by the middle of the seventeenth century in England, the term would be used officially and exclusively to refer to the respective criteria or warrants to which Catholic and Protestant theologians appealed in order to authorize their competing visions of salvation.[16]

What is the significance of the shift from the Trinity to Scripture as the rule of faith in Protestantism? It is not simply that Protestants chose Scripture over the historic creeds. Rather, the significance of the shift from the creeds to Scripture has to do with the primary *function* of Scripture as the rule of faith. In the early church the rule of faith functioned primarily to support the use of the triune name for God in baptism, worship, and the like. It functioned as a *means of grace* to assist people in a complex range of activities through which they came to know, love, interact with, and have communion with the triune God. In the context of the Reformation, the rule of faith was now being asked to function primarily as an *epistemic criterion* by which the true vision of salvation could be determined. Thus the shift was not merely a shift in the *identity* of the rule of faith, a shift from the great Trinitarian creeds to Scripture; it was also a deep shift in the kind of *activities* for which the rule of faith was thought to be important, a shift from *doxological* to *epistemological* activities.

The Rule of Faith and Assurance
in Early Seventeenth-Century England

Like the Continental Reformation before it, the English Reformation began life with a robust commitment to the Trinity. At no point do the

---

sions, 2:282). Indeed, the first five articles of the First Helvetic Confession have to do with the identity, authority, interpretation, and purpose of Scripture. Thus the doctrine of God does not show up until article six.

16. For one of the earliest and best examples of this usage of "rule" by Protestants and Catholics, see William Laud, *A Relation of the Conference between William Laud and Mr. Fisher the Jesuit* (London: Macmillan, 1901). We will highlight several prominent features of Archbishop Laud's argument below. The nineteenth-century Russian Orthodox theologian Alexei Khomiakov was one of the first to perceive that Catholic and Protestant theologians conceived of tradition and Scripture primarily as epistemic criteria or warrants in theology. See Alexei Khomiakov, *Ultimate Questions,* ed. Alexander Schmemann (Crestwood, NY: St. Vladimir's, 1975), pp. 50-51.

Magisterial English Reformers — Thomas Cranmer, William Jewel, and Richard Hooker — ever abandon the Trinity. On the contrary, their robust commitment to the Trinity is clearly reflected in the prominent place it was given in the Thirty-Nine Articles of Religion, which begin with the Trinity and then go on to affirm the Apostles', Nicene, and Athanasian creeds.[17] Likewise, in the Book of Common Prayer, the Trinity plays a prominent role in the church year, the prayers of the people, and in baptism and the Eucharist. Furthermore, the Trinity occupies a central place in early English Protestant catechetical materials, hymns, and poetry.[18] Thus it is clear that the Trinity was still functioning as the rule of faith in liturgical or doxological settings in the early years of the English Reformation. In these settings, as they had done in the early church, Trinitarian confessional materials shaped in deep and profound ways the most basic conception of the nature and purposes of God in the minds and hearts of early English Protestants. The God they called on in their prayers was none other than the God identified in the great historic creeds of Christianity.

a bigger story

While the early English Reformers were deeply committed to the Trinity, they also inherited from the Continental Reformation the appeal to Scripture as warrant for the Protestant church and for the Protestant vision of salvation. As reflected in the Articles of Religion, the Magisterial English Reformers insisted that all doctrine had been derived from Scripture and that the decisions of ecumenical councils were to be accepted only to the extent that they could be shown to derive from Scripture. What the Articles did not provide was a theory or method of derivation. Just how doctrines were to be derived would become a key issue in the disputes over the Trinity that lay ahead. But it is important not to get ahead of ourselves at this point. We can readily see in English Protestant theology that Scripture was operating as a second rule of faith alongside the Trinity from very early on. As one

17. Gerald Bray, *Documents of the English Reformation* (Minneapolis: Fortress, 1994), pp. 284-311.

18. For the Trinity in early English Protestant catechetical materials, see Ian Green, *The Christian's ABC* (Oxford: Oxford University Press, 1996). For the Trinity in early English Protestant hymnody, see J. R. Watson, *The English Hymn* (Oxford: Oxford University Press, 1997). For an excellent review of the Trinity in English poetry of the late sixteenth and early seventeenth centuries, see Philip Dixon, *Nice and Hot Disputes: The Doctrine of the Trinity in the Seventeenth Century* (London: T&T Clark, 2003), pp. 21-25.

scholar puts it, by the turn of the seventeenth century, the Bible was "thought to be a stable foundation that could support a structure of any size."[19]

At the beginning of the seventeenth century, the debate between Catholic and Protestant theologians over the identity of the rule of faith had reached a fever pitch. The volume and variety of literature on the rule of faith during this period is truly astonishing. On both sides, bishops, professors, parish priests, and even laity set forth and defended the rival rules of faith not only in lengthy treatises but also in shorter letters, pamphlets, and sermons. Almost every notable Protestant theologian wrote a major treatise on the subject. Often unable to publish anything beyond anonymous pamphlets for much of the century, Catholic theologians relied on treatises smuggled in from Antwerp and Paris.[20] In the vast majority of cases, the rule of faith was clearly thought of as an epistemic criterion, not a means of grace. This was equally true of Protestant and Catholic arguments.

As the controversy wore on, each side placed increasing emphasis on the importance of an unwavering commitment to its rule of faith. Eventually, Catholic and Protestant identities came to be inextricably tied to the appeal to Scripture and tradition mediated by the church and to Scripture alone respectively.[21] Thus, as early as the 1630s, English

19. David Katz, *God's Last Words: Reading the English Bible from the Reformation to Fundamentalism* (New Haven: Yale University Press, 2004), p. 74.

20. The two most influential Catholic theologians whose works were imported from Paris and Antwerp were Francois Veron and Edward Worsley, both of whom were Jesuits. See François Verón, *The Rule of Catholick Faith: Sever'd from the Opinions of the Schools, Mistakes of the Ignorant, and Abuses of the Vulgar* (Paris, 1660); and Edward Worsley, *Protestancy without Principles or, Sectaries Unhappy Fall from Infallibility to Fancy* (Antwerp, 1668). See also Edward Worsley, *Reason and Religion, or the Certain Rule of Faith, Where the Infallibility of the Roman Catholick Church is Asserted, against Atheists, Heathens, Jews, Turks, and all Sectaries* (Antwerp, 1672). Verón was a Jesuit controversialist who deeply influenced John Sergeant's skeptical arguments for the Catholic rule of faith (see n. 23 below for Sergeant's work). For an account of Veron's appeal to the skeptical tradition in defense of the Catholic rule of faith, see Richard H. Popkin, *The History of Skepticism from Erasmus to Spinoza* (Berkeley: University of California Press, 1979), pp. 70-79.

21. The traditional notion that classical Anglican theology was based on a triad of Scripture, reason, and tradition is simply false. At best, Anglican theology was derived from the dyad of Scripture and reason. See Abraham, *Canon and Criterion*, pp. 188-214. See also Hugh Trevor-Roper, *Catholics, Anglicans, and Puritans: Seventeenth Century Essays* (Chicago: University of Chicago Press, 1988), p. 45.

Protestant theologians used the term "rule of faith" to refer exclusively to Scripture. From this point on, it is increasingly rare to find English Protestant theologians making reference to any of the historic creeds as the rule of faith.

Throughout the rule of faith controversy in seventeenth-century England, Catholic propagandists pressed Protestants to secure the appeal to Scripture in a noncircular and nonregressive way. But near the beginning of the seventeenth century, Catholic theologians developed a devastating second line of attack against the adequacy of Scripture as the rule of faith. With increasing frequency, they pointed out that, on the basis of Scripture alone, Protestants had not been able to agree on matters of doctrine and ecclesial practice.[22] Therefore, even if Protestants could secure the appeal to Scripture as the rule of faith, they also had to demonstrate that the results of such an appeal would not be disastrous for unity of Christian belief and practice. Nor did this argument go away quickly. For example, in the second half of the century, John Sergeant declared that the books of Scripture were "mere black spots on paper," and an infallible judge was needed in order to determine not only which books were canonical but also to interpret the meaning of the black spots.[23]

While Catholic Counter-Reformation theologians were attacking the English Protestant rule of faith from without, a deep pastoral crisis of assurance was threatening to erode the authority of the English Protestant vision from within. In an effort to ensure that salvation would remain wholly a matter of divine grace and mercy, Luther and Calvin had made the absolute transcendence of God and the epistemic poverty of human beings with regard to the knowledge of God and of

22. Concerning disagreement among Protestants in seventeenth-century England, see G. R. Cragg, *From Puritanism to the Age of Reason: A Study of Changes in Religious Thought within the Church of England 1660 to 1700* (London: Cambridge University Press, 1950). Cragg says: "Within the dominant theological school there were innumerable shades of opinion, and the various sects could fight bitterly amongst themselves, in spite of the Calvinism common to the all" (Cragg, *From Puritanism*, p. 17).

23. John Sergeant, *Sure Footing in Christianity, or Rational Discourses on the Rule of Faith* (London, 1665), p. 68. For a very helpful analysis of Sergeant's arguments, see Beverley C. Southgate, "'Beating Down Skepticism': The Solid Philosophy of John Sergeant, 1623-1707," in *English Philosophy in the Age of Locke*, ed. M. A. Stewart (Oxford: Clarendon Press, 2000), pp. 281-315.

salvation touchstones of Protestant theology.[24] On the one hand, Luther had developed these emphases in his theology of the cross and in his doctrine of the hiddenness of God. On the other hand, Calvin had developed the doctrines of the inscrutable will of God and of unconditional double predestination in order to emphasize the transcendence of God and to safeguard the tradition against any and all residual forms of Pelagianism. (no original sin)

To be sure, the dual emphasis on the transcendence of God and on the utter incapacity of human beings to obtain knowledge of things divine was intended to drive home the point that humans were utterly dependent on the grace and mercy of God for salvation. However, the crisis of faith these doctrines were meant to induce proved too much for many of those in early seventeenth-century England to bear. Given the dark inscrutability of the will of God, many worried that they were not among the elect.[25] Madeleine Gray offers a powerful summary of this development:

> The Protestant emphasis on the priesthood of all believers and the importance of personal faith stripped away the helpful communal rituals of late medieval Catholicism and left people defenseless before an omnipotent God. The doctrine of predestination gave them no assurance of salvation. Some were themselves driven to despair and even to suicide.[26]

24. For a helpful account of these aspects of the Magisterial Reformers' theology, see William Placher, *The Domestication of Transcendence: How Modern Thinking about God Went Wrong* (Louisville: Westminster, 1996), chs. 3-4. See also Brian Gerrish, "To the Unknown God: Luther and Calvin on the Hiddenness of God," *Journal of Religion* 53 (1973): 263-92.

25. For how dark the Calvinist God could be, see James Hogg, *The Private Memoirs and Confessions of a Justified Sinner* (New York: Oxford University Press, 1969). Known as "The Ettrick Shepherd," Hogg (1770-1825) was a self-educated lay Christian from Ettrick Hall in the Scottish Borders. In a most telling passage, Hogg says: "From the moment, I conceived it decreed, not that I should be a minister of the gospel, but a champion of it, to cut off the enemies of the Lord from the face of the earth; and I rejoiced in the commission, finding it more congenial to my nature to be cutting sinners off with the sword than to be haranguing them from the pulpit, striving to produce an effect which God, by his act of absolute predestination, had for ever rendered impracticable" (Hogg, *Private Memoirs*, p. 116).

26. Gray, *Protestant Reformation*, p. 38.

Thus English clerics during this period were faced with a twofold dilemma. On the one hand, they needed to respond to the twofold Catholic objection concerning the grounds and adequacy of the appeal to Scripture as the rule of faith. On the other hand, they had to address the problem of assurance brought on by the doctrine of election in orthodox Calvinism.

Leading English Protestant theologians discovered, to their delight, help coming from abroad in the work of the Dutch theologian Jacob Harmensen (1560-1609), the Latin form of whose name was "Arminius."[27] English Protestant theologians found in the writings of Arminius the makings of a promising solution to both sides of the dilemma they now faced.[28] Initially, they picked up on and developed those features in Arminius's theology that spoke directly to the problem of assurance triggered by the orthodox Calvinist vision of salvation. Frederick Beiser provides a splendid summary of these features:

> The theology of Arminianism was essentially a rejection of the Calvinist doctrine of predestination, with its rigid determinism, "dark and inscrutable decrees," and eternal separation of mankind into the elect and the reprobate. Against this severe and forbidding doctrine, the Arminians defended a moderate Pelagianism, the doctrines of universal redemption, free will, and good works.[29]

27. Arminius's theology made its way to England primarily through the work of Hugo Grotius. For an account of Grotius's contribution, see Frederick Beiser, *The Sovereignty of Reason: The Defense of Rationality in the Early English Enlightenment* (Princeton: Princeton University Press, 1996), pp. 91-94.

28. A "neo-Erasmian" movement, whose twin doctrines were "free will" and the availability of salvation for all, emerged in the late sixteenth century at both Oxford and Cambridge and helped to prepare the way for Arminianism. Among the chief proponents of these doctrines were Peter Baro, "a Huguenot who had escaped from the massacre of St. Bartholomew in France," and Baro's best students at Cambridge, Lancelot Andrewes, master of Pembroke College, and John Overall, master of St. Catharine's College and Regius professor of divinity.

29. Frederick Beiser, *Sovereignty of Reason*, p. 90. For a helpful summary of Arminian theology, see esp. Nicholas Tyacke, *Anti-Calvinists: The Rise of English Arminianism c. 1590-1640* (Oxford: Oxford University Press, 1987). For brief but helpful summaries, see Roger Lockyer, *The Early Stuarts* (London: Longman, 1989), pp. 307-24, and Gerald Cragg, *Freedom and Authority: A Study of English Thought in the Early Seventeenth Century* (Philadelphia: Westminster, 1975), pp. 76-126.

Adopting those features of Arminius's theology enabled English Protestant theologians to address the problem of assurance brought on by Calvin's doctrine of the inscrutable will of God clearly and head-on. Above all, Arminianism promised to restore to human agents a determining role in the drama of salvation.[30] In doing so, however, Arminianism put back on the table the two great questions that had given rise to the Protestant Reformation in the first place. First, just how determining was the human role in salvation? Second, and more importantly, what was the precise nature of the human role in salvation? What was it, exactly, that humans needed to do in order to be saved?

The question about the nature of the human role in salvation came into sharp focus when Archbishop William Laud (1573-1645) set out to address the Catholic challenge to Protestant authority.[31] As things turned out, Laud's solution to the problem of ecclesial authority suggested a powerful and, for many, deeply convincing solution to the problem of personal assurance. In the end, however, Laud's solution would also precipitate a subtle but immensely powerful shift in the English Protestant vision of God and of salvation — a shift that remains with us to this day.

By the early seventeenth century, Luther's and Calvin's responses to the Catholic challenge concerning the appeal to Scripture as the rule of faith had come under considerable strain. Catholic theologians had repeatedly argued in a skeptical fashion that the standard arguments in defense of Scripture as the rule of faith were guilty of circular reasoning. And if they were not guilty of circular reasoning, then the proponents of the arguments on behalf of Scripture could easily be forced into a regress *ad infinitum*.[32] Appeals to conscience or to the inner wit-

---

30. I should note that the Arminians in the Netherlands paid a heavy price for this after the Synod of Dordrecht. For example, Grotius himself was sentenced to life in prison and confined to the castle of Loevestein.

31. The need to address the Catholic challenge came to a head for Archbishop Laud when, in April 1622, by the king's orders, Laud took part in a controversy with Percy, a Jesuit, known as John Fisher, the aim of which was to prevent the conversion of the Countess of Buckingham to Romanism. A record of the debate was later published as *A Relation of the Conference between William Laud and Mr. Fisher the Jesuit*. For the best introduction to the life and work of Archbishop Laud, see Hugh Trevor-Roper, *Archbishop Laud, 1573-1645* (London: Macmillan, 1988).

32. For a general account of the Catholic use of skeptical arguments, see Popkin, *The History of Skepticism*, pp. 1-17.

ness of the Holy Spirit were essentially appeals to private judgment and thus not open to criticism. A solution was needed that was equally available to everyone and hence did not involve circular reasoning or an infinite regress.

For Archbishop Laud, the appeal of Arminianism lay precisely here: Arminianism recaptured a role for the human agent in salvation, as I have already noted. In a brilliant move, Laud took this to mean that, with regard to the problem of authorizing Scripture, the solution did not have to be exclusively divine in nature. Thus, while recognizing that in some sense Scripture bears witness to itself, and while not rejecting the inner witness of the Holy Spirit, Laud argued that all clear-thinking and intellectually virtuous people could *by reason* discern that Scripture was the Word of God.[33] He says:

> For though this truth, that Scripture is the word of God, is not so demonstratively evident *a priori*, as to enforce assent; yet it is strengthened so abundantly with probable arguments, both from the light of nature itself and human testimony, that he must be very wilful and self-conceited that shall dare to suspect it.[34]

This is truly an extraordinary development within English Protestantism. If Arminianism had insisted on a determining role for the human agent in salvation, then Laud had argued that at least one aspect of that role had to do with the use of reason to secure Scripture. On orthodox Calvinist grounds, this would have been unthinkable: the epistemic consequences of sin were simply too great for reason to perform such a task.[35]

Laud disagreed with the Calvinist insistence on the radical epistemic consequences of sin, and he argued that reason must be capable of recognizing that Scripture was the Word of God so pagans would be "without excuse." On a more positive note, he argued that God had given reason to humans precisely so that they would have access to salvation. He says:

33. Laud, *Relation of the Conference*, pp. 71, 87-88, 119-32.

34. Laud, *Relation of the Conference*, p. 88.

35. See Merold Westphal, "Taking St. Paul Seriously: Sin as an Epistemological Category," in *Christian Philosophy*, ed. Thomas Flint (Notre Dame, IN: University of Notre Dame Press, 1990), pp. 200-26.

And certainly God did not give this admirable faculty of reasoning to the soul of man for any cause more prime than this, to discover, or to judge and allow, within the sphere of its own activity . . . of the way to Himself, when and howsoever it should be discovered.[36]

At this stage, Laud realized that his argument that reason secures the appeal to Scripture as the rule of faith also suggested a solution to the problem of assurance that had been triggered by the orthodox Calvinist doctrine of double predestination. If humans could discern that Scripture is the Word of God by way of their reason, then clearly salvation was in some way tied to the exercise of reason. Laud posited that, for reason to apprehend that Scripture is the Word of God, it must first be able to apprehend the meaning of the propositions contained therein. Accordingly, he argued that, on discerning Scripture to be the Word of God, humans must simply give their "full and firm assent" to those things contained in or deduced from Scripture in order to secure their salvation by faith. In a fateful moment for English Protestant theology, Laud concluded, "This assent is called faith."[37]

In taking this direction, Laud laid the groundwork for a new conception of salvation in English Protestantism. Instead of salvation having primarily to do with the invocation of the triune God in repentance, demon exorcism, baptism, and the Eucharist, and in worship, thanksgiving, and praise, it now had to do with the cognitive or rational activity of giving assent to propositions contained in or deduced from Scripture. Together with the rule of faith, salvation was being relocated from the domain of doxology to the domain of epistemology. Thus Laud concluded his argument concerning the exercise of the faculty of reason by insisting that, in the giving of assent to the propositions contained in Scripture, people would "grow up into a most infallible assurance."[38]

In an eloquent passage worth quoting at length, Peter Harrison

---

36. Laud, *Relation of the Conference,* p. 90. In the coming centuries, the emerging instability in the Calvinist tradition that we are tracing here would pull that tradition apart. Thus, in the nineteenth and twentieth centuries, the Dutch Calvinist tradition preserved the appeal to the inner witness of the Holy Spirit, while B. B. Warfield and the Princeton School championed the appeal to reason.

37. Laud, *Relation of the Conference,* p. 121.

38. Laud, *Relation of the Conference,* p. 131.

summarizes the outcome of these developments in early seventeenth-century English Protestant theology.

> Of the Five Arminian Articles, the first is of most concern to us. It states simply that God determined to save those who chose to believe in Jesus Christ. This deceptively bland declaration has a significance that goes well beyond the theological controversy it engendered. For now, effectively, the whole business of salvation no longer falls under divine jurisdiction. From the inaccessible reaches of the inscrutable will of God, it enters the realm of human affairs, of objective knowledge and human assent . . . . Certainly, the Calvinist emphasis on saving knowledge set the process in motion, but in removing the safeguard of divine initiative, in lifting the veil from the incomprehensible divine will, Arminianism had unwittingly transformed the divinely inspired saving knowledge into just another species of information. God's place as the object of faith had been subtly usurped by a set of doctrines. Faith was no longer a precarious balancing act between *assensus* and *fiducia:* assent had triumphed over trust. Saving knowledge had begun a descent from the heavens to take its place in human discourse.[39]

After Laud, the appeal to reason to authorize Scripture as the rule of faith became a regular fixture in English Protestant theology. Indeed, arguments from reason on behalf of Scripture grew increasingly sophisticated throughout the remainder of the seventeenth century, culminating first with Edward Stillingfleet's *Origines Sacrae* and later with John Locke's *The Reasonableness of Christianity*.[40] In each of these

---

39. Peter Harrison, *'Religion' and the Religions in the English Enlightenment* (New York: Cambridge University Press, 1990), pp. 23-24. See also Placher, *The Domestication of Transcendence,* chs. 5 and 6.

40. See Edward Stillingfleet, *Origines Sacrae, or a Rational Account of the Grounds of Christian Faith, as the Truth and Divine Authority of the Scripture, and the Matters therein contained* (London, 1662); John Locke, *The Reasonableness of Christianity: As Delivered in the Scriptures,* ed. John C. Higgins-Biddle (Oxford: Clarendon Press, 1999). Perhaps more than anyone else, Stillingfleet sought to secure the authority of Scripture over against the Catholic rule of faith by appeal to reason. He went on to publish two additional treatises on the matter, including *A Rational Account of the Grounds of the Protestant Religion* (London, 1664), and *A Second Discourse, in Vindication of the Protestant Grounds of Faith* (London, 1673). When quoting Stillingfleet, I will at times cite the first edition of a spe-

works, and in many others like them, the chief arguments had to do with the reliability of testimony and the evidential force of miracles.[41]

While Laud's appeal to reason to secure Scripture as the rule of faith won wide appeal, it was not an all-encompassing solution. On the contrary, Laud's appeal to reason did little to respond to the second challenge presented by Catholic theologians, namely, that on the basis of Scripture, Protestants had been unable to secure agreement in crucial areas of belief and practice. As Irene Simon puts it, Catholic propagandists were increasingly fond of pointing out that "by exercising reason men far from reaching truth were led to an *impasse* in which contradictory propositions could be supported by equal arguments from reason."[42]

Thus, while arguments from reason may have helped to stem the tide concerning the security of the appeal to Scripture, new arguments were needed to address the question of whether or not Scripture could be successfully used as the rule of faith. Moreover, the matter of assurance with regard to personal salvation was still very much up in the air. If assurance depended on assent to the propositions contained in Scripture, then the Protestant inability to agree on what those propositions were or on how they were to be understood was no small problem.

---

cific work; at other times I will simply cite the collected works of Stillingfleet. For the collected works, see Edward Stillingfleet, *Works,* 6 vols. (London, 1707-10). For a discussion of Stillingfleet's conception and use of reason in each of these treatises, see M. A. Stewart, "Stillingfleet and the Way of Ideas," in *English Philosophy in the Age of Locke,* pp. 245-80. See also Robert Todd Carroll, *The Common-Sense Philosophy of Religion of Bishop Edward Stillingfleet, 1635-1699* (The Hague: Martinus Nijhoff, 1975), pp. 62-70.

41. For arguments concerning the reliability of testimony, see Stillingfleet, *Works,* 2:68-69, 180-81, 188-89. See also *A Rational Account of the Grounds of the Protestant Religion,* in *Works,* 4:302-24. John Sergeant replied to Stillingfleet's arguments from testimony and miracles in an appendix to his *Sure-Footing in Christianity.* Stillingfleet replied to Sergeant in an appendix to John Tillotson's *The Rule of Faith* (London, 1666). For an extended analysis of Stillingfleet's arguments on behalf of miracles, see Carroll, *Common-Sense Philosophy of Religion,* pp. 70-77. For a good overview of arguments from testimony and miracles in late seventeenth-century England, see Gerard Reedy, *The Bible and Reason: Anglicans and Scripture in Late Seventeenth Century England* (Philadelphia: University of Pennsylvania Press, 1985), pp. 46-62.

42. Irene Simon, *Three Restoration Divines: Barrow, South, Tillotson* (Paris: Les Belles Lettres, 1967), p. 79. For a summary of Roman Catholic arguments of this kind, see L. I. Bredvold, *The Intellectual Milieu of John Dryden* (Ann Arbor: University of Michigan Press, 1934), ch. 4.

The task of addressing both of these issues would fall first to William Chillingworth (1602-1644) and later to Archbishop John Tillotson (1630-1694).

Salvation by Assent: The (Mis-)Fortunes of *Sola Scriptura*

In *The Religion of Protestants,* William Chillingworth followed Archbishop Laud's lead in two crucial respects: first, he used the "rule of faith" exclusively to refer to Scripture; second, he conceived of faith as assent to the propositions contained therein.[43] However, in an effort to respond both to the Catholic charge that the appeal to Scripture had led to disunity among Protestants and to the ongoing problem of assurance, Chillingworth advanced Laud's argument in a way that solidified the subtle but powerful shift in the English Protestant doctrines of God and of salvation that were already underway.

Chillingworth's strategy for dealing with the Catholic objection that the appeal to Scripture had led to significant disagreements among Protestants was simple and straightforward. Drawing on Richard Hooker, Chillingworth developed what Gerard Reedy has aptly named a "doctrine of essential doctrines."[44] He simply insisted that Protestants did not "differ at all in 'matters of faith,' if you take that word in its highest sense, and mean by 'matters of faith' such doctrines as are absolutely necessary to salvation to be believed, or not to be disbelieved."[45] With regard to the things necessary to be believed for salvation, Protestants were in complete agreement with one another. Chillingworth went so far as to insist that such agreement was not only

---

43. William Chillingworth, *The Religion of Protestants: A Safe Way to Salvation* (London, 1638). Chillingworth's work is a detailed response to the Catholic theologian Matthew Wilson's *Mercy and Truth, or Charity Maintayned* (London, 1634). Wilson's work was written in response to the Protestant theologian Christopher Potter's *Want of Charity justly Charged* (London, 1633), which itself was a response to Wilson's original work, *Charity Mistaken* (London, 1633). Chillingworth was one of several leading intellectuals who met at Great Tew (the Lord Viscount Falkland's estate) in the 1630s to discuss philosophy and theology. In what follows, I will cite from the 1870 edition of Chillingworth's work.

44. Reedy, *The Bible and Reason,* p. 15.

45. Chillingworth, *Religion of the Protestants,* p. 272.

possible but was, in fact, to be expected. God had made Scripture utterly clear and plain with regard to the things pertaining to salvation. Consider the following passage from *The Religion of the Protestants:*

> [Scripture is] sufficiently perfect and sufficiently intelligible in things necessary, to all that have understanding, whether learned or unlearned. And my reason hereof is convincing and demonstrative, because nothing is necessary to be believed but what is plainly revealed. For to say, that when a place of Scripture, by reason of ambiguous terms, lies indifferent between divers senses, whereof one is true and the other false, that God obliges men, under pain of damnation, not to mistake through error and human frailty, is to make God a tyrant; and to say, that he requires us certainly to attain that end, for the attaining whereof we have no certain means; which is to say, that, like Pharaoh, he gives no straw, and requires brick, that he reaps where he sows not; that he gathers where he strews not . . . that he will not accept of us according to that which we have, but requireth of us what we have not.[46]

Chillingworth's argument at this point is significant for two reasons. First, he supports his claim that Protestants agree on things "absolutely necessary to salvation to be believed, or not to be disbelieved" by appeal to the clarity and perspicuity of Scripture.

Second, he addresses the issue of personal assurance of salvation in a most attractive fashion. The image of God as a tyrant is a thinly veiled reference to the Calvinist God whose will was dark and inscrutable. Unlike the tyrannical God of Calvinism, the God of the Great Tew Circle and of the Latitudinarians who were to follow them "would not allow the believer's salvation to depend on such ambiguities [in Scripture]; he had inspired the sacred writers to be eminently clear about the all-important truths." After Chillingworth, "this assumption formed the basis for all Anglican discussion of Scripture."[47]

46. Chillingworth, *Religion of the Protestants,* pp. 129-30.

47. Reedy, *The Bible and Reason,* pp. 13-15. I should point out that an emphasis on the clarity and perspicuity of Scripture was a hallmark of Protestant theology from the beginning. Thus Luther declared, "No clearer book has been written on earth than the Holy Scripture" (as quoted in Abraham, *Canon and Criticism,* p. 129). The quotation is from "Exposition of Psalm 37," in *What Luther Says: An Anthology,* trans. Ewald M. Plass (St. Louis: Concordia, 1959), vol. I, sec. 222.

Chillingworth had met the problem of personal assurance by arguing God had given all things necessary to be believed for salvation in
clear and intelligible propositions in Scripture.[48] He responded to the
Catholic charge simply by insisting that Protestants were in complete
agreement with regard to the things necessary to be believed for salvation.[49] Furthermore, he supported these moves by appealing to the justice and equity of God. In doing so, he set afoot a subtle but powerful
shift in the English Protestant understanding of God. Above all, the
God of the Bible was the kind of God who spoke in a manner all people, regardless of education or social status, could understand. No vi-

48. The problem of assurance precipitated by the emergence of a rival church to
Rome manifested itself in a powerful way in Chillingworth's own life. Born into a
Protestant family, Chillingworth would eventually become convinced that assurance of
salvation could only be had in the Catholic Church. As a result, Chillingworth would
leave the Church of England for Rome only to change his mind and return to the
Protestant fold again. In 1638, the same year that he published *The Religion of Protestants,*
Chillingworth took holy orders in the Church of England. For an account of
Chillingworth's pilgrimage to Rome and back, see Trevor-Roper, *Catholics, Anglicans, and
Puritans,* pp. 169-70. See also Carroll, *The Common-Sense Philosophy,* p. 7. Simon notes how
pervasive the concern was at this time that English Protestants were attracted to the as-
surance provided by the doctrine of papal infallibility (Simon, *Three Restoration Divines,*
pp. 79-83).

49. It is thus fitting and deeply ironic that, upon Chillingworth's untimely death in
1644, Francis Cheynell allegedly placed a copy of *The Religion of the Protestants* on top of
the late reverend's corpse, so that, as Carroll put it, "both might rot together" (Carroll,
The Common-Sense Philosophy, p. 5). Cheynell, who would go on to become President of St.
John's College, published an account of Chillingworth's death entitled *Chillingworth's
novissima, or the Sicknesse, Heresy, Death, and Buriall of William Chillingworth, (in his own
Phrase) Clerk of Oxford, and in the conceit of his Fellow Soldiers the Queen's Arch-Engineer and
Grand Intelligencer. Set forth in a letter to his eminent and learned Friends; a Relation of his Apprehension at Arundell; a Discovery of his Errours in a brief Catechism; and a short Oration at the
Burial of his heretical Book* (London, 1644). Standing over Chillingworth's grave, Cheynell
remarked: "If they please to undertake the burial of his corpse, I shall undertake to bury
his errors, which are published in this so much admired yet unworthy book: and happy
would it be for the kingdom, if this book and all its fellows could be so buried. Get thee
gone, thou cursed book, which has seduced so many precious souls! Get thee gone,
thou corrupt, rotten book! Earth to earth, and dust to dust! Get thee gone into the
place of rottenness, that thou mayest rot with thy author, and see corruption."
Cheynell's remarks quoted in Edward Augustus George, *Seventeenth Century Men of Latitude: Forerunners of the New Theology* (London: T. Fisher Unwin, 1908), pp. 59-60. For another account of this incident, see Margaret L. Wiley, *The Subtle Knot, Creative Scepticism
in Seventeenth Century England* (London: George Allen & Unwin Ltd., 1952), pp. 99-100.

sion of God would be more ideally suited to the modern democratic world that was to come.

In the years that lay ahead, Chillingworth's arguments became a part of the standard intellectual furniture of English Protestant theology.[50] For example, almost thirty years later, in a work entitled simply *The Rule of Faith,* Archbishop Tillotson reinforced and defended Chillingworth's proposal for a whole new generation of Protestant theologians.[51] Moreover, one can detect the direct influence of Chillingworth on Locke's *The Reasonableness of Christianity,* most notably in his conception of and use of Scripture as the rule of faith and in his vision of God and salvation.[52] Thus, if in the work of Archbishop William Laud "saving knowledge" began to make its way "from the heavens to take its place in human discourse," then in the work of William Chillingworth it took up permanent residence there.

With Chillingworth's *Religion of Protestants,* the shift in both the identity and function of the rule of faith was complete. He used the term "rule of faith" exclusively to refer to Scripture, declaring at one point that Scripture is the "perfect rule of faith" (p. 94). As for function, Chillingworth clearly conceived of the rule of faith as a formal criterion in theology, arguing that Scripture is the rule by means of which Christians must judge "what they are to believe, and what they

50. Reedy notes that Chillingworth's position on Scripture "became extremely influential after 1660" (*The Bible and Reason,* p. 1). For a similar judgment, see Thomas Birch, "Life of Mr. William Chillingworth," *Works of William Chillingworth, M.A.,* 10th ed. (London, 1762), p. iii.

51. The full title is *The Rule of Faith: Or an Answer to the Treatise of Mr. I. S. Entitled, Sure-footing, etc.* (London, 1666). As the title indicates, Tillotson was responding to John Sergeant's *Sure-footing in Christianity, or Rational Discourses on* The Rule of Faith. *With Short Animadversions on Dr. Pierce's Sermon; Also on some passages in Mr. Whitby and Mr. Stillingfleet, which concern That Rule* (London, 1665). Tillotson's treatise was published with a rejoinder to Sergeant from Edward Stillingfleet (see Chapter 3 below for more on this). Tillotson himself took holy orders in the Church of England in 1661 and was briefly rector of Kedington, Suffolk, in 1663 before becoming preacher at Lincoln's Inn in 1664. In 1670 he was made prebendary of Canterbury, and in 1672 he became dean of Canterbury. Finally, in 1689 he became dean of St. Paul's Cathedral, and from 1691 to 1694 he served as the Archbishop of Canterbury.

52. For Chillingworth's influence on Locke, see Higgins-Biddle's introduction to *Reasonableness,* pp. xxii, lvii–lxiv. Locke would appeal directly to Chillingworth in his lengthy dispute with Stillingfleet. John Locke, *Second Reply to the Bishop of Worcester,* in *The Works of John Locke,* 10 vols. (London, 1823; reprint, Aalen: Scientia Verlag, 1963), 4:275.

are not to believe" (p. 129). This is a textbook definition of an episte-mic criterion.

Chillingworth even came close to repudiating the notion that creeds or confessions were to be thought of as the rule of faith. He maintained that it was not by any confession of faith but by Scripture alone that people could be certain of their beliefs. In a notorious passage, he says:

> [B]y the Religion of Protestants, I do not understand the doctrine of Luther, or Calvin, or Melanchthon; nor the Confession of Augusta or Geneva, nor the Catechism of Heidelberg, nor the Articles of the Church of England, no, nor the Harmony of Protestant Confessions; *but that wherein all agree, and which they all subscribe with a greater Harmony, as a perfect Rule of their Faith and Actions — that is, the BIBLE.* The BIBLE, I say, the BIBLE only is the religion of Protestants! . . . I, for my part, after a long and (as I verily believe and hope) impartial search of "the true way to eternal happiness," do profess plainly that I cannot find any rest for the sole of my foot but upon this rock only. . . . In a word, there is no sufficient certainty but of Scripture only for any considering man to build upon. This therefore, and this only, I have reason to believe: this I will profess, according to this I will live, and for this, if there be occasion, I will not only willingly, but even gladly, lose my life, though I should be sorry that Christians should take it from me. (p. 463; italics in original)

Archbishop Tillotson would later reiterate Chillingworth's position on the identity and function of the rule of faith almost verbatim, declaring: "The opinion then of the Protestants concerning the Rule of Faith, is this in general, That those Books which we call the Holy Scriptures, are the means whereby the Christian Doctrine hath been brought down to us."[53] As for the function of Scripture as the rule of faith, Tillotson agrees that it is "something according to which we may judge what we are to assent to, as the Doctrine of Christ, and what not." Tillotson adds that it is crucial to have such a rule "so that when any Question ariseth about any particular Proposition, whether this be part of Christ's Doctrine, we may be able by this *Rule* to resolve it."[54]

53. Tillotson, *The Rule of Faith*, p. 16.
54. Tillotson, *The Rule of Faith*, p. 7.

By shifting the focus of their attack from the problem of securing Scripture as the rule of faith to the problem of the ineffectiveness of Scripture for securing agreement in doctrine and ecclesial practices, Catholic theologians had sought to gain a decided advantage in the rule of faith controversy.[55] Despite the deep doctrinal and liturgical divisions emerging within Protestantism, it had often been merely assumed that agreement would eventually be secured. History would prove otherwise.

As we have just seen, Chillingworth sought to answer the Catholic challenge by arguing that Protestants agreed on all things neces-

---

55. Catholic theologians were fond of challenging the effectiveness of Scripture as a criterion by raising a network of objections concerning issues like the unreliability of translations, the unreliability of the transmission process, and related historical and textual problems. Chillingworth treats the issue of the reliability of the translation and transmission of the biblical text at some length (*Religion of the Protestants*, pp. 101-20, 185-92). Catholic theologians increasingly pressed arguments against the reliability of translation and transmission after 1660. One of the most popular later works to do this was Richard Simon's *Histoire critique du vieux testament*. Simon's work was translated into English by H. Dickinson and published in 1682 under the title *A Critical History of the Old Testament*. For a summary of Simon's arguments, see Reedy, *The Bible and Reason*, pp. 104-6, 120-24. For Stillingfleet's response to Simon, see Reedy, *The Bible and Reason*, Appendix I. Also influential was a series of letters published in about 1687 by John Sergeant. Carroll says: "In the *Letters*, Sergeant appealed to the numerous hindrances preventing the discovery of an accurate text of the divine revelations through historical research alone. Given the variance of the ancient texts, the errors of the copyists and printers, and all the discrepancies found in collating the ancient copies of the Scriptural texts, Sergeant claimed *per non sequitur* that all ought to defer to the infallible Catholic Church" (*The Common-Sense Philosophy*, p. 41). Similarly, Katz summarizes Sergeant's position this way: "His argument was that even if the Latitudinarians were correct in their assumption that reason and the Bible could be joint rules of faith, the sheer number of biblical manuscripts which has survived, not to mention the problems of translation and interpretation, render this excessive devotion to human powers of comprehension unreasonable" (Katz, *God's Last Words*, p. 118). Stillingfleet replied to Sergeant's arguments in a work entitled *A Reply to Mr. Serjeant's Third Appendix* (London, 1665). Ironically, it was Catholic objections to the Protestant rule of faith in seventeenth-century England that forced Protestants to investigate historical and textual issues in greater detail than ever before, thereby helping to inaugurate the modern historical-critical investigation of Scripture. Having helped to invent the discipline, it would only be with the issuance of Pope Pius XII's encyclical *Divino Afflante Spiritu* in 1943 that the Roman Catholic Church would officially endorse the historical-critical investigation of Scripture.

sary to be believed for salvation. He calculated that this move would put to rest once and for all the problems surrounding the personal assurance of salvation. The argument would not hold. Protestant theologians after Chillingworth would all agree *that* the things necessary to be believed for salvation were contained in clear and intelligible propositions in Scripture; but they would disagree considerably over precisely *which* propositions were so contained and thus necessary to be believed.

Chillingworth himself had admitted that some passages in Scripture were ambiguous, having "divers senses." For Edward Stillingfleet, a few years later, sorting out clear from unclear propositions in Scripture was a relatively straightforward and simple matter.

> Can any Man in his senses imagine, that Christ's coming into the World to dye for Sinners, and the Precepts of the holy Life which he hath given, and the motives thereto from his second coming to judge the World, are not more plain than the Apocalyptic Visions, or the proofs for the Church of *Rome's* infallibility?[56]

But what was simple and straightforward for Stillingfleet was not so straightforward for others. Ever present on the horizon was a nagging question: What does it mean when disagreements arise over whether a particular proposition is intelligible or clear? In Chillingworth's terms, such disagreements would seem to count against the proposition in question's belonging to the list of things "necessary to be believed" for salvation.[57]

In the years that lay ahead, the all-important category "things necessary to be believed for salvation" would come under enormous strain. Indeed, for the remainder of the seventeenth century, the category would undergo a systematic "thinning out" process that would culmi-

---

56. See Edward Stillingfleet, *Works,* 5:71 (italics in original).

57. It is crucial to note that Chillingworth himself did not draw this conclusion. On the contrary, Chillingworth retained enough of the Calvinist notion of the epistemic consequences of sin that he actually anticipated that people would disagree with one another over religious matters. For this aspect of Chillingworth's argument, see Robert Orr, *Reason and Authority: The Thought of William Chillingworth* (Oxford: Clarendon Press, 1967), p. 152. For a general account of Chillingworth's recognition of the limits of human reason in matters of religion, see Carroll, *The Common-Sense Philosophy,* pp. 9-11.

nate in Locke's *The Reasonableness of Christianity.*[58] Most notable was the disagreement among Protestant theologians over the meaning of propositions related to the Trinity, which would result in quite a few reaching the conclusion that the Trinity was not contained in clear and intelligible propositions and hence was not necessary to be believed for salvation.

By now it should be clear that there are important differences between Scripture as the rule of faith in seventeenth-century English Protestantism and the Trinitarian rule of faith of early Christianity. The difference in content is obvious enough. Far more crucial is the difference between how Scripture and Trinitarian confessional materials *function* as the rule of faith. In the early church, Christian theologians designated Trinitarian confessional materials the rule of faith because those materials helped to identify the God whom Christians invoked in prayer, demon exorcism, baptism, worship, and the like. The rule of faith was especially important in helping catechumens to see that, to invoke "Father, Son and Holy Spirit," was to call upon a God whose nature is "to come to the aid of those in need." As such, it functioned ontologically: it helped Christians know and commune with their God.

By contrast, Protestant theologians in seventeenth-century England appealed to Scripture as the rule of faith because they needed a criterion by which to secure the truthfulness of the Protestant vision of salvation. More specifically, they appealed to Scripture as the rule of faith in order to identify which propositions were necessary to be be-

58. Locke would eventually declare that the only thing necessary to be believed is that "Jesus of Nazareth is the Messiah." He says: "For that this is the sole doctrine pressed and required to be believed in the whole tenor of Our Saviour's and his apostles' preaching, we have shewed through the whole history of the evangelists and the Acts. And I challenge them to shew, that there was any other doctrine, upon their assent to which, or disbelief of it, men were pronounced believers or unbelievers . . . . This was the only gospel-article of faith which was preached to them" (*The Reasonableness of Christianity,* pp. 43-44). Locke then concludes: "For to preach any other doctrines necessary to be believed, we do not find that anybody was sent" (p. 44). We will take up Locke's position more fully in the conclusion of this work. John Marshall has shown that Philipp van Limborch and William Popple were particularly instrumental in "pushing Locke towards the notion that very few doctrines indeed were plainly taught in Scripture as required to be believed." John Marshall, "Locke, Socinianism, 'Socinianism', Unitarianism," in *English Philosophy in the Age of Locke,* p. 153.

lieved for salvation. Thus what the rule of faith secured materially in the early church, it now secured only formally and provisionally. As such, it functioned epistemologically, assisting Christians in the sorting out of true from false beliefs.

In the early church, the rule of faith set forth the Christian vision of God to which everything else was held accountable. For seventeenth-century Protestant theologians, the rule of faith enabled one to pick out the propositions necessary to be believed for salvation. The latter conception of the rule of faith, in principle at least, made it possible to call into question the view of God embedded in the historic creeds. In principle, someone could accept the Protestant rule of faith but challenge doctrines traditionally held by Catholics and Protestants alike, including the doctrine of the Trinity. Chillingworth himself made this very point:

> Nothing can challenge our beliefe, but what hath descended to us from Christ by Originall and Universall Tradition: Now nothing but Scripture hath thus descended to us, therefore nothing but Scripture can challenge our beliefe.[59]

If substantial enough disagreement over the doctrine of the Trinity should arise, then the rule of faith required that advocates of that doctrine either prove it was contained in clear and intelligible propositions in Scripture or lower the status of the doctrine to something unnecessary to be believed for salvation. Regarding the long-haul consequences of this shift in the function of the rule of faith, Mark Pattison would later quip: "Christianity appeared made for nothing else but to be 'proved'; what use to make of it when it was proved was not much thought about."[60]

Even more important was the fact that, in an effort to secure Scripture as the rule of faith, Chillingworth had effected a subtle but extremely powerful shift in the English Protestant doctrines of God and salvation. In the early church, salvation had to do principally with human participation in and response to the divine actions of the economic Trinity in creation, the incarnation, and in the presence and

---

59. Chillingworth, *Religion of the Protestants,* p. 115.

60. Mark Pattison, "Tendencies of Religious Thought in England, 1688-1750," in *Essays,* 2 vols. (Oxford: Clarendon Press, 1889), 2:48.

work of the Holy Spirit in the full range of practices around which the life of the church revolved. For English Protestant theologians after Chillingworth, salvation was chiefly a matter of giving assent to propositions in Scripture, propositions that, because they were given by a God of equity and justice, were clear and intelligible enough for all to understand.

Among the many things lost in this shift in the conception of salvation, none was more crucial than the presence and work of the Holy Spirit. The appeal to reason meant that the presence and work of the Holy Spirit was no longer needed in the discernment of divine revelation and in the interpretation of Scripture. To the degree that assent to clear and intelligible propositions in Scripture was all that was needed for salvation, even the work of the Holy Spirit in ecclesial practices such as baptism, worship, and the Eucharist was not sufficiently emphasized. Observing these developments, Francis Cheynell, a Presbyterian minister and president of St. John's College, called for a recovery of a more robust doctrine of the Holy Spirit in the life of the believer.[61] Unfortunately, Cheynell's call went largely unheeded. By 1650, the doctrine of the Trinity and the vision of salvation that had for so long been prominent in the church was well on its way to being displaced by another doctrine of God and another vision of salvation.

Given that Scripture as the rule of faith was now pivotal for the assurance of personal salvation, it would be difficult for any English Protestant to imagine giving it up. This was true even when the commitment to *sola Scriptura* threatened the doctrine of the Trinity. As one scholar observes, the controversy over the Trinity in the 1690s would reveal that "the divines' commitment to the literal sense [of Scripture] was deep, even when the price of maintaining that commitment was controversy which the doctrine of essential doctrines was partly forwarded to avoid."[62]

While Chillingworth's solution clearly struck English Protestant theologians like Stillingfleet and Tillotson as satisfactory, Catholic theologians continued to press questions concerning Scripture's ability to secure agreement among Protestants in matters of belief

---

61. See Francis Cheynell, *The Divine Triunity of the Father, Son and Holy Spirit* (London, 1650).

62. Reedy, *The Bible and Reason*, p. 15.

and practice. These Catholic theologians understood that, in principle, the Protestant rule of faith made even the most cherished doctrines subject to change or even rejection. Thus they were constantly
on the lookout for disagreements among Protestants over doctrinal
and liturgical matters. Nevertheless, even the most optimistic Catholic propagandists could not have anticipated what would happen
next.

Unlikely Allies: Catholic Propagandists Enlist the Socinians

What the Protestant rule of faith made possible in principle actually
happened. During the 1630s the Socinian literature that had first made
its way into England in about 1609, from Poland by way of Amsterdam,
began to gain wider circulation.[63] To the delight of Catholic propagandists everywhere, the most prominent feature of Socinian literature was
a rule of faith that was strikingly similar, if not identical, to the one developed by Laud and Chillingworth. John McLachlan describes the
core commitments of Socinianism: "Its two leading characteristics
were its scrupulous and vigorous biblicism and its acknowledgement
of the rights of reason."[64]

Even a casual glance at the literature shows that Socinians combined these commitments into something very much like the rule of
faith developed by Laud and Chillingworth. The Socinian conception
of Scripture as the rule of faith is manifest in the two most important
early Socinian documents, the *Racovian Catechism* (1601) and the *Brevis
Disquisitio* (1633). The *Racovian Catechism* declares:

> [Reason] is, indeed, of great service, since without it we could neither
> perceive with certainty the authority of the sacred writings, under-
> stand their contents, discriminate one thing from another, nor apply
> them to any practical purpose. When therefore I stated that the Holy

63. Dixon recalls that the Catechism arrived in England "complete with a dedica-
tion to James I, whom the Socinians mistakenly believed to be a model of religious toleration." He adds: "James was appalled and the book was burnt by the hangman" (Dixon,
Nice and Hot Disputes, p. 40).

64. H. John McLachlan, *Socinianism in Seventeenth-Century England* (London: Oxford
University Press, 1951), p. 11.

Scriptures were sufficient for our salvation, so far from excluding right reason, I certainly assumed its presence.[65]

Similarly, the *Brevis Disquisitio* says:

Right reason is sufficient for everyone to judge with . . . . I say to judge the authority of Scripture, and by the Scripture . . . . For by the judgement of right Reason it is discovered, what every one meaneth, of what force his testimony is, and how much it recedeth from truth and falsehood. . . . Whatsoever doubts are discarded, whatsoever controversies are composed [it is] by the judgement of Reason.[66]

The similarities between these statements and the proposals set forth by Laud and Chillingworth were impossible to miss. What had gone largely unsaid but not entirely unacknowledged by both Laud and Chillingworth — that as a matter of principle their conception of the rule of faith made even the most well-established doctrines subject to change or rejection — was made painfully and unavoidably obvious by the arrival of the Socinians. The Socinians themselves wore this principle like a badge of honor. Thus the architects of the *Racovian Catechism* declared: "While we compose a Catechism, we prescribe nothing to any man."[67] What they meant was that they did not presume that any doctrines were true prior to examining them on the basis of the rule of faith.

Given the striking similarities between the Socinian and the English Protestant rule of faith, it is easy to see why Chillingworth, Tillot-

---

65. *The Rakovian Catechism,* trans. Thomas Rees, (London, 1818), p. 15.

66. *Brevis Disquisitio* (London, 1653), p. 10, as quoted by Frederick Beiser, who notes: "This tract was written by Joachim Stegmann, a German Socinian, and was first published in Amsterdam in 1633. It was translated by the English Socinian John Biddle, who published it anonymously in 1653, adding his own preface, 'To the Reader.' In both its Latin and English versions the work became notorious. It was mentioned among 'some most dangerous and reproveable books' by a committee appointed by the Lords, March 1640-1641, to consider innovations in religion" (Beiser, *The Sovereignty of Reason,* p. 101).

67. *The Rakovian Catechism* (Preface). To be sure, much Socinian teaching opposed the doctrine of the Trinity, especially as it is instantiated in the Nicene and Athanasian creeds. However, this had more to do with Socinian opposition to dogmatism than it did with the doctrine of the Trinity.

son, and many other Protestant theologians in seventeenth-century England would be intrigued by, if not sympathetic to, Socinianism.[68] Beginning with Laud and Chillingworth, many English Protestants found it increasingly difficult not to agree with the Socinians that it was only by reason that one could "perceive with certainty the authority of the sacred writings, understand their contents, discriminate one thing from another, [and] apply them to any practical purpose." Thus Chillingworth himself says:

> Whatsoever Man that is not of a perverse Mind, shall weigh with serious and mature Deliberation, those great Moments of Reason which may incline him to believe the Divine Authority of Scripture, and compare them with the light Objections, that in Prudence may be made against it, he shall not chuse but find sufficient, nay abundant Inducements to yield unto it firm Faith, and sincere Obedience.[69]

As for the use of reason to understand the contents of Scripture, Chillingworth's impact was equal to Laud's on arguments for the authority of Scripture:

> For my part, I am certain that God hath given us our reason to discern between truth and falsehood; and he that makes not this use of it, but believes things he knows not why, I say, it is by chance that he believes the truth, and not by choice; and I cannot but fear that God will not accept of this sacrifice of fools.[70]

In the latter half of the seventeenth century, Protestant theologians found the appeal to reason especially helpful in the controversy with Catholic theologians over transubstantiation. They repeatedly argued that transubstantiation was contrary to sense experience, and

68. For an account of these sympathies, see Frederick Beiser, *The Sovereignty of Reason*, pp. 100-103.

69. As quoted in Carroll, *The Common-Sense Philosophy*, p. 8.

70. Chillingworth, *Religion of the Protestants*, 2:113. Carroll calls attention to Chillingworth's evidentialism: "In matters of religion, as in matters of law, one took account of all the available and pertinent evidence. The assent given to the correctness of the decisions made in either case was to be made in proportion to the evidence" (*The Common-Sense Philosophy*, p. 11).

thus that they should seek another interpretation of Scripture.[71] Here and elsewhere, one can readily see the spread of Baconian sensibilities regarding the use of language and the appeal to mystery in natural philosophy.

With the influx of Socinian literature, which opposed the Trinity in the name of reason, English Protestant theologians found themselves in an increasingly uncomfortable position. Having appealed to reason in their arguments against transubstantiation, how could they oppose the appeal to reason by the Socinians in their arguments against the Trinity and the incarnation? Stillingfleet was the first to see the problem that now loomed on the horizon. In an especially prescient moment in 1662, he wrote:

> Who hath fixed the bounds of that which men call reason? How shall we know that thus far it will come, and no further? If no banks be raised against it to keep it in its due channel, we may have cause to fear it may overthrow not only the Trinity, Incarnation, Resurrection of the dead, but all other articles of the creed too.[72]

Stillingfleet had good cause to be concerned. On the basis of a rule of faith almost identical to the one formulated by Chillingworth, the Socinians had already rejected the Trinity. It was for this reason that

---

71. For the appeal to reason against transubstantiation, see Jeremy Taylor, *The real presence and spirituall of Christ in the blessed sacrament proved against the doctrine of transubstantiation* (London, 1653); William Hutchinson, *A rational discourse concerning transubstantiation in a letter to a person of honor from a Master of Arts of the University of Cambridge* (London, 1676); John Cosin, *The history of popish transubstantiation to which is premised and opposed the catholic doctrin of Holy Scripture, the antient fathers and the reformed churches about the sacred elements, and presence of Christ in the blessed sacrament of the Eucharist* (London, 1679); John Tillotson, *A Discourse Against Transubstantiation* (London, 1684); and Henry More, *A Brief Discourse of the Real Presence of the body and blood of Christ in the Celebration of the Holy Eucharist* (London, 1686). It is worth noting that it was about Tillotson's appeal to sense experience against transubstantiation that David Hume would later remark: "There is, in Dr. Tillotson's writings, an argument against the *real presence,* which is concise, and elegant, and strong an argument as can possibly be supposed against a doctrine, so little worthy of a serious refutation." Hume went on to transfer Tillotson's argument to the evidence for miracles. David Hume, *An Enquiry Concerning Human Understanding,* ed. L. A. Selby-Bigge and P. H. Nidditch (Oxford: Clarendon Press, 1975), p. 109.

72. Stillingfleet, *Origines Sacrae,* p. 237.

Socinian literature, almost as soon as it arrived in England, was condemned as heretical, along with all those who made common cause or otherwise sympathized with it. Before long, heresy hunters were frequently accusing Chillingworth and the other members of the Great Tew Circle of being sympathetic to, if not supportive of, Socinianism. Later on, leading Protestant theologians like Tillotson and Stillingfleet himself would also come under attack for allegedly having a favorable disposition toward Socinianism. Both Tillotson and Stillingfleet would seek to clear their names of these charges by insisting that belief in the Trinity was necessary.[73]

There can be no doubt that, if Chillingworth, the members of Great Tew, Tillotson, and other Protestant theologians were attracted to Socinianism, it was because of the deep similarities between the Socinian and English Protestant conceptions of the rule of faith on the one hand, and because of the common cause against rigid Calvinism on the other. These similarities are most certainly what lay behind the suggestion that Chillingworth and the others were themselves "Socinians." Thus John Marshall observes:

> [T]he accusation of "Socinianism" was one of the most commonly used accusations in the seventeenth century, and it was employed polemically to associate many thinkers with heresy, or to identify heretical tendencies in their thought. Those associated included John Hales, William Chillingworth, and many Latitudinarians such as John Tillotson. The accusation was directed against their emphases on free will, on moralism, and on the need for a working faith, which

73. See John Tillotson, *A Sermon Concerning the Unity of the Divine Nature and the Blessed Trinity* (London, 1693). Charles Leslie would later take up the attack on Tillotson in *The charge of Socinianism against Dr. Tillotson Considered* (Edinburgh, 1695). Leslie's attack came after Tillotson's death, and Stillingfleet came quickly to the late Archbishop's defense. See Edward Stillingfleet, *Works*, 3:446-47, 470-71. It was the Dominican Hugh Cressy who accused Stillingfleet of Socinianism in a work entitled *Fanaticism fanatically Imputed to the Catholic Church* (London, 1672), which was a response to Stillingfleet's *Discourse on Idolatry* (London, 1671). In turn, Edward Hyde, the Lord Clarendon, came to Stillingfleet's defense by publishing *Animadversions upon a Book Entitled Fanaticism fanatically imputed to the Catholic Church by Dr. Stillingfleet* (London, 1674). For an account of the debate between Cressy and Stillingfleet, and of the Lord Clarendon's defense of Stillingfleet, see B. H. G. Wormald, *Clarendon* (Cambridge, UK: Cambridge University Press, 1951).

were in contrast to the Calvinist emphases on man's extreme inherited depravity, Christ's merit transferred to humans, and justification through faith before works; or against their emphases on the role and capacity of reason; or against *the omission from* or form of defense in specific of their works on the Trinity, original sin, and the atonement; or against their arguments that Christianity included only a very few fundamental doctrines, belief in which was absolutely necessary for salvation, most notably those contained in the non-Trinitarian Apostles' Creed.[74]

Despite numerous accusations of "Socinianism," it proved very difficult to show that either the members of Great Tew or Latitudinarians such as Tillotson and Stillingfleet were ever openly or even privately opposed to the Trinity. From 1630 to 1680, Protestant theologians who were sympathetic to the Socinian conception of the rule of faith showed comparatively little, if any, interest in Socinian conclusions about the Trinity. Indeed, Socinian objections to the Trinity survived primarily as an underground movement for most of the seventeenth century. To be sure, a major reason for this was the political atmosphere during this period. For example, when Parliament passed the Act of Uniformity in 1662, the use of the Prayer Book was once again mandated. As a result, over seventeen hundred "nonconforming" ministers were evicted from their dwellings for "their refusal to accept the requirements of the act, many becoming the victims of poverty and petty persecution."[75] Furthermore, the Test Act of 1673 required all persons holding civil or military offices to receive Holy Communion according to the rites of the Church of England, to denounce transubstantiation, and to take oaths of supremacy and allegiance. Clearly, allegiance to the Church of England meant allegiance to the Thirty-Nine Articles of Religion, which, in turn, meant allegiance to the Trinity.

While the political atmosphere certainly discouraged any public

---

74. Marshall, "Locke, Socinianism," p. 112 (italics added). On the account of the structure and content of early Christian creeds and confessions presented in Chapter 1 of this work, it is difficult to understand what Marshall has in mind when he says that the Apostles' Creed is non-Trinitarian.

75. Dixon, *Nice and Hot Disputes*, p. 99. For an extended analysis of the consequences of the Act of Uniformity, see John Spurr, *The Restoration Church of England* (London: Yale University Press, 1991).

denials of the Trinity on the part of English clerics, that is no reason to question the sincerity of leading Protestant theologians' declarations of allegiance to the Thirty-Nine Articles of Religion, including the articles on the Trinity. From 1630 to 1680, it is difficult to find English clerics seriously questioning or opposing the doctrines enshrined in the Thirty-Nine Articles of Religion.[76] Moreover, it is difficult to prove that English clerics during this period maintained their allegiance to the Thirty-Nine Articles of Religion strictly for political reasons. On the contrary, the working assumption was that the doctrines enshrined in the Thirty-Nine Articles were clearly contained in and derived from Scripture.

There are two additional reasons not to overestimate the degree to which Protestant theologians questioned the Trinity during this period. First, their primary interests clearly lay elsewhere. For example, during the large middle portion of this period, they were primarily concerned to defend the Laud-Chillingworth model of the rule of faith over against the theologians of the Puritan Commonwealth. After all, Archbishop Laud himself had only recently been put on trial and executed by the Puritans. When worries about God did arise, those worries had to do with the very existence of God, since Protestants were far more concerned with atheism than with anti-Trinitarianism at this time.[77] Indeed, it is a testimony to the high degree to which Protestants maintained their allegiance to the Trinity during this period that, in their response to the atheist problem, the Cambridge Platonists did not think it sufficient to defend belief in a generic deity or in the deity of the classical attributes, but they argued instead for belief in the triune God.[78]

---

76. To be sure, a few did challenge the doctrine of the Trinity during this period, the most notable of whom was John Biddle; but the opposition to them was always swift, strong, and decisive. Biddle published his objections in two separate works: *A Confession of Faith Touching the Holy Trinity according to the Scripture* (London, 1653) and *Twelve arguments drawn out of the Scripture wherein the commonly received opinion touching the deity of the Holy Spirit is clearly and fully refuted* (London, 1654).

77. See, esp., John Redwood, *Reason, Ridicule, and Religion: The Age of Enlightenment in England 1660-1750* (London: Thames and Hudson, 1976), ch. 1. See also Beiser, *The Sovereignty of Reason*, ch. 4.

78. See Ralph Cudworth, *The True Intellectual System of the Universe* (London, 1678), "The Preface to the Reader," pp. 574-75, 618-22.

The second reason not to overestimate anti-Trinitarian sentiment during this period is simply that Socinian literature was hard to obtain. Thus Dixon is correct when he observes that, while the Racovian Catechism "had an influence on certain thinkers," its "popular impact was slight."[79] Even this comment is unduly cautious, because the evidence is scant at best that "certain thinkers" before the 1680s were familiar with the details of Socinian arguments against the Trinity.[80] Sometime in the 1680s, however, the situation changed drastically.

The mid-1680s to late 1680s witnessed a growing trend toward freedom and toleration of religious belief. One can observe an increasing reluctance to enforce laws requiring allegiance to the Thirty-Nine Articles of the Church of England, more than anywhere else, in the freedom of the presses granted during this period. Therefore, despite the fact that the Toleration Act was not passed until 1689 (and even then, it did not extend privileges to Catholics and Unitarians), a truly astonishing amount of Catholic and Socinian literature was published beginning in 1686.[81] By 1687, if not earlier, one of the two standard works of Polish Unitarianism, namely, Christopher Sandius's *Bibliotheca Anti-Trinitariorum* (1684), was in circulation in England.[82] Even more important, Stephen Nye published *A Brief History of the Unitarians* in 1687: together with the *Bibliotheca Anti-Trinitariorum* and a collection of earlier continental Socinian texts, this work made the arguments against the Trinity readily available to all. When the freedom of the presses made Socinian and Unitarian literature more widely available, those who were members of the emerging "Republic of Letters" were duty bound to read and promote them. Thus, even after 1680, the mere fact that someone was familiar with Socinian or Unitarian arguments is not suf-

---

79. Dixon, *Nice and Hot Disputes*, p. 15.

80. To be sure, "Socinian" became a term of derision well before 1680. However, it is extremely difficult to tell exactly what was meant by the term: for example, it was often used interchangeably with "atheist." Clearly, Socinians were not atheists. The evidence suggests that few were familiar with actual Socinian arguments against the Trinity prior to 1680.

81. John Marshall describes "the Unitarian Controversy of 1687-c.1700" as "a debate over the Trinity which flared up when the Unitarians took advantage of the relaxation of the press under James II to disseminate their views" (Marshall, "Locke, Socinianism," p. 118).

82. The other standard work, the eight-volume collection *Bibliotheca fratrum Polonorum,* was circulating in England by 1688.

ficient evidence to show that he or she was sympathetic to or in agreement with the arguments.[83]

With the sudden increase in the publication and open circulation of Socinian and Unitarian literature, Catholic theologians discovered the ultimate weapon in the long-running debate over the rule of faith. The Socinian and Unitarian arguments against the Trinity contained in these publications were carried out on precisely the same grounds that Protestants had argued against the doctrines of transubstantiation and the ubiquity of Christ, namely, the authority of Scripture established and interpreted by reason. Seeing this, several astute Catholic propagandists began producing literature intended to undermine the Protestant rule of faith. In these works, composed as dialogues, Catholic theologians insisted that Protestants must, like the Socinians, assess the Trinity on the same grounds on which they had rejected transubstantiation.[84]

From the standpoint of Catholic Counter-Reformation propagandists, the conclusion to be drawn was clear. On submitting the Trinity to reason, Protestants would discover they could reject the Trinity along with transubstantiation and join ranks with the Socinians; or they could discard the Protestant rule of faith and return to the Catholic Church, where the Trinity was secure. In short, Protestants would now have to choose between Rome and Rakow.

Rightly understood, the Trinitarian controversy of the 1690s was the last phase in the great debate over the rule of faith that had spanned

83. This is especially important in the case of John Locke. John Marshall observes: "There are many reasons to associate Locke with this ethos of discussion . . . and, more generally, with participation in the republic and its ethos of civility; and to argue that the value of conversation about disputed matters was much more important to Locke than attachment to specific theological positions, while simultaneously associating him with the causes of the best critical scholarship and tolerationism, and thus with an unusually open-minded consideration of Unitarianism. Locke's central group of friends for discussion of theological issues thus included many Unitarians, several very irenic trinitarians, and several who seem to have thought it best to avoid focus on the Trinity whatever their own views; and almost all of these individuals elevated over almost all specific doctrinal commitments a series of other commitments, including most notably those to toleration, modesty or humility in interpretation, and civility in learned discussion" (Marshall, "Locke, Socinianism," p. 140).

84. Here the grounds have to do with Baconian sensibilities regarding the need for meaning in language to reflect sense experience.

the seventeenth century.[85] English Protestant theologians agreed that Scripture was the rule of faith and that salvation was primarily a matter of rational assent to clear and intelligible propositions contained therein. They would now have to show that the Trinity could be explained in clear and intelligible propositions. If they could not do so, they would have to admit, on pain of contradiction, that the Trinity was not necessary to be believed for salvation.

85. Thus I take issue with M. A. Stewart, who says: "But a number of unitarian tracts, claiming no special allegiance to continental Socinians and oriented more to the specific anomalies of the Trinity, started to surface in the late 1680s, distracting the Anglican church from its mission against the Catholics, and the movement gathered momentum in the 1690s" (Stewart, "Stillingfleet and the Way of Idea," pp. 246-47). While I agree that the Unitarian literature being published in the late 1680s focused on the Trinity in a way that earlier continental Socinian literature had not done, I disagree with Stewart's suggestion that Anglican theologians suddenly turned their attention from Catholic objections about the rule of faith to Unitarian objections to the Trinity. On the contrary, as I will show, the Trinitarian debate of the 1690s should be seen as an extension of the debate over the rule of faith between Protestants and Catholics. In the next chapter I will show that it was primarily Catholic polemics concerning the rule of faith that left Protestant theologians with little choice but to confront the Unitarians. M. A. Stewart's views are found in Stewart, "Stillingfleet and the Way of Ideas," pp. 245-280. Similarly, while Dixon is clearly aware of the role that Catholic apologetics played in bringing about the Trinitarian controversy, he fails to see the extent to which the controversy over the Trinity was precipitated by Protestant efforts to defend Scripture as the rule of faith.

CHAPTER 3

The Protestant Dilemma

*No, no, I will believe no pretended revelation, which contra-
dicts the plain dictates of reason, which all mankind agree in,
and were I persuaded, that those books, which we call the
Holy Scriptures did so, I would not believe them.*

William Sherlock

As the last episode in the seventeenth-century debate over the rule of
faith, the Trinitarian controversy of the 1690s constitutes the beginning
of modern Christian theology in the West. In the wider context of the
debate over the rule of faith, the Trinitarian controversy exhibits a distinguishing feature of Christian theology in the modern West, namely,
granting primacy to epistemology over ontology. From the late seventeenth century to the early twenty-first century, English Protestant
theologians have been heavily preoccupied with epistemological considerations, including the assessment of the rationality, justifiability, and
truthfulness of Christian beliefs. On the one hand, the preoccupation
with epistemology yielded a rich and respected tradition in analytic philosophy of religion, a tradition that includes the likes of John Locke, David Hume, John Henry Newman, F. R. Tennant, Austin Farrer, Lesslie
Newbigin, and Richard Swinburne, to name a few. On the other hand, it
has at times been disastrous for Christian theology and doctrine, and
most notably for the doctrine of the Trinity.

To their credit, Protestant theologians in seventeenth-century England were reluctant to subject the Trinity to criticism. Unfortunately,

they had tied both the legitimacy of the Church of England and the assurance of salvation directly to the epistemic conception and use of Scripture as the rule of faith. In doing so, they simply assumed that the doctrine of the Trinity was either contained in or derived from clear and intelligible propositions in Scripture. If challenged to do so, they would defend the doctrine of the Trinity accordingly. With the arrival of Polish Socinianism and the spread of its distinctively English variant, Unitarianism, such a challenge loomed large on the horizon.

In the mid- to late 1680s, the marked increase in the publication and circulation of Socinian literature gave Catholic propagandists a devastating weapon to deploy in their ongoing efforts to undermine the Protestant rule of faith.[1] The problem that Socinianism posed was plain to see: Socinians openly denied that the Trinity was either contained in or derived from clear and intelligible propositions in Scripture. Thus English Protestant theologians had three choices: they could (1) maintain their commitment to Scripture as the rule of faith and prove the Socinians were wrong about the Trinity; (2) maintain their commitment to Scripture as the rule of faith and admit that the Socinians were right about the Trinity; or (3) acknowledge that only the Catholic rule of faith could secure the Trinity.[2]

---

1. When James II took the throne in 1685, he ignored the Test Act of 1673, and from 1685 to 1688, Catholic propagandists took full advantage of hitherto unprecedented freedom of the press.

2. Many scholars overlook the crucial role played by Catholic polemics concerning the rule of faith in the early stages of the Trinitarian controversy, often depicting the controversy as a straightforward confrontation between Protestants and Unitarians. As I noted at the end of Chapter 2, M. A. Stewart goes so far as to say that the publication of Unitarian materials distracted the Protestants from their dispute with the Catholics over the rule of faith. See M. A. Stewart, "Stillingfleet and the Way of Ideas," in *English Philosophy in the Age of Locke*, ed. M. A. Stewart (Oxford: Clarendon Press, 2000), pp. 246-47. G. R. Cragg is one of the few scholars to have recognized that the Trinitarian controversy was the last episode in the seventeenth-century rule of faith controversy. He says: "At times, the struggle with Romanism flared up into fierce activity, but guerilla fighting was constantly in progress. . . . The Roman Catholics believed they could impale their Protestant opponents on the horns of a dilemma. There were only two alternatives, they said; you could accept the authority of an infallible church, or you could subside into deism. It was of no avail to appeal to Scripture; unless authenticated by a church which could not err, the Bible had no decisive voice in religious controversy." G. R. Cragg, *From Puritanism to the Age of Reason: A Study of Changes in Religious Thought within the Church of England, 1660 to 1700* (London: Cambridge University Press, 1950), p. 64.

Discerning the dilemma posed by Socinianism, Catholic theologians pounced, publishing a host of propaganda materials aimed at undermining the Protestant rule of faith once and for all. In these materials, Catholic theologians challenged English Protestant theologians to respond to Socinian objections to the Trinity by securing the Trinity on the grounds now enshrined in the Protestant rule of faith.[3] Had this new round of Catholic propaganda materials been confined to the universities, Protestant theologians might simply have ignored the situation. It was precisely at this time, however, that the Jesuits were stepping up their evangelistic efforts in England, and with some success.[4]

One of the byproducts of Jesuit evangelistic success was the publication of a growing number of conversion narratives.[5] Among the most well known of these conversion narratives was a set of three papers: two of them were allegedly written by Charles, the brother of the king, James II; the third was written by James's first wife, Anne Hyde. These papers gave accounts of the conversion to Catholicism of Charles and Anne, the former just before his death.[6] Nor did it help Protestant theologians that some of the authors of Catholic propaganda were former members of the Church of England. For example, Abraham Woodhead (1609-1678), sometime fellow of University College, Oxford, published two treatises in which he argued the case for the Catholic

---

3. For a bibliography of the pamphlets published between 1685 and 1688, see Louis I. Bredvold, *The Intellectual Milieu of John Dryden* (Ann Arbor: University of Michigan Press, 1934), appendix.

4. For Jesuit proselytizing activity at this time, see Robert Todd Carroll, *The Common-Sense Philosophy of Religion of Bishop Edward Stillingfleet, 1635-1699* (The Hague: Martinus Nijhoff, 1975), pp. 50-57.

5. The conversion narrative had been popular in England throughout the seventeenth century. For an early example, see Hugh Cressy, *Exomologesis* (Paris, 1647). Cressy went on to publish a defense of the Catholic rule of faith and vision of salvation entitled *Fanaticism fanatically Imputed to the Catholic Church* (London, 1672), a work he wrote in response to Edward Stillingfleet's *Discourse on Idolatry* (London, 1671).

6. Edward Stillingfleet responded to the publication of these papers in a treatise entitled *An Answer to Some Papers Lately Printed, Concerning the Authority of the Catholick Church in Matters of Faith, and the Reformation of the Church of England* (London, 1686). The poet John Dryden, in turn, responded to Stillingfleet with *Defense of the Papers Written by the Late King . . . and Duchess of York* (London, 1686). For an account of this exchange, see Carroll, *Common-Sense Philosophy*, pp. 46-49. Carroll observes: "The central religious issues in the Stillingfleet-Dryden controversy were the rule of faith and the justification of the Reformation" (p. 47).

rule of faith over against Archbishop Laud and Stillingfleet.[7] As the publication of Catholic propaganda materials increased dramatically during the mid- to late 1680s, Protestant theologians were understandably concerned.

In a brilliant move, Catholic propagandists carried out their new strategy through a series of fascinating and highly creative theological dialogues designed to force English Protestants to side with either Rome or Rakow.[8] Particularly inflammatory among these dialogues were two anonymously published tracts entitled *The Protestants Plea for a Socinian*[9] and *A Dialogue Between a New Catholic Convert and a Protestant.*[10] These popular tracts argued persuasively that only the Catholic rule of faith could safeguard the Trinity from Socinian objections.

Not surprisingly, Protestant theologians responded with dialogues of their own, which was, in all likelihood, exactly what the Catholic propagandists wanted. The Protestant response drew immediate fire from the Unitarians, which, in turn, ignited the Trinitarian controversy of the 1690s. In the end, the Trinitarian controversy would dramatically confirm the Catholic point. After all, even if Protestants managed to gain an upper hand in the debate, the very fact that the Trinity was so widely disputed meant that, according to the Protestant rule of faith, the Trinity was not among the things necessary to be believed for salvation.

Given the extent to which these dialogues helped to precipitate the Trinitarian controversy of the 1690s, it will help to examine them closely. In what follows, I will analyze closely the arguments in *The Protestants Plea for a Socinian* and in *A Dialogue Between a New Catholic Convert*

7. See Abraham Woodhead, *The Guide in Controversies of Religion: Reflecting on the Later Writings of Protestants; Particularly Archbishop Laud and Dr. Stillingfleet on this Subject* (n.p., 1666); see also Woodhead, *Dr. Stillingfleet's Principles, Giving an Account of the Faith of Protestants by N. O.* (Paris, 1671).

8. These dialogues were at the core of the Catholic strategy for undermining the Protestant rule of faith in late seventeenth-century England. Despite this, they have received very little attention from scholars.

9. The full title is *The Protestants Plea for a Socinian: Justifying His Doctrine from being opposite to Scripture or Church-Authority; And Him from being Guilty of Heresie, or Schism. In five Conferences* (London, 1686).

10. The full title is *A Dialogue Between a New Catholic Convert and a Protestant Shewing the Doctrine of Transubstantiation to be as Reasonable to be Believ'd as the Great Mystery of the Trinity by all Good Catholicks* (London, 1686).

and a Protestant. Next I will examine the attempts by Edward Stillingfleet and William Sherlock to respond to these dialogues by making a crucial midcourse adjustment to rules for applying the Protestant rule of faith. Finally, I will show that those attempts by Stillingfleet and Sherlock failed precisely because their own background theological commitments preempted the adjustment they were now seeking to make.

The Catholic End Game[11]

The longer of the two treatises, *The Protestants Plea for a Socinian* (hereafter the *Plea*), set forth a sharp either/or contrast. On the basis of the Protestant rule of faith, the Socinians or Unitarians openly denied the "consubstantiality of the Son with God the Father" (*Plea*, p. 4). By contrast, the Catholic rule of faith prohibited the heterodox from tampering with the doctrine of the Trinity. The conclusion to be drawn was clear: a rule of faith that secured the doctrinal commitments of Christianity, most notably the doctrine of the Trinity, was to be preferred over a rule of faith that made those commitments vulnerable.

The *Plea* was constructed as a dialogue between a Socinian and a Protestant, and its purpose was to show "the invalidity of such a Guide as Protestants have framed to themselves for preserving the true Faith, and suppressing Heresies." What made the Protestant guide or rule of faith invalid was that the Socinians, "who tho' denying the Trinity, and our Saviors Deity, yet, most zealously [urge] Scripture, and its plainness in all necessaries, as if it justified [their] own Errors; or that they Erred only in matters not necessary." Having said this, the author of the *Plea* correctly clarified that he did not intend "hereby to equal all Protestant Opinions" with Socinianism. To put it another way, he was not claiming that all Protestants were anti-Trinitarian. Rather, he was simply observing that the Protestant rule of faith could "as rationally justifie the *Socinian* as the Protestant" with regard to the Trinity (p. 2). The goal of

11. In what follows, I have envisioned the rule-of-faith debate on the eve of the Trinitarian controversy as the closing rounds of a century-long theological chess match between Catholics and Protestants. Thus we begin with the Catholic strategy for ending the match.

the *Plea* was not to undermine the Trinity itself, but to show that the Protestant rule of faith could not finally secure the Trinity.

The dialogue proper begins when the Protestant interlocutor asks the Socinian:

> Why do you, to the great danger of your soul, and salvation, not believe, *God the Son to be of one, and the same essence, and substance with God the Father,* it being so principal an Article of the *Christian* faith, delivered in the *Holy Scriptures?* (p. 2)

To this question, the Socinian offers a threefold response. First, he believes "with other Christians, that the Scriptures are the Word of God; and, with other Protestants, that they are a perfect *Rule* of my Faith." Second, whether he believes "truly, or falsly" concerning the oneness of Christ with God the Father, he is "secure that [his] Faith is entire, as to all *necessary* points of Faith," implying that the Trinity is not among the things necessary to be believed. Third, quoting directly from Chillingworth's *Religion of the Protestants,* the Socinian interlocutor says, "He that believes all that is in the Bible, all that is in the Scriptures (as I do) believes all that is necessary there" (pp. 2-3).

The Socinian's position is clear. With regard to the rule of faith, he is Protestant to the core. However, he denies that the doctrine of the Trinity is either contained in or derived from clear and intelligible propositions in Scripture. On the Protestant rule of faith, it is thus not among the things necessary to be believed for salvation. At this stage, the Protestant informs his Socinian opponent that he has not in fact believed "all the Scriptures" unless he has believed them according to their "true sense." In denying that Christ is "of one, and the same essence, and substance, with God the Father," the Socinian has mistaken the "true sense of something *necessary.*" Apparently, the problem with Socinianism is simply a matter of the misinterpretation of Scripture.

The Socinian's response incorporates two extracts from Chillingworth and is worth quoting at length:

> *I believe, that that sense of [the Scriptures] which God intendeth whatsoever it is, is certainly true . . . . I do my best endeavour to believe Scripture in the true sense thereof. [By my best endeavour I mean, such a measure of industry, as human prudence, and ordinary discretion (my abilities, and opportunities,*

my distractions, and hindrances, and all things considered) shall advise me unto in a matter of such consequence. Of using which endeavour also, I conceive, I may be sufficiently certain: for otherwise, I can have no certainty of any thing I believe from this compleat Rule of Scriptures; this due endeavour being the condition, which Protestants require, that I shall not be, as to all necessaries, deceived in the sense of Scripture.] Now, being conscious to my self of such a right endeavour used: *For me, to believe, further, this or that to be the true sense of some Scriptures; or to believe the true sense of them, and to avoid the false, is not necessary, either to my faith or salvation. For, if God would have had his meaning in these places certainly known, how could it stand with his wisdom, to be so wanting to his own will and end, as to speak obscurely? Or how can it consist with his justice to require of men to know certainly the meaning of those words which he himself hath not revealed? For my error or ignorance in what is not plainly contained in Scripture, after my best endeavour used; to say that God will damn me for such errors, who am a lover of him, and lover of truth, is to rob man of his comfort, and God of his goodness; is to make men desperate, and God a Tyrant.* (pp. 3-4)[12]

In keeping with the Protestant rule of faith as developed by Laud and Chillingworth, the Socinian interlocutor maintains that the only condition for apprehending the true sense of Scripture with regard to all things necessary to salvation is simply doing one's epistemic best. Moreover, a person's epistemic best is sufficient for getting at the true sense of Scripture precisely because it would be inconsistent with the wisdom and justice of God to make salvation dependent on her ability to grasp something "obscurely" spoken. Finally, the Socinian adds (again quoting Chillingworth), "The Scripture is a Rule, as sufficiently perfect, so sufficiently intelligible in things necessary, to all that have understanding; whether learned, or unlearned. . . . [W]here Scriptures are plain, as they are in necessaries; they need no infallible Interpreter, no further explanation" (p. 4).

Not surprisingly, the Protestant interlocutor agrees entirely with this line of argument: after all, the Catholic author of the dialogue has borrowed virtually the whole of the argument from the greatest champion of the Protestant rule of faith in seventeenth-century England,

12. The extracts from Chillingworth are in italics.

namely, Chillingworth himself. Having secured the Protestant's agreement, the Socinian declares that the "Consubstantiality of the Son
with God the Father" is "not clear, and evident in Scripture." Therefore,
on pain of contradicting the Protestant rule of faith, he cannot hold it
to be among the things necessary to be believed for salvation. Of
course, the situation with regard to the Trinity is even worse than that.
Thus the Socinian asserts that he "can produce most clear and evident
places out of Scriptures . . . that the contrary is so" (p. 5).

With the appearance of Socinianism, what the Protestant rule of
faith made possible in principle has become reality. The Protestant interlocutor is in a very bad bind. Indeed, he seems to have only three options: he can show that the Trinity is a plain teaching of Scripture; he
can concede that a belief in the Trinity is not necessary to salvation; or
he can maintain the Trinity and give up his rule of faith, returning to
the Catholic Church.

Instinctively, the Protestant pursues the third option, appealing to
tradition as warrant for a Trinitarian interpretation of the relevant passages in Scripture. Consequently, after a dispute over several biblical
texts, the exasperated Protestant interlocutor argues that, because "so
great a part of the Christian world (doubtless rational men), in the
sense of these very Scriptures" differs from the Socinian, there must be
a "defect" in the Socinian's "due industry" (p. 8). With this move, the
Protestant has now introduced a Catholic interpretive principle into
the rules governing the application of the Protestant rule of faith.

The Socinian's threefold response is devastating. First, he rightly
maintains that the same criticism could be turned against the Reformers themselves. Second, he argues that there never has been "an
unanimous consent of the Church Catholick of all ages" concerning
"the aforementioned Consubstantiality" (pp. 13-14). Third, he reminds
the Protestant interlocutor (quoting Edward Stillingfleet to good effect) that, even if the majority of the "Church Catholick" could be
shown to support the doctrine, "the sense of the Church Catholick is
no infallible rule of interpreting Scripture in all things which concern
the Rule of Faith" (p. 14).

The irony here is not to be missed: in the face of Unitarian opposition, the Protestant has instinctively sought safety behind the Catholic
rule of faith. Consequently, the Socinian has to remind the Protestant
that the interpretation of Scripture by reason and not by tradition is

the Protestant rule of faith. And thus the dialogue ends. The exasperated Protestant has no choice but to confess that he is a closet Catholic, relying unconsciously on the Catholic rule of faith in his interpretation of Scripture. Moreover, he admits that only the Catholic rule of faith can safeguard the Trinity from Socinian opposition.

The second dialogue, *A Dialogue Between a New Catholic Convert and a Protestant* (hereafter the *Dialogue*),was even more rhetorically persuasive than the first. Recalling the Protestant insistence that Scripture be understood in accordance with reason in the recent debates over transubstantiation, the author of this dialogue argues that the Trinity is even more difficult to secure by reason than transubstantiation. Once again, the Protestant's options are clear: he can maintain his argument against transubstantiation and give up the Trinity, or he can recognize that reason is not a sufficient ground on which to reject either transubstantiation or the Trinity and return to the Catholic Church.

The Catholic interlocutor begins the dialogue by claiming that the mysteries under consideration, the Trinity and transubstantiation, "have equal ground from Scripture, Reason, and Tradition." As such, he claims, there is "the same obligation of your receiving the one, as well as the other." Of course, the fact that he has already asserted that reason is of no help for understanding the mysteries of the Christian religion suggests that the statement regarding Scripture, reason, and tradition is really a rhetorical straw man. The author is clearly setting a trap, strategically moving the Protestant interlocutor into a corner.

After listening to the Catholic's argument from tradition, the Protestant interlocutor reminds his opponent that he is committed to *sola Scriptura*:

> Well, Sir, 'tis true, we cannot so well plead Tradition to what you have urg'd; and especially when I call to mind, that Arianism was confirm'd by a General Council: But we alledge an higher ground; we stand on the Authority of the Scriptures, and indeed that is the true Touchstone of all Doctrine. (*Dialogue*, p. 3)

Once again, the debate ultimately comes to turn on the interpretation of Scripture. It is here that the Catholic author of the dialogue wittingly enlists the Arians and Socinians in his cause:

'Tis true, if you will follow the Catholic Church, and take the Scriptures literally, you may discover the Mystery of the Holy Trinity in them; but if you once yield to Figurative Allusions and Interpretations, the Arians will be as much too hard for you, as you imagine your selves to be for the Catholic Church. In short, both Doctrins will be at a loss, and both equally require the Authority of the Church to support them. (pp. 3-4)

Though the Protestant interlocutor does not yet realize it, the argument is over. With regard to the interpretation of Scripture, the Protestant has two choices: on the one hand, he can interpret Scripture literally, in which case he must affirm transubstantiation alongside the Trinity; on the other, he can dismiss transubstantiation by interpreting passages related to it figuratively. But if he does that, he will have to explain why Arians and Socinians cannot do the same with respect to passages related to the relationship between Jesus and God the Father. Thus the Catholic observes:

'Tis as reasonable to take *This is my Body* literally as it is to take these Texts *I and my Father are one God ever all blessed for ever,* and *by him all things were made,* without reference to other Scriptures, and a Figurative Interpretation. (p. 6; italics in original)

Next, the Catholic interlocutor argues that the parallel between the Trinity and transubstantiation is the easiest to maintain with regard to reason. "'Tis strange new Arithmetic to a Man," he says, "to tell him, Three distinct Persons are one and the same Individual Nature." He continues: "For my part, I cannot tell well how the Prejudice of Education could possibly digest a thing so unreasonable, were it not a Divine Mystery." Moreover, he is sure that by his "Carnal Reason, there may be as well Three hundred Persons in the Godhead, as Three," and he cannot fathom "what can be said of Transubstantiation that is . . . more absurd than That" (p. 5). He concludes: "[It is] as equally unreasonable, and as seemingly repugnant, to say One is Three, as it is to say a Body is not what it appears" (p. 6).[13]

13. It is worth noting that the Catholic propagandist could have made an even stronger case here. For example, he could have argued that the Trinity is considerably more irrational or contrary to reason than transubstantiation. While transubstantia-

As the dialogue draws to a close, the Protestant interlocutor is left with two options. First, now that the Catholic has removed his objections to transubstantiation with an argument from analogy with the Trinity, he can return home to the Catholic Church, where the Trinity is safe from Arian, Socinian, and Unitarian objections. Second, he can maintain his allegiance to Scripture as the rule of faith and, rejecting both transubstantiation and the Trinity, join ranks with the Unitarians. The problem is clear: transubstantiation and the Trinity rise or fall together; Rome is the only alternative to Rakow. Thus the author of the *Dialogue* concludes by urging the Protestant interlocutor to follow his example and become "a new Catholic convert."[14]

Maneuvering for a Stalemate: The Protestant Rejoinder

Leading Protestant theologians in the mid-1680s were in no mood to abandon their hard-won rule of faith. The rule of faith was indispensable both as a warrant for the Protestant vision of salvation and as a way for Protestants to obtain assurance of salvation. Therefore, when William Sherlock and Edward Stillingfleet published responses to the Catholic dialogues quoted above, their primary objective was to show that the Protestant rule of faith did not make the Trinity vulnerable to Unitarian objections.[15] In reality, Sherlock and Stillingfleet were ma-

---

tion seems to be contrary to the empirical evidence acquired through sense perception, the Trinity appears to violate the principle of noncontradiction known by intuition. On the one hand, we know that sense perception is not always reliable; indeed, we can think of instances where sense perception has failed us. On the other hand, we know of no instances where the principle of noncontradiction has failed us. Therefore, one could make the case that the Trinity is more problematic with regard to reason than is transubstantiation. Indeed, the Catholic propagandist may even have considered making this a stronger case; after all, he does make the negative case that transubstantiation cannot be "more absurd" than the Trinity. In my judgment, it is likely that the Catholic propagandist held back from making a stronger positive claim because his goal was to argue on behalf of the Catholic rule of faith and not, as Tillotson would suggest, to undermine the Trinity.

14. It is doubtful that the author really was a "new Catholic convert." Rather, his identity should be seen as part of a brilliant rhetorical strategy.

15. See William Sherlock, *An Answer to a Late Dialogue Between a New Catholick Convert and a Protestant, To Prove the Mystery of the Trinity to be as absurd a Doctrine as Transub-*

neuvering for a stalemate. Well aware that they now had enemies on two fronts, they were keen not to say too much.[16] Wary of overcommitting themselves, the two carefully measured their responses, a strategy in keeping with the general tenor of the Latitudinarian movement of which they were a part.[17]

---

stantiation. *By way of short Notes on the said Dialogue* (London, 1687). Stillingfleet actually went so far as to publish a two-part response. See Edward Stillingfleet, *The Doctrine of the Trinity and Transubstantiation Compared, as to Scripture, Reason, and Tradition. In a New Dialogue between a Protestant and a Papist. The First Part. Wherein an Answer is given to the late Proofs of the Antiquity of Transubstantiation, in the Books called Consenses Veterum, and Nubes Testium, etc.* (London, 1686); and *The Doctrine of the Trinity and Transubstantiation Compared, as to Scripture, Reason, and Tradition. In a New Dialogue between a Protestant and a Papist. The Second Part. Wherein the Doctrine of the Trinity is shewed to be agreeable to Scripture and Reason, and Transubstantiation repugnant to both* (London, 1687). In response to *The Protestants Plea for a Socinian,* Thomas Tenison (1636-1715), the future Archbishop of Lincoln, also published a response. Tenison tried to turn the tables on the Catholic interlocutor by arguing that it was Catholicism rather than Protestantism that had led to the Socinian heresy in the first place. Unfortunately, even if all of Tenison's historical arguments were sound, he failed to take seriously the charge that the Protestant rule of faith could not secure the Trinity against Socinian or Unitarian objections. In short, Tenison had misidentified the nature of the Catholic argument. The full title of Tenison's response is *The Difference Betwixt the Protestant and Socinian Methods: In Answer to a Book Written by a Romanist, and Intituled The Protestants Plea for a Socinian* (London, 1687).

16. In chess, a stalemate is a tie that results when one player manages to maneuver her king into a position that is the only "safe" one available. In other words, the other player cannot move his king anywhere else without moving into "checkmate" and losing the match. The analogy is especially fitting because maneuvering for a stalemate is something that skilled chess players can do intentionally when the odds of winning the match outright are not especially good.

17. The Latitudinarians were deeply aware of the extent to which their theological predecessors had, in overcommitting themselves to reason, helped to trigger many of the present dangers. The spirit of the Latitudinarian theologians was one of conciliation and mediation. Their aim was often to soften and refine the stance taken by, among others, the Cambridge Platonists. However, it is important to note that the term "latitudinarian" can be problematic. Carroll says: "In its broadest sense, the term generally designated the moderate wing of the Church, though the term itself can be deceptive, since 'moderation' only gets its meaning in terms of the excesses at the time that the term is deployed to describe . . . . Thus, a latitude-man in the age of Stillingfleet does not appear as broadminded as a latitude-man in the age of Chillingworth. The moderate Anglican view fifty years after Chillingworth's death in 1644 became much more conservative." Carroll, *The Common-Sense Philosophy,* p. 6. For the various applications of the term "latitudinarian," see John Tulloch, *Rational Theology and Christian Philosophy,* 2 vols. (Germany: Georg Olms Verlagsbuchhandlung, 1966; repr. of 1823 ed.), 2:6-35.

For his part, Sherlock began by arguing that the author of *A Dialogue Between a New Catholick Convert and a Protestant*, in the name of demonstrating the superiority of the Catholic rule of faith, had admitted that neither the Trinity nor transubstantiation "are reasonable, or have any Authority." In one sense, Sherlock was simply calling attention to the fact that Catholic propagandists were actively promoting Socinian arguments against the Trinity. In Sherlock's eyes, this alone was enough to make these new dialogues unworthy of serious consideration: it was one thing for Catholics to argue that transubstantiation contradicts reason; it was quite another for them to "[d]ishonour . . . common Christianity, by exposing the most sacred and venerable Mystery of it to the Scorn and Derision of Infidels and Hereticks." Indeed, it was mind-boggling that these Catholic authors thought it a "great credit to the Doctrine of the Trinity; that it cannot be proved, either by *Tradition, Scripture, or Reason*" (*An Answer*, p. 2; italics in original).

Of course, Sherlock knew only too well that the purpose of the treatise was "to bring men to rely on the Authority of the Church." Thus he rather sarcastically observes that the point of the dialogue is to persuade Protestants "to fling away Sense, and Reason, and Scripture, and [their] own private Judgment, and to rely wholly on the Authority of the Church." For Sherlock, such a move was unthinkable, "for when these are out of the way, we may believe the Church in any thing" (p. 2). Indeed, Sherlock does not scruple about the depth of his commitment to reason. He says: "I can't believe that which is unreasonable and absurd, whoever tells it me" (p. 2).

Far from demonstrating that the Protestant rule of faith did not, as the Socinians claimed, render the Trinity unnecessary to be believed for salvation, Sherlock's argument appeared to raise the stakes. He clearly did not think the Socinian objection to the Trinity was sufficiently problematic to warrant abandoning the Protestant rule of faith and returning to the Catholic Church. As Sherlock certainly understood, this left only two options. He would either have to prove that the Trinity was contained in clear and intelligible propositions in Scripture, or he would have to adopt a soft Unitarian position, conceding that the Trinity was not necessary to be believed for salvation.

In Sherlock's mind, there was an easy solution to the problem posed by the Catholic dialogues. One simply needed to distinguish things subject to reason from things above reason. Transubstantiation had to do with things subject to reason; by contrast, the Trinity had to do with things above reason. At bottom, this move presupposed a neat separation between the natural and supernatural realms. In the natural realm, reason was both reliable and sufficient, providing people with sound knowledge. With regard to the supernatural realm, reason was of little use: humans were dependent on divine revelation. Thus Sherlock says:

> For though God reveals things to us, as Natural Reason could not discover; and cannot comprehend, yet Revelation cannot contradict plain Reason; for Truth can never contradict it self; what is true in Revelation, can never be false in Reason; and what is true by Natural Reason can never be false in Revelation.[18]

Stillingfleet agreed, arguing that the Trinity was above reason and transubstantiation contrary to it. According to Stillingfleet, reason and sense experience were completely sufficient for understanding the properties of physical bodies. Indeed, he had made this point rather forcefully in an earlier debate concerning transubstantiation:

> There is far greater ground why we should reject Transubstantiation and ubiquity, as inconsistent with reason . . . because the grounds of reason on which we reject those opinions are fetched from those essential and inseparable properties of bodies, which are inconsistent with those opinions; now these are things within the reach of our understandings (in which case God himself sometimes appeals to reason).[19]

However, in his response to *A Dialogue Between a New Catholick Convert and a Protestant,* Stillingfleet went further, arguing not only from the reliability of sense perception but also from the inability of God to contradict the laws of nature:

18. William Sherlock, *A Vindication of the Doctrine of the Holy and Ever Blessed Trinity, and the Incarnation of the Son of God, Occasioned by the Brief Notes on the Creed of St. Athanasius, and the Brief History of the Unitarians, or Socinians; and containing an Answer to both* (London, 1690), p. 147.

19. Stillingfleet, *Origines Sacrae, or a Rational Account of the Grounds of Christian Faith, as the Truth and Divine Authority of the Scripture, and the Matters therein contained* (London, 1662), pp. 238-39.

Those things are by the ordinary Course of Nature, which cannot be changed but by Divine Power, but imply no repugnancy for God to alter that Course; but those are by the unchangeable Order of Nature, which cannot be done without overthrowing the very Nature of the things; *and such things are impossible in themselves, and therefore God himself cannot do them.*[20]

Stillingfleet's appeal to reason and sense experience as reliable guides for understanding the natural realm was perfectly in keeping with the language and logic of learned discourse in seventeenth-century England. Virtually all people of learning in late seventeenth-century England wanted to restrict knowledge of the natural realm to reason and sense experience.[21] Sherlock and Stillingfleet stood at the end of a long and complex process, the primary aim of which had been to eliminate appeals to mystery or divine revelation from everyday explorations of the natural world. This process had begun when many of England's leading intellectuals became convinced that approaching nature from within theological and philosophical frameworks prevented genuine understanding of the "things" of nature.[22] Inspired by the work of Francis Bacon, English natural philosophers regarded the sacramental view of the natural world and the Aristotelian categories used to support it as especially problematic.[23] Moreover, the Baconian quest to understand the natural world without the distorting influences of theological or philosophical categories had led to the formation of the

---

20. Edward Stillingfleet, *Works*, 6 vols. (London, 1707-10), 4:601 (italics in original).

21. For the emerging confidence in reason for apprehending the nature of things in the natural world, see Barbara Shapiro, *Probability and Certainty in Seventeenth-Century England: A Study of the Relationships between Natural Science, Religion, History, Law, and Literature* (Princeton: Princeton University Press, 1983). See also Cragg, *From Puritanism to the Age of Reason*, pp. 87-113, and John Redwood, *Reason, Ridicule and Religion: The Age of Enlightenment in England 1660-1750* (London: Thames and Hudson, 1976), pp. 93-115.

22. For an outstanding analysis of the developments that brought about this conviction, see Peter Harrison, *The Bible, Protestantism, and the Rise of Natural Science* (New York: Cambridge University Press, 1998).

23. For an assessment of Bacon's worries about the distorting effects of Aristotelian categories, see William S. Babcock, "The Commerce Between the Mind and Things," *The Unbounded Community: Papers in Christian Ecumenism in Honor of Jaroslav Pelikan*, ed. William Caferro and Duncan G. Fisher (New York and London: Garland Publishing, 1996), pp. 163-86.

Royal Society, the chief aim of which was to promote the study of the natural world through reason and sense experience alone.[24] Thus, when Stillingfleet invoked the reliability of natural reason against transubstantiation, it was against the backdrop of increasingly widespread agreement that appeals to mystery and divine revelation had no place in the quest for knowledge of the natural realm.

Having maintained that sense experience and reason were sufficient for knowledge of the natural realm, Stillingfleet went on to argue that reason was not equipped to make judgments about things in the supernatural or divine realm. The doctrines of the Trinity, the nature of Christ, and the manner of our salvation, he urged, were "above reason." Nor was this an entirely new proposal. On the contrary, Stillingfleet's position concerning reason's inability to obtain knowledge of the supernatural realm reflected a similar position enshrined in the earliest creeds and confessions of English Protestantism. Beginning with the earliest English Protestant confessions, the Trinity, the incarnation, and the atonement were matters of "saving knowledge," which by definition meant that they were inaccessible by natural reason. Thus the Scotch Creed of 1560 declares:

> For of nature we are so dead, so blind, and so perverse, that neither can we feill when we are pricked, see the licht when it shines, nor assent to the will of God when it is revealed, unless the Spirit of the Lord Jesus quicken that quhilk is dead, remove the darnesse from our myndes, and bow our stubborn hearts to the obedience of his blessed will.

Similarly, the Thirty-Nine Articles of Religion (1563) deny that saving knowledge could be obtained by natural reason:

> They also are to be had accursed that presume to say, That every man shall be saved by the Law or Sect which he professeth, so that he be diligent to frame his life according to that Law, and the light of Nature.

---

24. Richard H. Popkin, "The Philosophy of the Royal Society of England," in *The Columbia History of Western Philosophy*, ed. Richard H. Popkin (New York: Columbia University Press, 1999), pp. 358-62.

Finally, the architects of the Westminster Confession (1647) had been careful to say that the light of nature was "not sufficient to give that knowledge of God, and of his will, which is necessary unto salvation."[25] Against this backdrop of creedal and confessional consensus, Stillingfleet declared that the Trinity was above reason. The core of his argument was straightforward enough: those who objected to the Trinity and incarnation simply failed "to keep [reason] in its due channel."[26] Thus, Stillingfleet complained that the Socinians "send us to created Beings for the Rules and Measures of our Judgment concerning a Being acknowledged to be Infinite."[27]

Sherlock made a very similar move, arguing that the real problem was not with the Trinity, but rather with the Socinians' failure to recognize and respect the limits of human reason. The Socinians had simply failed to exercise proper epistemic humility with regard to the scope of reason. Sherlock says:

> [It] is an impudent Argument, which brings Revelation down in such sublime Mysteries to the level of our Understandings, to say, such a Doctrine cannot be contained in Scripture, because it implies a Contradiction; whereas a modest man would first inquire, whether it be in Scripture or not, and if it be plainly contained there, he would conclude, how unintelligible soever it appeared to him, that yet there is no Contradiction in it, because it is taught by Scripture: We must not indeed expound Scripture contrary to common Sense, and to the common Reason of Mankind, in such matters as every man knows, and every man can judge of; but in Matters of pure Revelation, which we have no natural idea of, and know nothing of but what is revealed, we must not pretend some imaginary Contradictions to reject the plain and express Authority of a Revelation; for it is impossible to know, what is a Contradiction to the Nature of Things, whose Natures we do not understand.[28]

---

25. The excerpts from the Scotch Creed, the Thirty-Nine Articles, and the Westminster Confession are quoted here as they appear in Peter Harrison, *'Religion' and the Religions in the English Enlightenment* (New York: Cambridge University Press, 1990), pp. 20-21.

26. Stillingfleet, *Origines Sacrae*, p. 237.

27. Stillingfleet, *Works,* 4:633.

28. Sherlock, *Vindication*, pp. 141-42.

The position of Sherlock and Stillingfleet with regard to reason amounted to a *via media* between the Catholic view of the relationship between reason and revelation on the one hand, and the Socinian and Unitarian view of that relationship on the other. In the Catholic view, as shown by the doctrine of transubstantiation, divine revelation could "correct" or "enhance" human understanding not only of things divine but also of things in the natural realm.[29] In the Socinian or Unitarian view, as shown by the rejection of the doctrine of the Trinity, reason was a reliable judge of assertions about things in both the natural and the supernatural realm.

The proposals by Sherlock and Stillingfleet naturally generated several questions. What grounds did they have for arguing that reason reaches to a certain point but no further? What was to prevent a Socinian or Unitarian from simply replying that Sherlock and Stillingfleet had underestimated the scope and power of reason? Was it by reason or revelation that humans could know where reason left off and divine revelation began?

The temptation at this point is to dig deeper into the arguments of Sherlock and Stillingfleet concerning the limits of reason. But there are at least two problems with this strategy. First, neither Sherlock nor Stillingfleet offered anything like an extensive philosophical analysis of the limits of human reason or understanding. Indeed, such extensive analysis would have to await the publication of John Locke's *Essay Concerning Human Understanding* (1689).[30] Second, and more important, views of the relationship between reason and revelation supervened on theological commitments. In other words, how people thought about both the capacity and the limits of reason was dependent on prior theological commitments concerning the nature of God, humans, and salvation. For example, the Catholic view of the limits of reason super-

---

29. Medieval Catholic theologians developed the notion that divine revelation "corrected" or "enhanced" natural reason's apprehension of the meaning and nature of "things" in the natural world by drawing on and developing Augustine's theory of signs. For an account of this development, see Harrison, *The Bible*, pp. 28-37. For Augustine's theory of signs, see esp. Rebecca Weaver, "Reading the Signs," *Interpretation* 58, no. 1 (2004): 28-34. See also Frances Young, "Augustine's Hermeneutics and Postmodern Criticism," *Interpretation* 58, no. 1 (2004): 42-55.

30. John Locke, *An Essay Concerning Human Understanding*, ed. Peter H. Nidditch (Oxford: Clarendon Press, 1975).

vened on theological commitments having to do with the doctrine of the incarnation.[31] Thus, in order for us truly to understand and appreciate the position of Sherlock and Stillingfleet on the limits of reason, it is important to identify the theological commitments that supported their views.

Theological Commitments and the Suprarationality of Saving Knowledge

While developments in English natural philosophy and the English Protestant creedal and confessional tradition provide the immediate backdrop and support for the position of Sherlock and Stillingfleet on the limits of reason, their position goes back at least to the Continental Reformers. For example, Luther says:

> Plainly, three and two are five, are they not? Again, if a man makes a coat, is he not wise to make it of cloth, or foolish to make it of paper? . . . This is all true, but it is necessary to make a distinction between spiritual and temporal things . . . . [In] divine things, the things concerning God, and in which we must conduct ourselves acceptably with him . . . human nature is absolutely blind, staring stone-blind, unable to recognize in the slightest degree what these things are.[32]

The Magisterial Continental Reformers had developed an entire network of epistemic doctrines in an effort to secure and support the

---

31. We see this especially in the theological rationale for transubstantiation. Peter Harrison says: "As the body is sanctified by Christ's full participation in fleshly humanity, this physical world takes on a new positive light as the locus of divine redemptive activity . . . . This theological emphasis on Christ's body was also reflected in sacramental practice. In the mass, the centerpiece of medieval religion, priests were to rehearse the process of incarnation by transforming the matter of bread and wine into the very substance of God. The elements of the mass were not simply naked signs, significant for what they symbolised: now they were vested with intrinsic importance for what they literally were — the body and blood of Christ. Participants in the eucharist saw themselves as 'eating God'" (Harrison, *The Bible*, pp. 36-37).

32. Martin Luther, "Sermon for Epiphany on Isaiah 60:1-6," in *Sermons of Martin Luther*, ed. John Nicholas Lenker (Grand Rapids: Baker Book House, 1988), 6:319.

all-important doctrine of justification by faith alone, including the doctrines of *sola Scriptura,* the inner witness of the Holy Spirit, and a doctrine of illumination. These epistemic doctrines gave rise to the argument that "saving knowledge" was "above reason." However, while these doctrines served as warrants for the Protestant vision of salvation, they were also closely tied to a network of theological commitments designed to support that vision, including Luther's doctrine of the hiddenness of God and Calvin's doctrines of total depravity, double predestination, and the *Deus absconditus.* Indeed, the epistemic doctrines of *sola Scriptura,* the inner witness, and divine illumination supervened on these foundational theological commitments, especially the doctrine of total depravity.

No theological commitment was more essential for securing the doctrine of justification by faith alone than the doctrine of total depravity. In developing the doctrine of total depravity, the Reformers emphasized that humans are not just morally and spiritually depraved; they are also epistemically depraved.[33] As Luther put it, humans are "stone-blind, unable to recognize in the slightest degree" the "things concerning God."

Calvin brought the epistemic consequences of sin into even sharper focus. To be sure, Calvin's emphasis on the epistemic consequences of sin was intended primarily to support the doctrine of justi-

---

33. For an analysis of the noetic effects of sin, see Alvin Plantinga, *Warranted Christian Belief* (New York: Oxford University Press, 2000), pp. 199-240. Following Calvin, Plantinga says: "Our original knowledge of God and of his marvelous beauty, glory, and loveliness, has been severely compromised; in this way the narrow image of God in us was destroyed and the broad image damaged, distorted. In particular, the *sensus divinitatus* has been damaged and deformed; because of the fall, we no longer know God in the same natural and unproblematic way in which we know each other and the world around us. Still further, sin induces in us a *resistance* to the deliverances of the *sensus divinitatus,* muted as they are by the first factor; we don't want to pay attention to its deliverances. We are unable by our own efforts to extricate ourselves from this quagmire" (Plantinga, *Warranted Christian Belief,* p. 205). See also Merold Westphal, "Taking St. Paul Seriously: Sin as an Epistemological Category," in *Christian Philosophy,* ed. Thomas Flint (Notre Dame, IN: University of Notre Dame Press, 1990), pp. 200-26. Westphal highlights three aspects of Calvin's doctrine of the epistemic consequences of sin: first, the consequences are universal (i.e., "all of us are involved"); second, it is not "simply a matter of ignorance or weakness," but we deliberately turn our thoughts away from God; finally, the result is not a "spiritual vacuum" but "idolatry" (p. 201).

fication by faith alone. After all, if humans could identify and understand Scripture as the Word of God without God's help, then in some sense they could be said to have some role in bringing about their salvation. In this way, the doctrine of justification by faith alone could be understood in a way that allowed meritorious works to sneak in through a back door. While the doctrines of the inner witness and illumination of the Holy Spirit served as warrants for the formal appeal to Scripture, they also worked hand in hand with a doctrine of total depravity to give material support to the doctrine of justification by faith alone. If people could not identify and understand the Word of God without the help of the Holy Spirit, then they could not think — in recognizing the doctrine of salvation by faith alone contained in it — that they had done something to merit their salvation.

Despite having developed and used the doctrines of total depravity, the inner witness, and divine illumination to prevent people from thinking they could merit salvation through identifying and understanding the Word of God, Calvin wasn't finished supplying safeguards for the doctrine of justification by faith alone. On the contrary, he was concerned that the desire to find a way to merit salvation was so strong that creative minds would simply find another way to God. Thus, taking a direction that was designed to cut off all unaided access to God, Calvin eliminated the possibility that humans might discover God through reason or through the apprehension of the natural world. For example, this is the way Calvin concludes his long discourse on the inability of both natural reason and the "light of nature" to lead us to God:

> It is therefore in vain that so many burning lamps shine for us in the workmanship of the universe to show forth the glory of its Author. Although they bathe us wholly in their radiance, yet they can of themselves in no way lead us to the right path . . . . [A]lthough the Lord does not want for testimony while he sweetly attracts men to the knowledge of himself with many and varied kindnesses, they do not cease on this account to follow their own ways, that is, their fatal errors.[34]

34. John Calvin, *Institutes of the Christian Religion*, ed. John T. McNeill (Louisville: Westminster John Knox Press, 1960), vol. 1, p. 68.

What are the fatal errors that prevent us from apprehending God either through reason or the light of nature? William J. Abraham observes:

> [Calvin] was thoroughly opposed to attempts to arrive at knowledge of God from observation of, or inference from, the natural order. Although human beings have a natural awareness of God, an implanted understanding of God's majesty, they do not foster this understanding, repelling all remembrance of God from their minds. Not even the continued testimonies of God's wisdom avail to remedy human ignorance; on the contrary, they are met with ingratitude and with a tendency to twist the truth by the ravings of evil imaginations of our flesh, corrupting by vanity the pure truth of God.[35]

For Calvin the epistemic consequences of sin are so devastating that humans can neither identify nor understand the Word of God, nor can they come to know God through natural reason or the light of nature. Thus the constitutive components of the Protestant vision of salvation necessarily lie above unaided reason. Moreover, an entire network of theological commitments lie behind and support the view that "saving knowledge," including knowledge of the Trinity and incarnation, is beyond the grasp of unaided human reason.

Sacrificing the Last Line of Defense

When Sherlock and Stillingfleet invoked the distinction between things above reason and things contrary to reason, they did so knowing that the official creeds and confessions of English Protestantism were on their side. It is true that the creeds and confessions had preserved Calvin's argument that "saving knowledge" could not be obtained by natural reason or by the "light of nature." However, what has been "confessed" in official Christian creeds and confessions down through the ages has not always been reflected in what Christian theologians have actually believed and taught. Moreover, there have been more than a few times when what theologians have believed and taught

35. William J. Abraham, *Canon and Criterion in Christian Theology: From the Fathers to Feminism* (Oxford: Clarendon Press, 1999), p. 131.

has been more influential and widely held than what is confessed in official creeds and confessions.[36]

As things turned out, this was precisely the situation in late seventeenth-century English Protestantism. Sherlock and Stillingfleet severely underestimated the extent to which the material theological commitments had given rise to and supported the Magisterial Reformers' declaration that saving knowledge was above reason had been eroded. Laud, Chillingworth, the Cambridge Platonists, and the Latitudinarians, including Sherlock and Stillingfleet themselves, had embraced Arminianism as a way of putting an end to a twofold crisis of assurance. They had argued throughout the seventeenth century that unaided reason could secure two of the three constitutive components of the Reformation doctrine of salvation, namely, the identification and understanding of the Word of God. In doing so, they took a major step toward undermining the English Protestant creedal and confessional position concerning reason's inability to obtain saving knowledge.

The only thing that now put the divine world beyond the reach of reason was reason's inability to discover God either through innate ideas or by the light of nature. So long as humans were dependent on divine revelation for knowledge of the existence and nature of God, saving knowledge could in some sense be said to be above reason. In this analysis, God simply gives divine revelation in a form that human reason can apprehend. As Chillingworth had said, to suggest otherwise would be "to make God a tyrant." Yet, apart from God's self-disclosure in divine revelation, humans would by the light of nature know nothing of God. Unfortunately, by the time Sherlock and Stillingfleet sought to secure the doctrine of the Trinity by locating it above reason, this final protective barrier between the divine world and human reason had already been sacrificed, like so many pawns in the early stages of a chess match. Sherlock and Stillingfleet were now on the run, desperately trying to maneuver for a stalemate.[37]

Sherlock and Stillingfleet had themselves been instrumental in sacrificing Calvin's stand against the natural knowledge of God. When

36. Jaroslav Pelikan, *The Emergence of the Catholic Tradition*, vol. 1 of *A History of Christian Doctrine* (Chicago: University of Chicago Press, 1971), pp. 1-10.

37. Anyone who has played chess knows that pawns are the most dispensable pieces in the early going. But if a match runs long, pawns can be surprisingly valuable, even indispensable.

they eventually discovered that they had no choice but to show that the
Trinity did not contradict reason, they had no one to blame but themselves. The Trinitarian controversy of the 1690s would be a case of
"death by one's own hand."

The classical Reformed position against the natural knowledge of
God was sacrificed very early in English Protestantism. Beginning with
Hooker's theory of natural law, there emerged a long and rich tradition
in English theology whereby people could know the will of God by the
light of reason.[38] However, in the middle of the seventeenth century
there emerged a deep tension between *revealed* religion, on the one
hand, and *natural* religion, on the other. The emergence of the latter
form of religion in the theology of the Cambridge Platonists and Latitudinarians thoroughly undermined the classical Reformed opposition to natural theology. Peter Harrison summarizes this development:

> Up until the middle of the seventeenth century, the truth of revela-
> tion was contrasted with the light of nature. Almost from the mo-
> ment of its birth, the propositional "religion" was divided into two
> types, based on the two modes of divine knowledge. The "religion"
> witnessed to by Scripture became "revealed religion," a mode of reli-
> gion which was contrasted with "natural religion." Following the
> emergence of the two kinds of religion, there ensued a debate over
> which form was superior. Strict reformed orthodoxy posited a fun-
> damental opposition between the two, claiming the superiority of
> revealed religion in all respects. At the other extreme, "deism" as-
> serted the sufficiency and universality of natural religion. Between
> these two poles were the Cambridge Platonists and "Latitudinarian"
> divines who were willing to concede that natural religion, though de-
> ficient, was a necessary preparation for revealed religion.[39]

38. For examples of the natural-law tradition in seventeenth-century English theology, see Edward Stillingfleet, *Irenicum: A Weapon-Salve for the Churches Wounds: or the Divine Right of Particular Forms of Church Government, Discussed and examined according to the
Principles of the Law of Nature, the positive Laws of God, the Practice of the Apostles, and the Primitive Church, and the Judgment of Reformed Divines. Whereby a Foundation is laid for the
Church's Peace, and the Accommodation of our present Differences* (London, 1659). See also
John Locke, *Essays on the Laws of Nature,* ed. W. von Leyden (Oxford: Clarendon Press,
1988).

39. Harrison, *'Religion' and the Religions,* p. 24. Harrison's is the best available account of the relationship between natural and revealed religion in seventeenth-century

Among the most notable Cambridge Platonists were Henry More (1614-1687), Ralph Cudworth (1617-1688), and Benjamin Whichcote (1609-1680). Indeed, More's *Antidote Against Atheisme* (1659), Cudworth's *The True Intellectual System of the Universe* (1678), and Whichcote's *Moral and Religious Aphorisms* were some of the most influential and controversial works of the early Restoration period. As the title of More's book suggests, the Cambridge Platonists turned to and embraced natural religion as an "antidote against atheism." Above all, the Cambridge Platonists sought to demonstrate by reason the three things that atheists had called into question in seventeenth-century England, namely "the existence of God, providence, and immortality."[40]

With regard to the existence of God, the appeal to reason took the form of a straightforward appeal to the "innate" idea of God. Thus More argued for the "Existency of the God-head from the naturall *Idea* of God, inseparably and immutably residing in the Soul of Man."[41] Moreover, like Laud and Chillingworth before them, the Cambridge Platonists appealed to reason to alleviate their worries about personal assurance that Calvin's *Deus absconditus* and the doctrine of unconditional double predestination were still engendering in and around Cambridge at that time.[42] To resolve this problem, they argued that

---

England. See also Peter Byrne, *Natural Religion and the Nature of Religion: The Legacy of Deism* (New York: Routledge, 1989).

40. Frederick Beiser, *The Sovereignty of Reason: The Defense of Rationality in the Early English Enlightenment* (Princeton: Princeton University Press, 1996), p. 142. For a full account of the Cambridge Platonists' conception and use of reason, see *The Sovereignty of Reason*, pp. 134-83; see also Harrison, *'Religion' and the Religions*, pp. 28-39. For the Cambridge Platonists' concern with atheism, see John Redwood, *Reason, Ridicule and Religion*, pp. 29-69. For an older but still exceptional analysis of the overall thought of the Cambridge Platonists, see Ernst Cassirer, *The Platonic Renaissance in England*, trans. James P. Pettigrove (London: Nelson, 1953). For a solid general introduction to Cambridge Platonism, see Cragg, *From Puritanism to the Age of Reason*, pp. 37-60.

41. Henry More, *An Antidote Against Atheisme* (London, 1653), p. 29.

42. G. R. Cragg says: "The Cambridge Platonists never fell into the facile rationalism which repudiates mysteries simply because they are mysteries, but they deprecated too great an occupation with obscure and unintelligible doctrines. But there was one of the dogmas of Calvinism which they directly and unequivocally attacked. Predestination, they claimed, was neither intellectually nor morally defensible. More bluntly called it 'the black doctrine of absolute reprobation', and Whichcote declared that 'it is not worth the name of religion to charge our consciences with that, which we have not reconciled to the reason and judgment of our minds, to the frame and temper of our

"reason could provide a safe guide to salvation . . . because it could grasp those eternal moral rules that even God himself followed on the day of judgement."[43]

In the end, the Cambridge Platonists took the appeal to reason well beyond the appeal to innate ideas to establish the existence of God and the notion that reason could grasp God's "eternal moral rules." To put it another way, they took the appeal to reason well beyond the development of a natural theology on the one hand and a theory of natural law on the other. Indeed, they developed the appeal to reason into a transmuted version of the appeal to divine speaking. Whichcote put the matter bluntly: "To go against reason is to go against God; it is the selfsame thing, to do that which God Himself doth appoint; reason is the divine governor of man's life; it is the very voice of God."[44]

Finally, in *The True Intellectual System of the Universe*, Ralph Cudworth went so far as to argue that the ancient Platonists had discovered the Trinity by reason.[45] To be sure, Cudworth argued that the Trinity discovered by Platonists had to be conformed to the Trinity as revealed in Scripture and Christian tradition. He says:

> Wheresoever this most Genuine Platonick Trinity, may be found to differ, not only from the Scripture it self (which yet notwithstanding is the single Rule of Faith) but also from the Form of the Nicene and Constantinopolitane Councils; and further from the Doctrine of Athanasius too, in his Genuine Writings . . . [it] is there utterly disclaimed and rejected by us. (p. 620)

Despite these concessions, the very fact that Cudworth thought that the Platonists had secured the Trinity by reason is indicative of just how far the Cambridge Platonists were willing to go in extending reason's reach beyond the so-called natural realm. Thus John Marshall

---

souls'. It is [therefore] not surprising that a rigid Calvinist like Thomas Goodwin regarded the Cambridge Platonists with horror" (*From Puritanism to the Age of Reason*, p. 40). Harrison agrees: "If the Cambridge Platonists denied the Calvinist view of natural religion, they were even less eager to affirm the dark doctrine of double predestination" (*'Religion' and the Religions*, p. 29).

43. Beiser, *The Sovereignty of Reason*, p. 149.

44. Benjamin Whichcote, *Moral and Religious Aphorisms . . . to which are added Eight Letters which passed between Dr. Whichcote . . . and Dr. Tuckney* (London, 1753), p. 76.

45. Ralph Cudworth, *The True Intellectual System of the Universe* (London, 1678).

says: "The Unitarians could not have wished for better ammunition for their association of the Trinity with a Platonic corruption of Christianity, and they made much of Cudworth's claim."[46]

As so often happens, it was the students of the Cambridge Platonists and not the Cambridge Platonists themselves who would have to respond to Unitarian objections. Chief among the students who would later take up this task of responding were none other than Sherlock and Stillingfleet, both of whom were educated at Cambridge during the heyday of Cambridge Platonism. Not surprisingly, Sherlock and Stillingfleet readily embraced the Cambridge Platonists' confidence in reason.[47]

Like the Cambridge Platonists before him, Stillingfleet, a fellow at St. John's College, Cambridge, published numerous works that extended reason's reach well beyond the natural realm. In *Origines Sacrae* (1662) and *A Rational Account of the Grounds of the Protestant Religion* (1664), Stillingfleet argued that reason could demonstrate the existence of God, establish the divine authority of Scripture, and provide assurance of salvation.[48] Indeed, Stillingfleet repeatedly claimed that "the idea of God is most consonant to Reason."[49]

46. John Marshall, "Locke, 'Socinianism, Socinianism', Unitarianism," in *English Philosophy in the Age of Locke,* edited by M. A. Stewart (Oxford: Clarendon Press, 2000), p. 123. For the Unitarian use of Cudworth's argument against the Trinitarians, see Herbert McLachlan, *The Religious Opinions of Milton, Locke, and Newton* (New York: Russell and Russell, 1972), pp. 105-6.

47. Beiser says: "Among the disciples of the Cambridge school were some important latitudinarian divines: Simon Patrick (1626-1707), Edward Fowler (1632-1714), John Tillotson (1630-1694), John Moore (1646-1714), Gilbert Burnet (1643-1715), Edward Stillingfleet (1635-1699), and Thomas Tenison (1636-1715)" (Beiser, *The Sovereignty of Reason,* p. 134). Not surprisingly, virtually every person in Beiser's list would go on to play a role in the Trinitarian controversy of the 1690s. William Sherlock should be added to Beiser's list.

48. Cragg declares: "Stillingfleet was continually defending revelation by appeal to reason. He proved that the Mosaic history must be true because it was reasonable, and he established the credibility of the whole idea of revelation on purely rational grounds" (*From Puritanism to the Age of Reason,* pp. 68-69). For a summary of Stillingfleet's various arguments from reason for the existence of God, see Carroll, *The Common-Sense Philosophy,* pp. 114-35.

49. See Stillingfleet, *Origines Sacrae,* pp. 367, 371. It is important to note that in using arguments from reason for the existence of God, Stillingfleet was one of the early pioneers of what would become the distinguishing characteristic of Anglican theistic epis-

The same can be said for Sherlock. For example, in the opening
section of *A Vindication of the Doctrine of the Holy and Ever Blessed Trinity*, Sherlock provides an argument from reason for the existence of
God:

> As unconceivable the Notion of Eternity is, yet all Mankind, even
> Atheists themselves, must confess, that something was from Eter-
> nity; for if ever there was nothing, it is impossible there ever should
> have been anything; for that which once was not, can never be with-
> out a Cause, and therefore whatever Difficulties there may be in the
> Notion of an Eternal Being, we must acknowledge something Eter-
> nal . . . and I am sure the Notion of a first Eternal Cause, is much
> more easie and natural, than to make either Matter, or the World,
> and all the Creatures in it Eternal.[50]

On the one hand, Sherlock and Stillingfleet followed in the Cambridge Platonists' footsteps in their appeals to reason to demonstrate
the existence of God, providence, and immortality. On the other hand,
they were also deeply worried that the appeal to reason would get out
of hand. As we have seen in the preceding chapter, Stillingfleet in particular wanted to put the brakes on reason. In an effort to stem the ris-
ing tide of natural reason, Stillingfleet developed the following principle: "The immediate dictates of natural light are not to be the measure
of divine revelation" (*Origines Sacrae*, p. 25). It was not clear in what

---

temology right down to the present day, namely, the "cumulative-case" argument. Thus
Carroll says: "But, although one might object to each of his arguments for the existence
of God because they failed to *prove* the truth of God's existence, Stillingfleet claimed
that when *taken as a whole*, his defense of theism possessed a strength which was greater
than the sum of its parts. Each argument he had to offer may be weak when taken by itself, but taken in its context, and in relation to all his other arguments taken in their
contexts, the overall argument for God would be sufficient to convince any reasonable
and unprejudiced man" (*The Common-Sense Philosophy*, p. 116). Anglican philosophers and
theologians to make use of cumulative-case arguments include Richard Hooker, William Chillingworth, John Locke, Bishop Butler, John Henry Newman, William Tennant,
J. R. Lucas, Basil Mitchell, Richard Swinburne, and Caroline Franks Davis. For an analysis of the nature and use of cumulative-case arguments, see William J. Abraham, "Cumulative Case Arguments," in *The Rationality of Religious Belief: Essays in Honor of Basil
Mitchell*, ed. William J. Abraham and Steven Holtzer (New York: Oxford University Press,
1987), pp. 17-38.

50. Sherlock, *Vindication*, p. 5.

sense, if any, Stillingfleet, having established this principle, could himself abide by it. The Latitudinarians, including Stillingfleet and Sherlock, customarily made a twofold appeal to reason. Like Laud and Chillingworth, they regularly appealed to reason to secure the identity and correct interpretation of Scripture as the Word of God. Like the Cambridge Platonists, they appealed to reason to prove the existence of God.

What Stillingfleet did not realize at the time was that the Unitarians only needed this twofold appeal to reason — and not the excesses of Whichcote and Cudworth — to deny the doctrine of the Trinity. Thus the Unitarians challenged the doctrine of the Trinity by combining the rationalist hermeneutics of Laud and Chillingworth and the natural theology developed by the Cambridge Platonists and later endorsed by the Latitudinarians themselves. Having abandoned the classical Reformed opposition to natural theology in their attacks on atheism, Stillingfleet and Sherlock had already helped to sacrifice the last line of defense behind which they could maintain that the Trinity was a mystery of faith above reason.

The Protestant Counterattack Begins

It did not take long for the Unitarians to object to the Protestant response to the Catholic dialogues discussed above. In *Brief Notes on the Creed of St. Athanasius,* an anonymous Unitarian author challenged the argument of Sherlock and Stillingfleet that the Trinity was above reason. According to this author, Sherlock and Stillingfleet were denying to reason its proper role in the interpretation of Scripture.

> And the truth is, the Contest between the Unitarians and Trinitarians is not, as is commonly thought, a clash of Reason with Scripture; but it layeth here, whether, when the Holy Scripture may be understood as teaching only One God, or but One who is God, which agrees with the rest of Scripture, and with Natural Reason, we must notwithstanding preferr an Interpretation of it that is absurd, and contrary to it Self, to reason, and to the rest of Scripture, such as the Trinitarians Interpretation (exprest in this Creed) appears to be! In a word, the Question only is, *Whether we ought to Interpret Holy Scripture,*

*when it speaks of God, according to Reason, or not, that is, like fools, or like
wise Men.*[51]

Sherlock was infuriated by the suggestion that he and Stillingfleet
were refusing to interpret Scripture in accordance with reason, and he
set out to rebut the Unitarian challenge. The result was *A Vindication of
the Doctrine of the Holy and Ever Blessed Trinity.* Responding in a line-by-
line fashion to the argument in the *Brief Notes,* Sherlock distinguished
between two senses in which one can interpret Scripture according to
reason:

> Now this is all sham, and fallacy: For to expound Scripture by Rea-
> son, may signifie two very different things. 1. To use our own Reason
> to find out the true Sense and Interpretation of Scripture. 2. To ex-
> pound Scripture in Conformity with the Principles and Maxims of
> Natural Reason. In the first sense, he expounds Scripture according
> to Reason, who considers the Use and Propriety of Words, the Scope
> and Design of the Place, what goes before, and what follows, and
> how one place of Scripture is consistent with another . . . and he who
> does not thus expound Scripture by Reason, expounds it *like a fool;*
> that is, if he put such a Sense upon it, as the Words will not bear, or
> the Design of the Text will not admit, and as no Man would think of,
> who were not presupposed and prejudiced against what appears to
> be the plain and obvious Sense of the Text. (p. 146; italics in original)

Having distinguished between interpreting Scripture according to
discursive reason and interpreting it according to natural reason,
Sherlock went on to argue that Scripture should be interpreted in accordance with discursive reason. The role of reason in the interpretation of
Scripture, he said, is to identify the "plain and obvious Sense of the
Text." Sherlock then quickly added that Scripture must be interpreted
in accordance with natural reason as well. Otherwise, as Sherlock knew
only too well, Protestant theologians would be unable to refute Catholic
appeals to Scripture to secure transubstantiation. Thus he declares:

> As for the other Sense of expounding Scripture according to Reason;
> that is, in Conformity to the Principles and Maxims of Natural Rea-

---

51. Quoted in Sherlock, *Vindication,* p. 140.

son; we allow this too so far, that we must not expound Scripture to such a sense, as contradicts the plain and express Maxims of Natural Reason. (p. 147)

It is at this point that Sherlock began to come to grips with the heart of the Unitarian challenge: when combined with a rationalist hermeneutic, Protestant arguments that the existence of God can be known by reason circumvent arguments that the Trinity is "above reason." Sherlock summarizes the Unitarian position:

Natural Reason tells us, That there is, and can be but One Supreme God, the Sovereign Lord of the World, and should any Man pretend to prove from Scripture, that there are Three Gods, this would be an express Contradiction to the Natural Belief of One God, and therefore we must reject this sense of Scripture, as contrary to Reason: but to prove from Scripture, that there is but One God, this is no Contradiction to Reason, which teaches but One God. (p. 147)

However, in response to Unitarian objections, Sherlock claims that when reason proves the existence of God, it tells us nothing of the nature or personality of God.

Yes, you'll say, that there should be Three Persons, each of which is God, and yet but One God, is a Contradiction: But what Principle of Natural Reason does it contradict? Reason tells us, that Three *Gods* cannot be One God, but does Reason tell us, that Three Divine *Persons* cannot be One God? . . . Natural Reason teaches nothing about the Personality of the Godhead; it teaches One God, but whether this One God, be One or Three Persons, it says not, and therefore it may be either, without contradicting the Natural Notions we have of One God. (pp. 147-49; italics in original)

It is at this crucial moment in the debate that the Protestant rule of faith works against Sherlock and Stillingfleet. According to the Protestant rule of faith, the triune personality of God can only be among the things necessary to be believed for salvation if it is contained in clear and intelligible propositions. Thus the Unitarians maintained that, on the plain and intelligible sense of the word "person," "three divine persons" equals "three Gods." Unless Sherlock and

Stillingfleet could provide a plain and intelligible sense of the word "person" on which "three divine persons" did not equal "three Gods," then they would have to admit that the Trinity contradicts what is known by reason, namely, that there is one God.

In raising this objection, the Socinians and Unitarians were simply registering that there was a problem in the principle of individuation, a problem that the best medieval Catholic minds had been unable to resolve successfully. However, given the Protestant rule of faith, the doctrine of the Trinity could only be retained as necessary to be believed for salvation if Protestant theologians could provide a satisfactory solution to the problem. Thus Sherlock concluded that he had to take the Unitarian challenge head-on, providing a reasonable solution to the problem of individuation.

Together with Laud, Chillingworth, the Cambridge Platonists, and the other Latitudinarians, Sherlock was more deeply committed to maintaining Scripture as the Protestant rule of faith than he was to any particular material doctrine, including the doctrine of the Trinity. Thus, in a statement that marks both the beginning of the great Trinitarian controversy of the 1690s and, with it, the beginning of modern Christian theology, Sherlock says:

> But suppose then, that the Natural Construction of the Words, import such a Sense, as is contrary to some evident Principle of Reason? then I won't believe it. How not believe Scripture? No, no, I will believe no pretended Revelation, which contradicts the plain Dictates of Reason, which all mankind agree in, and were I persuaded, that those Books, which we call the Holy Scriptures did so, I would not believe them; and this is a fairer and honester way, than to force them to speak, what every impartial Man, who reads them, must think was never intended, that we may believe them. (p. 151)

Refusing to admit that the "Natural Construction of the Words" in Scripture was in any way contrary to "some evident Principle of Reason," Sherlock resolved to tackle the problem of the principle of individuation. The stakes could not have been higher. In his debate with the Catholics a few years earlier, he had made it clear that he would not give up the Protestant rule of faith under any circumstances. As far as Sherlock was concerned, salvation itself was dependent on rational assent to the clear and intelligible propositions contained in Scripture. A return to the Catholic rule of faith was thus, from Sherlock's point of view, impossible. He would either have to provide a clear and intelligible account of "person" on which three persons did not equal three Gods, or he would have to concede that the Trinity was not among the things necessary to be believed for salvation.

To his great credit, and to the great detriment of the doctrine of the Trinity, Sherlock rose to meet the Unitarian challenge head-on. At the outset of his *Vindication of the Doctrine of the Trinity,* he declared he would provide "a very easie and intelligible Notion of a Trinity in Unity."[52] In doing so, he sparked off a controversy over the Trinity that would last for the next two decades. He also set the terms on which the Trinity would either be secured or undermined. Indeed, John Wallis would follow Sherlock's lead in trying to secure the Trinity by resolving the problem of the principle of individuation. What few, if any, noticed at this stage was the degree to which Trinitarian theological reflection was now focused exclusively on the immanent Trinity. The economic Trinity was nowhere in sight.

---

52. Sherlock, *Vindication,* "To the Reader."

CHAPTER 4

Boethius's Ghost

And it is no more absurd or inconsistent, to say, that God the Father, God the Son, and God the Holy Ghost, are the same God; than to say, that God the Creator, God the Redeemer, and God the Sanctifier, are the same God.

John Wallis

As the last decade of the seventeenth century got under way, English Protestant theologians faced a difficult dilemma. On the one hand, they could maintain their commitment to Scripture as the rule of faith and concede that the Trinity was not among the things necessary to be believed for salvation. On the other hand, they could give up their conception of Scripture as the rule of faith (a conception that included a rationalist hermeneutics and a canon of essential doctrine) and return to the Catholic Church, where the Trinity was secured by the creed and where the creed made it possible to read Scripture in a Trinitarian way.

Suffice it to say, many English Protestants deemed neither of these options satisfactory. Instead, several prominent Anglican clergy decided to take the Unitarian challenge head-on, including the likes of William Sherlock, John Wallis, and Edward Stillingfleet. From Sherlock's perspective, the task was an easy one. They would demonstrate that the Trinity was rational or intelligible and thus necessary to be believed for salvation. To accomplish this, they simply needed to find an analogy or a definition of terms in which the Trinity makes sense, does not involve logical contradictions, and so on.

While it may not seem immediately obvious, English Protestant defenses of the Trinity in the 1690s let loose a way of thinking about the Trinity that continues largely unabated in English Protestantism to this day. Whatever else the Trinity might be, many English Protestant Christians are sure it is first and foremost a puzzle to be solved; it only requires the correct analogy. The Trinity is like cherry pie. It is like a triangle. It is like ice, water, and steam.

But what the late seventeenth-century divines did not see then and what we often do not see now is that attempts to find analogies or definitions of terms, whatever the level of sophistication, tend to be so utterly preoccupied with the immanent Trinity that it is not clear what, if anything, the Trinity has to do with creation or with human salvation. The economic Trinity is often nowhere to be seen. The Trinity is a network of rational propositions to be believed, not a personal God to be encountered, worshiped, feared, loved, and so on. Nor is this development especially surprising. Rather, it follows directly from a commitment to Scripture as the rule of faith in which Scripture is conceived of primarily, if not exclusively, as a network of rational or intelligible propositions and faith as an assent to those propositions.

It is possible, of course, to see Scripture as containing identifying descriptions having to do with the divine economy and hence as aiding people to encounter the triune God in worship and prayer. However, two things prevented most seventeenth-century English Protestant theologians from taking such a view. First, the appeal to Scripture as the rule of faith involved no intimate connection with the wider catechetical, sacramental, and liturgical life of the church in which the Trinity functioned first and foremost as the name for God. Second, the Unitarian challenge focused the attention of English Protestant theologians squarely on the problem of demonstrating that propositions having to do exclusively with the immanent Trinity — propositions presumably derived from Scripture — were intelligible.

In this chapter I will investigate two attempts during the 1690s to demonstrate the rationality or intelligibility of the immanent Trinity. First, I will examine William Sherlock's attempt to explain the Trinity via an appeal to a Cartesian notion of personhood. Second, I will take up John Wallis's efforts to provide an intelligible account of the Trinity by retrieving a pre-Boethian understanding of the term "person." I will examine Stillingfleet's efforts to demonstrate the rationality or intelligibility of the Trinity on Lockean grounds in the next chapter.

"What Is So Much Enquired After, the *Principium Individuationis*"[1]

English Unitarians wanted Protestant theologians simply to explain how three divine persons did not equal three gods. In other words, they were challenging English Trinitarians to provide what Locke would later call the *principium individuationis,* or principle of individuation. A good way to understand what is meant by the principle of individuation is to contrast it with the concept of *personal identity*. On the one hand, says Udo Thiel, individuation has to do with "what it is that makes an individual the individual it is and distinguishes it from all other individuals of the same kind." On the other hand, personal identity "concerns the requirements for an individual's remaining the same through time and partial change."[2] Individuation, one might say, has to do with what distinguishes Peter, James, and John from one another; personal identity, by contrast, seeks to name what it is that makes Peter the old man the same person as Peter the infant or Peter the child.

Before taking up Sherlock and Wallis's purported solutions, it will help to say a word or two about the history of the search for the principle of individuation, since the Unitarians were by no means the first to register concern over this issue. As with so many issues in modern philosophy, the quest for the principle of individuation first emerged among Christian theologians.[3] Indeed, philosophers *qua* philosophers did not take up the problem of individuation until after the Trinitar-

---

1. John Locke, *Essay Concerning Human Understanding,* ed. Peter H. Nidditch (Oxford: Clarendon Press, 1975), 2.27.3.

2. See Udo Thiel, "The Trinity and Human Personal Identity," in *English Philosophy in the Age of Locke,* ed. M. A. Stewart (Oxford: Clarendon Press, 2000), pp. 217-18.

3. Consider, for example, William J. Abraham's fascinating argument that the main issues and concerns in classical foundationalism emerged first in the theology of the Magisterial Reformers and were only later picked up and made a matter of philosophical concern by Descartes. William J. Abraham, *Canon and Criterion in Christian Theology: From the Fathers to Feminism* (Oxford: Clarendon Press, 1999), pp. 178-79.

ian controversy in late seventeenth-century England.[4] By contrast, questions concerning how to individuate persons emerged in Christian theology long before the 1690s, when theologians looked to individuate the Father, Son, and Holy Spirit in a way that would uphold the belief that the distinctions in God were real but did not compromise the oneness or unity of God, which the church had inherited from Judaism and to which it was so deeply committed. In fact, the quest for the principle of individuation emerged among Christian theologians as early as the third century C.E., when Tertullian suggested that the three divine persons might be individuated by analogy with either the internal relations within a person (e.g., memory, will, and intelligence) or by analogy with three different persons (e.g., Peter, James, and John). Later, Augustine set the pattern of thinking on the subject for the West by seizing on and exploring more fully than anyone before or after him the suggestion that the Father, Son, and Holy Spirit might be understood by analogy with the internal relations in a *single* person. Similarly, Gregory of Nyssa helped set the pattern of thinking for the East by exploring more fully the analogy with three *different* persons.

In addition to the analogies recommended by the early church fathers, ecumenical church councils developed and refined a series of technical terms designed to emphasize both the oneness of God and the distinctions between the Father, Son, and Holy Spirit. Since they were more exacting than analogies, the technical terms often generated more confusion and disagreement than clarity and consensus. Thus there emerged a long and complicated debate over how best to combine and use terms such as *hypostasis, hypostases, ousia, homoousios,* and *homoiousios.* After years of debate, the formula "three *hypostases* and one *ousia*" was officially endorsed at the Council of Constantinople in 381 C.E. In this formula the Father, Son, and Holy Spirit were three individual *hypostases* of one *ousia.* In time, the formula achieved at Constantinople would be rendered in Latin as *una substantia, tres personae* ("one

---

4. The history of individuation as a problem in philosophy can be rightly said to be the result of the Trinitarian controversy in late seventeenth-century England. For a succinct and helpful discussion of the link between the Trinitarian controversy in late seventeenth-century England and individuation as a problem in philosophy, see Udo Thiel's chapters entitled "Individuation" and "Personal Identity" in *The Cambridge History of Seventeenth Century Philosophy,* 2 vols., ed. Daniel Garber and M. R. Ayers (Cambridge, UK: Cambridge University Press, 1998), chs. 9 and 26 respectively.

substance, three persons"), making the Father, Son, and Holy Spirit three individual or distinct *personae* of one *substantia*.

The change in terminology set the stage for a reigniting of the debate over the principle of individuation in the Middle Ages. It is true, the issue of how to individuate the divine persons was a matter of concern from the very beginning of the Middle Ages.[5] However, the quest for the principle of individuation took a most unfortunate turn when medieval theologians began applying to the Latin Trinitarian formula a definition of "person" that Boethius had developed with christological issues in mind. William S. Babcock captures what was at stake in this development:

> In a christological treatise, [Boethius] proposed a definition of "person" designed to support the Chalcedonian claim that Christ is one person in two natures: *naturae rationabilis individua substantia* ("the individual substance of a rational nature"). The theologians of the medieval schools transferred Boethius' phrase from the christological to the trinitarian context and made it the standard definition of the three *personae* in the one *substantia* of God. The consequences are predictable. The transfer saddled trinitarian theology with the impossible task of explaining how the one divine substance could contain three individual substances; and it made the Trinity an all too easy target for its critics once they arose.[6]

As soon as they recognized the problem created by the transfer of Boethius's definition from the christological to the Trinitarian context, medieval scholastic theologians went to work on a solution.[7] Of

5. For a review of the issue of individuation in the early Middle Ages, see J. J. E. Gracia, *Introduction to the Problem of Individuation in the Early Middle Ages* (Washington, DC: The Catholic University of America Press, 1984).

6. William S. Babcock, "A Changing of the Christian God," *Interpretation* 45 (1991): 141-42. The translation of *naturae rationabilis individua substantia* is taken from Boethius, *The Theological Tractates: The Consolation of Philosophy*, rev. ed., trans. H. F. Stewart, E. K. Rand, and S. J. Tester, Loeb Classical Library (Cambridge, MA: Harvard University Press, 1973), p. 85. For an example of the transfer of Boethius's definition of person from the christological to the Trinitarian context, Babcock cites Thomas Aquinas, *Summa Theologiae*, 1:29.

7. For a treatment of the problem of individuation in late medieval scholastic theology, see J. J. E. Gracia, ed., *Individuation in Scholasticism: The Later Middle Ages and the Counter Reformation (1160-1650)* (Albany: State University of New York Press, 1994).

course, if they could not resolve the problem, they were not prepared to give up the Trinity. It was, after all, a matter of principle for medieval Catholic theologians that reason was to be conformed to divine revelation.[8] At this stage, saving knowledge was not yet tied to the literal meaning of propositions in Scripture.[9] Nevertheless, attempts to resolve the problem only made the apparent contradiction all the more obvious to future onlookers, not the least of whom were those "on the margins of the Reformation." Babcock continues:

> The *Rakovian Catechism*, produced by the anti-trinitarian Socinians in Poland in 1605, did not hesitate to make the apparent conclusion plain: Since a person is an individual intelligent essence, to assert three persons is to assert three essences; and to assert one essence, as Christians must (to avoid tritheism), is to assert one person.[10]

Finally, by way of introduction to the problem of the principle of individuation, it is important to note, while the patristic fathers developed analogies by which to think about the distinctions among the three divine persons, they were deeply concerned that neither the analogies they developed nor the technical terms they endorsed at Constantinople be regarded in any way as determinative of God. Indeed, the fathers were deeply aware of the dangers that accompanied the use of analogies in this case. In the first instance, the analogy with three distinct human beings, if pressed too far, could lead to tritheism. In the second instance, the analogy with the internal relations of a person's memory, will, and intelligence could easily lead to Sabellianism.

Therefore, in order to combat the tendency to take the analogies and the terminology too far, the fathers regularly emphasized that they wanted only to register the point that the Father was not the Son, the Son was not the Spirit, and the like, but there were, nonetheless, not

8. See Thomas Aquinas, *Summa Theologiae: Latin text and English translation, notes, appendices, and glossaries* (New York: McGraw Hill, 1964), 1.32.1.

9. There is a different set of problems concerning the interpretation of Scripture in the late medieval period. See Eleonore Stump, "Revelation and Biblical Exegesis: Augustine, Aquinas, and Swinburne," in *Reason and the Christian Religion: Essays in Honour of Richard Swinburne*, ed. Alan G. Padgett (Oxford: Clarendon Press, 1994), pp. 161-98.

10. Babcock, "A Changing of the Christian God," p. 142. Babcock cites *The Rakovian Catechism*, trans. Thomas Rees (1818; reprint, Lexington, KY: The American Theological Association, 1962), p. 33.

three gods. Thus they insisted that the analogies and the terms they used were utterly incapable of referring to God in an even remotely adequate or accurate way. In a passage worth quoting at length, Babcock captures this crucial facet of early Trinitarian theology:

> The great project of the patristic theologians who were the chief architects of the trinitarian doctrine was to restore the commerce of the mind and a God understood to transcend the world of things — and to disqualify a language that seemed to impede the restoration. Both our concepts and our discourse, on their view, have been formed by, and for, our dealings with those corporeal things, both persons and objects, that occupy with us the mutable world of space and time. For just this reason, they do not and cannot serve for God. It was commonplace of patristic theology that we are not to apply to God either the corporeal imagery or the corporeal terminology that we derive from and use in our intercourse with the material world. Only by freeing ourselves from these forms of thought and discourse will we be able to approach the divine. If we are to attain to God, our minds must finally be purged of their concepts, and our discourse must finally be reduced to silence.[11]

Given that human discourse cannot serve for God, patristic theologians were keen to argue that the Trinity must be retained regardless of the degree to which the analogies or the terminology succeed or fail. In other words, the Trinity must be retained regardless of whether human reason can provide a solution to the problem of the principle of individuation. Concerning the question of how to individuate the three divine persons without compromising the unity of God, Gregory of Nyssa declares:

> [I]t is very difficult to deal with the question. If indeed, we could find something to support the mind in its uncertainty, so that it no longer doubted and wavered in the face of this extraordinary dilemma, it would be well. But if our rather feeble powers of reason prove unequal to the problem, we must guard the tradition we have received from the Fathers, as ever sure and immovable, and seek from the Lord a means of defending our faith. If this should be dis-

11. Babcock, "A Changing of the Christian God," p. 139.

covered by anyone endowed with grace, we shall give thanks to Him who granted the grace. If not, we shall none the less hold on to our unchangeable faith in those points which have been established.[12]

Cartesian Modifications: Sherlock and the Boethian Definition of "Person"

Upon taking up William Sherlock's proposal for resolving the problem of the principle of individuation, one notices immediately how much the tone of Sherlock's treatise differs from the tone of Gregory of Nyssa's *Answer to Ablabius*. Whereas Gregory began by acknowledging that the problem is so difficult that there may not be an adequate solution to it, William Sherlock begins his defense of the Trinity on a note of supreme confidence, announcing to his readers that he is sure he has "vindicate[d] the Doctrines of the Trinity and Incarnation, from those pretended Absurdities and Contradictions, which were so confidently charged upon them." Moreover, he is certain that he has come up with "a very easie and intelligible Notion of a Trinity in Unity."[13] It is difficult to imagine the patristic fathers or even medieval scholastic theologians ever approaching the problem of individuation in such an overconfident way.

The supreme confidence with which Sherlock began the *Vindication* was a direct reflection of the difference between Sherlock's conception of the Trinity and that of the patristic fathers. For Gregory and the patristic fathers, the Trinity served first and foremost to designate the God they had come to know in and through the life, death, and resurrection of Christ and in and through the work of the Holy Spirit in the church, that is, in and through catechesis, baptism and the Eucharist, the liturgy, images, and the lives of the saints. For Sherlock, in contrast, the Trinity was first and foremost a doctrine contained in or derived

12. Gregory of Nyssa, *An Answer to Ablabius: That We Should Not Think of Saying There Are Three Gods in Christology of the Later Fathers*, ed. Edward R. Hardy (Philadelphia: Westminster, 1954), p. 257.

13. William Sherlock, *A Vindication of the Doctrine of the Holy and Ever Blessed Trinity, and the Incarnation of the Son of God, Occasioned by the Brief Notes on the Creed of St. Athanasius, and the Brief History of the Unitarians, or Socinians; and containing an Answer to both* (London, 1690), "To the Reader."

from intelligible propositions in Scripture that, like other intelligible propositions contained therein, were necessary to be believed for salvation. Moreover, the propositions necessary to be believed were to be so intelligible that almost anyone could readily understand them. Thus Sherlock began by emphasizing the fact that the "notion of a Trinity in Unity" was "very easie and intelligible." Anything less than this would have been, according to the Protestant rule of faith, grounds for excluding a doctrine from the list of doctrines necessary to be believed for salvation.

Despite Sherlock's promise to provide a "very easie and intelligible" explanation of the Trinity, his treatise turned out to be highly technical. It was hardly the kind of thing the common plowman would have understood. And this was not lost on Sherlock's critics, as we shall see below. Crucial to Sherlock's argument is his adoption of Boethius's definition of "person" as "an individual substance of a rational nature," that is, "as an Aristotelian first substance whose essence consists in rationality."[14] Nor was Sherlock unaware that it was precisely according to Boethius's definition of person as a "rational substance" that three persons appeared to be three gods to the Socinians and Unitarians. Sherlock simply believed that he could solve the problem of individuation by giving the Boethian definition of person a Cartesian update.[15] In

14. Thiel, "The Trinity and Human Personal Identity," p. 221. The following analysis of Sherlock's resolution to the problem of the principle of individuation is deeply influenced by Thiel's seminal essay. For a different reading of Sherlock's proposals, see G. Wedeking, "Locke on Personal Identity and the Trinity Controversy of the 1690s," *Dialogue* 29 (1990): 163-88.

15. William S. Babcock's contention that Sherlock "proposed a restatement of the doctrine of the Trinity in terms accommodated to Locke's view that all of our ideas are ultimately derived 'either from external impressions or internal sensations'" can be misleading ("A Changing of the Christian God," p. 142). Indeed, as Babcock points out, the quoted phrase from Locke does appear in Sherlock's *A Defence of Dr. Sherlock's Notion of a Trinity in Unity* (p. 6). Yet, as Thiel has shown, when Sherlock first set out to defend the Trinity in 1690, he did so by restating the doctrine of the Trinity in Cartesian, not in Lockean, categories. Moreover, as we shall see, when Sherlock defended his statement of the doctrine of the Trinity in 1694, he actually brought his restatement of the doctrine of the Trinity even further into line with Descartes's notions of "person" and "consciousness." Indeed, Sherlock only appealed to Locke in an effort to secure space for his Cartesian understanding of "person." Therefore, those most familiar with Sherlock's statement of the doctrine of the Trinity were quick to point out the overriding influence of Descartes on Sherlock (e.g., Robert South's *Animadversions,* p. 68; cf. p. 151). Ste-

order to see this clearly, we should take a moment to come to grips with
Descartes's notion of person.

After pointing out that, for Descartes, a person is an "individual
spiritual substance," or soul,[16] Udo Thiel gives the following summary
of Descartes's definition:

> Now Descartes argues that thought is the "principle property" of the
> soul: it is that which "constitutes its nature and essence, and to
> which all its other properties are referred", the soul or mind (or self)
> is essentially a thinking thing, a *res cogitans*. Thought itself is defined
> by Descartes in terms of *consciousness*. Our understanding of our-
> selves as thinking things is based on the consciousness which always
> accompanies thought. This self-understanding is in turn the basis of
> our knowledge of ourselves as individual selves.[17]

Thiel concludes his summary of Descartes's notion of person with
an observation that is absolutely crucial for an understanding of both
Sherlock's initial proposal for resolving the problem of individuation
and the dispute that followed with Robert South, the canon of Christ
Church, Oxford.[18] Thiel observes:

---

phen Nye even went so far as to label Sherlock's account the "Cartesian Trinity." Stephen Nye, *Considerations on the Explications of the Doctrine of the Trinity, By Dr. Wallis, Dr.
Sherlock, Dr. S — th, Sr. Cudworth, and Mr. Hooker; as also on the account given by those that say,
the Trinity is an Unconceivable and Inexplicable Mystery. Written to a Person of Quality* (London, 1693), pp. 10-13.

16. Thiel says: "For Descartes, in the Sixth Meditation, holds that the soul constitutes the essence of the self, whereas the body is something which the self merely 'has',
and to which it is 'very closely joined'" ("The Trinity," p. 222). Thiel cites René Descartes,
Oeuvres, ed. C. Adam and A. Tannery, 12 vols. (Paris, 1964-76), 7:78; Descartes, *Philosophical
Writings,* trans. J. Cottingham et al., 3 vols. (Cambridge, UK: Cambridge University Press,
1984-1991), 2:54.

17. Thiel, "The Trinity," p. 222.

18. Robert South was educated in Christ Church, Oxford; he took his M.A. there in
1657 (one year before Locke received his degree from Christ Church). South would go on
to become chaplain to the Chancellor of Oxford University and then canon of Christ
Church. His debate with Sherlock began when he published *Animadversions upon Dr.
Sherlock's book* (London, 1693). Sherlock responded with *Defense of Dr. Sherlock's notion of a
Trinity in Unity* in 1694, and South replied with *Tritheism charged upon Dr. Sherlock's new notion of the Trinity* in 1695. The dispute between them, observes Thiel, "created widespread
interest and controversy at the time and many other theologians and philosophers con-

Descartes does not say that consciousness is what individuates the soul; all he claims is that we derive our knowledge of the individuality of souls from the consciousness we have of our own thoughts. Descartes's argument implies that the individuality of the soul is given prior to the consciousness of thoughts. He does not even attempt to explain what brings about the individuality of souls. (Thiel, "The Trinity," pp. 222-23)

There is a striking resemblance between Descartes's and Sherlock's concepts of a person. For example, Sherlock says: "When we enquire into the strict Notion of Personality, that must be a simple uncompounded thing, as indivisible as self is, which cannot consist of Parts."[19] Later he simply says that "the soul makes or constitutes the Person." Finally, he adds:

Whatever change there be in the Body, the Person is the same still, which could not be, were the Body part of the Person, for then the change of the Body would be a partial change of the Person too; and yet our Bodies are in a perpetual Flux, and change every day.[20]

From these quotations it is clear that Sherlock, like Descartes, regarded a person, whether human or divine, not simply as "an individual substance" but as an "individual spiritual substance," or soul (Thiel, p. 222). Sherlock's concept of a person also resembles Descartes's concept insofar as he "accounts for the *individuality* of persons in terms of the notion of consciousness, or what he calls 'self-consciousness'" (Thiel, p. 223). But it is here that Sherlock goes beyond Descartes, arguing that "self-consciousness" is actually the principle of individuation in finite persons. For example, in his book *Vindication*, Sherlock says:

---

tributed to it" ("The Trinity," p. 220). In 1693, one anonymous author observed that "South upon Sherlock is in every Mouth [and South's *Animadversions*] is in almost every Shop, and Study, bought up and inquired for by most Men." See *A Letter to the Reverend Dr. South. Upon Occasion of a late book entituled, Animadversions upon Dr. Sherlock's book, in vindication of the Trinity* (London, 1693), p. 2. For a brief but helpful summary of the debate between Sherlock and South, see Gerard Reedy, *Robert South: An Introduction to His Life and Sermons* (New York: Cambridge University Press, 1992), pp. 137-42.

19. Sherlock, *Defence*, p. 45 (quoted in Thiel, "The Trinity," pp. 221-22).

20. Sherlock, *Defence*, p. 51.

> In finite created Spirits . . . numerical Oneness can be nothing else,
> but every Spirit's Unity with itself, and distinct and separate subsis-
> tence from all other created Spirits. Now this Self-unity of the Spirit
> . . . can be nothing but Self-Consciousness: That it is conscious to its
> own Thoughts, Reasonings, Passions, which no other finite Spirit is
> conscious to but it self: This makes a finite Spirit numerically One;
> and separates it from all other Spirits, that every Spirit feels only its
> own Thoughts and Passions, but is not conscious to the Thoughts
> and Passions of any other Spirit. (pp. 48-49)

Sherlock adds: "We know the Unity of a Mind or Spirit, reaches as far
as its Self-Consciousness does: for that is One Spirit, which knows and
feels itself, and its own thoughts and motions" (p. 50). He then articu-
lates his position on how to individuate persons most clearly and succinctly: "The self-consciousness of every Person to itself makes them
distinct Persons" (p. 68).

By making self-consciousness the principle of individuation,
Sherlock was arguing that a person as "an individual spiritual substance," or soul, is "numerically one and distinct from other spiritual
substances, because it alone is conscious of its thoughts and actions."
In other words, "the unity of a person reaches as far as this consciousness of thoughts and actions reaches."[21] Thus, in a very important passage in *Vindication*, Sherlock says: "In a created Spirit this consciousness
extends only to it self, and therefore self-consciousness makes it One
with it self, and divides and separates it from all other Spirits" (p. 68).

At this stage, the implications for the Trinity do not look promising. If the three divine persons are three centers of self-consciousness,
each of which "extends only to it self," and if self-consciousness makes
each person "One with it self, and divides and separates it from all
other Spirits," then in Sherlock's notion of person, it is difficult to see
how three persons do not equal three gods. Clearly, if Sherlock's appeal
to self-consciousness as the principle of individuation was to salvage
the Trinity, then he would need to modify it in a way that would enable
him to apply it to the three divine persons without dividing the substance. Sherlock's solution is intriguing, to say the least.

---

21. Thiel, "The Trinity," p. 223.

In the same passage from which the previous quotation comes, Sherlock develops the notion of "mutual consciousness":

> Nor do we divide the Substance, but unite these Three Persons, in One numerical Essence: for we know nothing of the unity of the Mind but self-consciousness . . . and therefore the self-consciousness of every person to it self makes them distinct Persons, so the mutual consciousness of all Three Divine Persons to each other makes them all but One infinite God: as far as consciousness reaches, so far the unity of a Spirit extends, for we know no other unity of a Mind or Spirit, but consciousness . . . . [B]ut could this consciousness extend to other Spirits, as it does to it self, all these Spirits, which were mutually conscious to each other, as they are to themselves, though they were distinct Persons, would be essentially One: And this is that essential unity, which is between Father, Son and Holy Ghost, who are essentially united by a mutual consciousness to whatever is in each other, and do by an internal sensation . . . feel each other, as they do themselves; and therefore are as essentially One, as a Mind and Spirit is One with it self. (p. 68)

With the principle of mutual consciousness, we have reached the heart of Sherlock's proposal. Indeed, there can be no question that, with self-consciousness as the principle of individuation, Sherlock believed that he had developed "a very easie and intelligible Notion of a Trinity in Unity." But Robert South's response was devastating. South realized almost immediately that Sherlock was attempting to solve the problems created by the Boethian notion of "person" by giving it a Cartesian update. However, South also discerned that Sherlock had departed significantly from Descartes's notion of consciousness, and it was with the manner of this departure and not with the appeal to "mutual consciousness" per se that South took issue. In his *Animadversions* on Sherlock's stance, he says:

> And . . . as poor and mean a Notion as [self-consciousness] is, it is Borrowed too. But you will say, From whom? Why? Even from Honest *Des Cartes,* and his *Cogito Ergo Sum.* Only with this unhappy difference in the Application of it, That this Proposition which *Des Cartes* lays as the Basis and Groundwork of his Philosophy, our Author places with its Heels upwards in his Divinity. For whereas *Des Cartes*

insists upon *Cogitation,* only to prove a Cause from its Effects, or rather an Antecedent from its Consequent: Our Author, on the contrary, makes *Cogitation* the very Cause and Principle of Being and Subsistence, by making it the Person who Thinks, or Reflects; than which nothing can be more false, and ridiculous.[22]

What did South take to be the problem with making self-consciousness not simply the means by which to account for the *individuality* of persons but also the *principle of individuation?* What was it about this move that made it supremely "false" and "ridiculous," from South's point of view? The answer to these questions comes at the outset of chapter 3 of *Animadversions:*

> According to the Natural Order of Things, *Self-Consciousness* in Persons, pre-supposes their Personality, and therefore is not, cannot be the Reason of it. The *Argument,* I conceive, is very plain. For whatsoever pre-supposes a Thing, is in Order of Nature Posterior and Subsequent to the Things so pre-supposed by it; and again . . . the formal Reason of any Thing is in Order of Nature, precedent to that Thing, of which it is the Reason . . . . So that there must be a Person before there can be an Act, or Action proceeding from, or attributable to a Person. In a word, there must be a Person in Being, before any Action issues from him . . . . But now *Self-Consciousness* does not only do this; but (which is more) it also pre-supposes another Act Antecedent to it self. For it is properly and formally a *Reflex Act* upon the Acts, Passions, or Motions of the Person whom it belongs to. (p. 71)

Later South revisits this point:

> The very word *Self-Consciousness* contradicts and overthrows its being the *ground,* or *Formal Reason* of *Personality.* For still *Self* must be before *Consciousness;* and *Self* imports *Personality;* as being that, by which a *Person* is said *to be, what he is;* and they both stand united in this one Word, as the *Act and the Object,* and therefore *Consciousness* cannot be the *Reason of it.* (pp. 96-97; italics in original)[23]

22. South, *Animadversions upon Dr. Sherlock's book,* p. 88.

23. Quoted in Thiel, "The Trinity," p. 232. Thiel notes that Richard Burthogge and Edward Stillingfleet identify the same problem in Sherlock's argument. For example, Burthogge says: "Now for that *Moment* of Reason, in which a Spirit is conceived *in Being,*

South's main argument was that "one's individual personality is logically prior to the consciousness of one's own thoughts and actions and, therefore, self-consciousness cannot constitute this individual personality."[24] This made it painfully obvious that Sherlock had not succeeded in providing a principle of individuation on which three persons did not equal three gods. If he had succeeded, it would only be because the appeal to self-consciousness had dissolved the real distinctions among the three divine persons.

If South was right to argue that individual personalities are logically prior to self-consciousness, then Sherlock's solution led directly to tritheism. In the light of South's objection, the mutual consciousness of the three divine persons secures epistemic unity at the cost of ontological unity. In other words, the unity of the three divine persons was secured by the fact that they were conscious of one another's thoughts and actions. However, if South's objection held, then the thoughts and actions themselves belonged to three distinct persons, whose existence logically preceded both self-consciousness and mutual consciousness. Moreover, it is difficult to see how Sherlock could argue that what he meant by self-consciousness was not distinguishable from a logically prior individual personality without dissolving the distinctions among the persons. Either way, Sherlock's solution was turning out to be anything but "an easie and intelligible Notion of a Trinity in Unity."

In response to South, Sherlock tried to rescue the appeal to self-consciousness as the principle of individuation by arguing that self-consciousness was not the same thing as self-knowledge or knowledge of one's own thoughts and actions. Self-consciousness was not, as

---

without being conceived to be acting, and in which it is conceived *Acting* before it becomes *Conscious* of its actings, in that precedent moment, (which speaks *order*, not *duration*) it must be conceived to be *one with it self*, and numerically different from every thing besides; and therefore that is *so*, cannot arise from self-consciousness, or its being conscious of its own actings." Richard Burthogge, *An Essay upon reason, and the nature of spirits* (London, 1694), p. 273 (italics in original). Edward Stillingfleet later echoes the judgment of South and Burthogge: "And nothing can be said to make that, which must be supposed to be before it self; for there must be a Mind in being distinct from all other Minds, before it can reflect upon it self." Stillingfleet, *A Discourse in Vindication of the Doctrine of the Trinity* (London, 1697), p. 71.

24. Thiel, "The Trinity," p. 231.

South had suggested, "Posterior to the Act reflected on by it." Rather, self-consciousness, Sherlock argued, differed from self-knowledge in the same way that sensation differs from speculation.

> *Self-Knowledge* properly signifies to contemplate our own Natures in their Idea, to draw our own Image and Picture as like the Original as we can, and to view our selves in it: But *Self Consciousness* is an *intellectual Self Sensation,* when we feel our selves, and all the Thoughts, Knowledge, Volitions, Passions of our Minds, and know what is Self, and what belongs to Self by feeling it.[25]

Prior to distinguishing self-consciousness from self-knowledge, Sherlock seems to anticipate South's response to this move. Indeed, Sherlock realized that, even according to this distinction, South could argue that self-consciousness remains "a second order act of perception" and an individual personality remains logically prior to what Sherlock was now calling "intellectual self-sensation."[26] Thus Sherlock tried to preempt South with an utterly surprising move, appealing to Locke in an effort to rescue his Cartesian update of the Boethian notion of person. At the outset of *Defence,* Sherlock says:

> For a Mind and Spirit is the truest Image of God, that is in Nature; for God is a Spirit, and therefore it is more likely to find some Image of the Unity of the Godhead in a Spirit, than in Matter, and yet we know nothing of a Spirit, but what we feel in our Selves, and can Philosophize no farther about it; for as Mr. *Lock* has truly observed, we can form no Idea but either from external Impressions or internal Sensations; and therefore we can know no more of the Unity of a Spirit nether, than what we feel. (p. 6)

This was an unexpected move. Sherlock was attempting to shore up his Cartesian update of the Boethian definition of a person by appealing to Locke's skepticism concerning our ability to know "things in themselves." As Locke himself put it, "Since *the Mind,* in all its Thoughts and Reasonings, hath no other immediate Object but its own *Ideas,* which it alone does or can contemplate, it is evident, that

---

25. Sherlock, *Defence,* p. 77, quoted in Thiel, "The Trinity," p. 233 (italics in original).
26. Thiel, "The Trinity," p. 234.

our Knowledge is only conversant about them."[27] Unfortunately, it was not clear how the appeal to Locke was supposed to salvage Sherlock's appeal to consciousness at this late stage in the debate. The answer appears to come in the following passage. Sherlock says:

> [A]n easie and obvious distinction between the Principle and the Act answers all: A Self-conscious Principle, without which we can't conceive a Mind, makes a Mind one with it self, and distinguishes it from all other Minds, and by the Acts of *Self-consciousness,* which suppose the Principle, every Mind feels it self to be One, and distinguished from all others.[28]

Apparently, Sherlock thought Locke's skepticism concerning our ability to apprehend things directly warranted the appeal to self-consciousness as a principle because it was "the only means available . . . for *discovering* our self-unity."[29] But what exactly did Sherlock mean by a "principle" of self-consciousness? In *Defence* he says: "The Soul is the seat of Personality, the only Principle of Reason, Sensation, and a Conscious life" (p. 67). The soul itself, then, as the principle of self-consciousness, and not actual self-consciousness, was that which could "distinguish between Self-conscious Persons" (p. 66).

Though he did not realize it, Sherlock had actually managed, in moving in this direction, to retreat to Descartes's original conception of person. In other words, he had retreated to a position in which he did not specify what the principle of individuation was. The soul was the "principle of self-consciousness," but since we cannot actually know what the soul is, we are forced into agnosticism concerning what it is that individuates the soul. Udo Thiel summarizes the problem this way:

> In attempting to explain the individuality of the person (=soul) in terms of the "principle of self-consciousness" (=soul), Sherlock quite obviously fails to account for the individuality of the person understood as an immaterial substance — just as Descartes himself fails to account for the individuation of the soul. And so, despite his un-

27. Burthogge, *Essay upon Reason,* 4.1.1 (italics in original).
28. Sherlock, *Defence,* p. 67 (quoted in Thiel, "The Trinity," p. 235).
29. Thiel, "The Trinity," p. 235.

Cartesian appeal to scepticism about essence, Sherlock's position on the self is very close to the standard Cartesian one. The self is conceived of as an immaterial thinking substance, and its individuality is said to be known on the basis of consciousness; but what constitutes this individuality is left unexplained. (p. 236)

By appealing to Locke, Sherlock had managed to undermine the very thing he had set out to do in *Vindication,* namely, to provide "a very easie and intelligible Notion of a Trinity in Unity." But that was not the end of it. There was an even more devastating problem with Sherlock's account; it went largely unnoticed by South, but Burthogge correctly discerned it:

> *Again,* in Dr. *Sherlock's* way of Discoursing, which is, that Three Persons do intimate to one another as he supposes, would become numerically one, I do not see but that instead of the *Three* Persons in the Blessed *Trinity* . . . we shall have but *one* Person (in number).[30]

Sherlock apparently believed that mutual consciousness did not "create the unity of *one* person, but the unity of the Godhead with three distinct persons." Thus the three divine persons were said to "remain distinct through their self-consciousness, and to retain this distinctness as persons despite their mutual consciousness of each other through which they become one Godhead." Yet it is not at all clear that their distinctness could be "retained in mutual consciousness." Sherlock never explained how mutual consciousness constituted "a different kind of unity from that of self-consciousness." But if mutual consciousness produced "the same kind of unity" as self-consciousness, then "mutual consciousness between two Spirits" would make them one person, so that "they would no longer be two distinct persons."[31]

Sherlock's solution to the problem of the principle of individuation had led to three conclusions concerning the Trinity, none of which were especially appealing. First, if Sherlock were simply to acknowledge South's distinction between self-consciousness and a prior individual personality, then mutual consciousness would not prevent the appeal to self-consciousness from running the Trinity into tritheism. Indeed,

30. Burthogge, *Essay upon Reason,* p. 274 (italics in original).
31. Thiel, "The Trinity," p. 242.

in this analysis, three persons would equal three Gods. Second, if Sherlock maintained his appeal to Lockean skepticism about essences, then the appeal to self-consciousness could not do what it was intended to do, namely, specify what individuates the three divine persons. Third, if Sherlock maintained his position that mutual consciousness produced the same kind of unity as self-consciousness, then his solution would appear to eliminate the distinctions between the divine persons altogether.

The most important thing to note regarding Sherlock's solution is that, on the doctrine of essential doctrines, the disagreement between Sherlock and South caused some who were not already Unitarian in outlook to conclude that the Trinity was not among those plain and intelligible things necessary to be believed for salvation. For example, Benjamin Furly, the Rotterdam Quaker, said he doubted whether he would ever see the Trinity "demonstrated to be of the number of those things, that are necessary to be beleeved in order to salvation, however it fare with the truth of the assertion." Referring specifically to the controversy between Sherlock and South, Furly added:

> If it be so intricate that the most learned, are so confounded in their explications of it, that they fly in one another's faces, charging each others systems with Idolatry or Heresy — sure I am there's no possibility for the simple hearted, and unlearned people, to be ever cleare in the point. And so their securest way [is] to passe it.[32]

Whatever might be said for or against Sherlock's solution to the problem of the principle of individuation, it proved in the end to be anything but the "easie and intelligible Notion of a Trinity in Unity" that he had promised. The fact that South, Burthogge, and Stillingfleet all disagreed with Sherlock made it only too evident that Protestants did not agree on how rightly to explain the Trinity. What was clearly needed was a simpler definition or understanding of "person" upon which all could agree. After all, the problem with Sherlock's proposal was that he had unduly muddied the waters by adopting the old Boethian definition of person. The time had come to resolve the

---

32. Benjamin Furly, *Correspondence*, 4: 1329, n. 1344; 5:1702, 1741, 1961, quoted in John Marshall, "Locke, Socinianism, 'Socinianism', Unitarianism," in *English Philosophy in the Age of Locke*, ed. M. A. Stewart (Oxford: Clarendon Press, 2000), p. 137.

problem of individuation by adopting a pre-Boethian understanding of person. This was precisely John Wallis's inclination.

John Wallis and the Etymology of *Persona*

A longtime "Oxford Professor of Geometry, Chaplain in Ordinary to the King, and sometime preacher at St. Mary's Church in Oxford," John Wallis found himself surrounded by a controversy over the publication of *The Naked Gospel*, a book clearly Unitarian in outlook and purpose.[33] When the controversy began, the book's author, Arthur Bury, was the rector of Exeter. Before the controversy was over, Bury himself was "expelled from his livings" by Trelawny, the Bishop of Exeter, and his book was publicly condemned by Convocation.[34] Later, Bury repented, but even then he retained his belief that "an understanding of the eternal generation of the Son of God was not essential to salvation."[35]

In the context of the dispute over Bury, Wallis set out to defend the Trinity in 1690 by publishing *The Doctrine of the Blessed Trinity briefly explained in a letter to a friend*. He followed this up with seven letters in the following year, which he subsequently published during 1691 and 1692. Wallis also preached three times on the subject at St. Mary's Church in 1691, and he published those three sermons later that same year under the title *Three Sermons concerning the Sacred Trinity*.

Like Sherlock, Wallis focused his attention on the problem of the principle of individuation. However, Wallis's solution turned out to be even more radical than Sherlock's. Whereas Sherlock had sought to give the Boethian definition of person a Cartesian update, Wallis sought to dispense with the medieval notion of person altogether and to begin again in a more humble, less assuming fashion. In particular, Wallis sought to provide a definition of person that was consistent with the early church fathers' conception and use of the Latin term *persona*.[36]

33. See John Redwood, *Reason, Ridicule and Religion* (London: Thames and Hudson, 1976), p. 159.

34. Redwood, *Reason, Ridicule and Religion*, p. 157.

35. Redwood, *Reason, Ridicule and Religion*, p. 158.

36. For Wallis's interest in getting at the correct "sense" of words, see John Wallis, *An Explication of the Athanasian Creed in a Third Letter Pursuant of Two former, Concerning the Sacred Trinity Together with a Postscript, in Answer to Another Letter* (Cheapside, 1691), pp. 55-56.

Before taking up Wallis's arguments on behalf of the Trinity, I find two things worth noting. First, Wallis was committed to the Protestant rule of faith and to the notion that the propositions contained in Scripture were of the most plain and intelligible sort. In his third letter he declared his desire that his explanations "may be so plain, and so familiar" that a "Tankard-bearer may apprehend them: and thence perceive It is not Impossible that Three may be One."[37] Second, Wallis's proposal occurs in its most orderly and accessible form in his second sermon of 1691, so we will focus our attention primarily on the arguments in that text.

In his second sermon on the Trinity, Wallis took as his starting point a Socinian objection concerning the interpretation of John 17:3, which he translated thus: "And this is life eternal, that they might know thee the onely true God and Jesus Christ, whom thou has sent." According to Wallis, the Socinians had argued that the word "Onely" was restrictive of the subject "Thee," and not of the predicate "the True God." Wallis says:

> The first and great Objection of the Socinians, from this place, against the Divinity of Christ, and the Doctrine of the Trinity, is this; If the Father be the onely true God; then the Son, or Holy-Ghost, is not God, or the True God; but the Father onely.[38]

Initially, Wallis insisted that the Socinian reading of the text "perverts the order of the words," and that "the placement of the restrictive 'monon' shows it to determine the predicate and not the subject." Next, Wallis argues that even "if it had been said (as it is not) Thee Onely; yet even this would not exclude any who is the same with Him," including the Son and the Holy Spirit since "they are One and the same God with Him" (*Three Sermons,* pp. 34-35).[39] Wallis then hastens to add: "[I]f it had been said (as it is not) Thee Onely, (as the Socinians would have it understood)," then it could still be argued that "This were an Essential Predication, rather than a Personal." What Wallis meant, of course, was that "the Predicate True God, is affirmed of him in regard

37. Wallis, *An Explication of the Athanasian Creed,* p. 41.

38. John Wallis, *Three Sermons* (Cheapside, 1691), p. 33.

39. Wallis cites John 10:30, which he translates, "I and the Father are One," and 1 John 5:7, which he translates, "These Three are One," as support.

of his Essence, rather than of his Personality . . . as belonging to the Essence, which is common to the Three Persons, not as peculiar to the Person of the Father" (p. 36). But what did Wallis mean by "Essential Predication"? Wallis answers this question by using an analogy from Scripture:

> Like as if it were said, David the King of Israel, or David the Father of Solomon, is a Reasonable Creature, or endued with Reason; this being endued with Reason, doth not belong to him as King of Israel, or as Father of Solomon; but, as he is a Man (though denominated by these Relations,) and is equivalent to this, The Man (who is Father of Solomon, and King of Israel) is endued with Reason. So if it had been said, that David King of Israel, and He onely, was Father of Solomon: it is not intended, that he was so as King of Israel (much less, in that capacity Onely,) but rather, as the Man who begot him; though designed by that Character. So here: and God the Creator is the Onely True God: and God the Redeemer likewise. Shall we therefore argue, That God the Redeemer is the Onely True God, and beside him there is no God, therefore not God the Creator? No we must not so argue. For it is not as Redeemer, or as Creator, that he is the Onely True God, but as God . . . . For he was the Onely True God from all Eternity; but it was in Time that he made the World, and was the Redeemer of Mankind. (pp. 36-37)

The second Socinian objection Wallis takes up is that, while the passage under consideration "doesn't deny the Son and Holy Ghost to be the True God . . . Yet neither doth it Prove them so to be." Wallis agrees, arguing that "the Proof of the Trinity must be fetched from other places in concurrence with this." He is simply answering objections regarding the passage of Scripture being considered. Thus Wallis goes on to provide a list of places from which the Trinity could be "proved" (he lists 1 John 5:17, 20; John 10:30).

This move served as the occasion for a third Socinian objection, namely, that some of the words in these other places are absent in some ancient translations or copies. To this objection, Wallis replies that many words were omitted in different copies, but we should not therefore put them out of the Bible. Wallis gives three reasons for retaining the words. First, he suggests that the fuller copy is likelier to be true because it is easier to leave out a line than to put one in. Second, he points to the way the Fathers cited or quoted texts as evidence that the text was then as it is now. Third, he uses a literary argument to the effect that the thesis/antithesis symmetry in 1 John 5:7-8 strongly suggests that verse 7 is not an insertion, and he concludes: "The latter clause would seem lame without the former" (pp. 39-47).[40]

Having dealt with three of six Socinian objections, Wallis paused long enough to develop further a part of his argument to this point. Picking up the argument concerning how to interpret John 17:3, Wallis insists that the verse does not exclude the Son from the true God any more than other texts that say only Christ is the Redeemer exclude God the Creator from Redeeming activity. He then adds: "That there is a God the Creator, a God the Redeemer, and a God the Sanctifier; and that these are the same God; I think cannot reasonably be denied" (*Three Sermons*, pp. 50-52). Wallis then takes the argument one step further: "Now this same God the Creator, God the Redeemer, and God the Sanctifier, I take to be *the same with* what we otherwise call, God the Father, God the Son, and God the Holy Ghost" (p. 53).

To support his claim that God the Father, Son, and Holy Spirit are the same God as God the Creator, Redeemer, and Sanctifier, Wallis appeals to the Trinitarian confessional materials embedded in the Church of England's Catechism.

> And our Church doth so expound it in her Catechism; First I learn to believe in God the Father, who hath Made me and all the World: Secondly, in God the Son, who hath Redeemed me and all Mankind: Thirdly, In God the Holy Ghost, who Sanctifieth me and all the Elect people of God. And it is no more absurd or inconsistent, to say, that God the Father, God the Son, and God the Holy Ghost, are the same God; than to say, that God the Creator, God the Redeemer, and God the Sanctifier, are the same God. (pp. 53-54)

40. We see here how the doctrine of essential doctrines can and did lead to what we might anachronistically call the historical-critical investigation of Scripture. Efforts such as Wallis's to show that the Trinity was among the doctrines contained in or derived from plain and intelligible propositions in Scripture contributed directly to the birth of the historical criticism of the Bible. Thus, of the various forms of criticism that would eventually emerge, we see here some early examples of textual and literary criticism.

I should observe at this point that, for one brief moment in the Trinitarian controversy of the 1690s, there was a suggestion that the Trinity had something to do with creation and with human salvation. Whatever else one makes of Wallis's proposal, Wallis himself deserves credit for reminding people that the Trinity was more than a network of rational propositions about God's nature or being. Whereas Sherlock and (later) Stillingfleet focused exclusively on the immanent Trinity, Wallis was at least mindful of the economic Trinity. Indeed, he went so far as to note the difference between the economic and the immanent Trinity:

> As they stand related to us, they are called God the Creator, God the Redeemer, and God the Sanctifier. As to the different Oeconomy, amongst themselves, one is called the Father, who is said to Beget; another the Son, who is said to be Begotten; and a third, the Holy Ghost, who is said to Proceed or Come forth; But all are the same God. (pp. 54-55)

While Wallis was clearly mindful of the economic Trinity, he could not escape the gravitational pull of the times. Having distinguished between God as God who is "related to us" and God as three divine persons related to one another from eternity, Wallis proceeded to a fourth Socinian objection. According to Wallis, the Socinians argued that, if God the Father, God the Son, God the Holy Ghost, and God the Creator, Redeemer, and Sanctifier are all the same God, then "they cannot be Three Persons: And if they be Three Persons, they must be Three Gods. For like as Three Persons, amongst Men, doth signifie Three Men; so Three Persons, who are God, must be Three Gods" (p. 55).

Like Sherlock, Wallis was well aware of the problem of the principle of individuation. However, unlike Sherlock, Wallis thought that the problem had to do with the conception or definition of person on which the whole debate traded. Whereas Sherlock thought the Boethian definition merely needed a Cartesian update, Wallis maintained that it needed to be scrapped altogether. From Wallis's perspective, what was needed was some strong etymological disinfectant. Therefore, at the core of Wallis's proposal is a careful etymological analysis of the English word "person" and the Latin *persona*. His analysis itself consists of six moves, the first three of which are designed simply to clear the decks for a recovery of the church fathers' conception and use of *persona.*

Having acknowledged the problem of the principle of individuation, Wallis asserts that the Socinians wished merely "to cavil over a word." More significantly, he insists that the word "person" is of little, if any, real importance. In a rhetorical flourish, he exclaims, "Change it to three things or three somewhats — give them another name besides persons or no name at all and this objection is at an end!" (p. 56).

In a second deck-clearing move, Wallis offers a close examination of the etymology of the English word "person": "Tis very true, that, in our English Tongue, by another Person, we sometimes understand another Man, (because that other Person is, very often, another Man also)." He then adds: "But it is not always so; nor is that the proper Signification of the Word; but an Abusive sense put upon it" (p. 56).

How was it, then, that the word "person" acquired another sense besides the proper one? According to Wallis, the problem had to do with the limitations of the English language. In reality, he claims, the English word "person" simply does not correspond to the Latin and Greek terms in Trinitarian theology.

And the reason of using the word Person in this abusive or improper sense; is, for want of an English word to answer the Latin word *Homo,* or the Greek *anthropos,* which might indifferently relate to both sexes. For the word Man doth properly relate to the Male, and Woman to the Female. And if the word Man be sometimes so used as to imply the Woman also; it is (by a Synecdoche) putting the Name of One Sex, to signifie Both. And 'tis for want of such a Word (which might indifferently relate to both Sexes) that we sometime make use of Person in a borrowed sense, rather than to use a Circumlocution of Man and Woman, by naming both Sexes. And if we should use such Circumlocution of Man and Woman; yet even this would not reach the whole Species. For we do not use to call them Man and Woman, till they be of a considerable Age; before which time they are called Children; and therefore to comprehend the whole Species, we say, Man, Woman, and Child. We do indeed, sometimes, to that purpose, make use of the word Mankind, (adding the word kind to that of Man, to Ampliate the Signification of it.) But this relates only *to Genus Humanum* in a Collective sense; not to *Homines* taken Distributively. For we do not say a Mankind, two Mankinds, etc., as we say *Homo, Homines*. We are fain, therefore, for the want of a proper English word, to make use of Person in a borrowed sense to answer the Latin *Homo*. (pp. 56-57)

According to this analysis, the problem with Socinian or Unitarian objections was that they were based on English formulations of Trinitarian doctrine. As Wallis puts it, "the Ancient Fathers, who first applied the word *Persona* to the Sacred Trinity, did not speak English." Consequently, it was simply not possible, "from the present use of the word Person in our Language," to conclude that the Trinity was either irrational or unintelligible. Before any of us could do that, we would have to pay close attention to the sense in which the early church fathers "used the word *Persona*" (p. 57).

In a third deck-clearing move, Wallis makes the etymological problem even worse by arguing that, where the Trinity is concerned, the conception and use of the word *persona* was badly corrupted long before it was translated into the English "person." At this point, Wallis's target is none other than Boethius's definition of "person."

The Schoolmen in later Ages have yet put another sense on the word *Persona*, peculiar to themselves; extending it indifferently to Men and Angels; (for want of a proper word of that Extent;) so as to signifie (with them) what they call *Suppositum Rationale*, or what we call a Reasonable Creature. (And, in imitation of them, some others have used it.) But this is a New sense, of later Ages, since the time of those Fathers, (nor do the Schoolmen, in this sense, without a Metaphor, apply it to the sacred Trinity.) We cannot therefore conclude from hence, What was the Fathers sense of it. (p. 58)

Having argued that neither the modern, seventeenth-century English nor the Boethian conception and use of "person" adequately captured what the early church fathers understood by *persona* when they applied it to the Trinity, Wallis is finally ready to recover the true meaning of the term.

To find out therefore the true sense of the word Person as applied to the Trinity; we are not so much to consider, what now-a-days the word doth sometime signifie in English; nor what sense the Schoolmen have put upon it since the time of those Fathers: As, what was the true sense of the word Persona, at or before their times, in approved Latin Authours. Which is quite another thing from either of these senses. (p. 58)

In a fourth move, Wallis began to recover "the true sense of the word *Persona* . . . in approved Latin Authours" by explaining what those authors did not mean by the term.

> For what in English we sometimes mean by Three Persons (taken indifferently for Men, Women, and Children,) the Latins would not have called *tres Personas,* but *tres Homines:* Though, if considered in such Relations, as Father, Mother, and Child. They might so be called *tres Personae* . . . . Nor do I find that in approved Latin Authours, the word *Persona* was wont to be attributed by them (as by the Schoolmen it hath since been) to Angels; nor to their Genii, or Heathen Gods. (pp. 58-59)

In a fifth move, Wallis undertook to show how the ancients conceived of and used the word *persona* in more modest or pedestrian contexts, saving the application of the term to the Trinity for his sixth and final move. In everyday life, Wallis notes, the term signifies "the State, Quality, or Condition of a Man, as he stands Related to other Men." He continues:

> Suppose, as a King, a Subject, a Father, a Son, a Neighbor, a Publick or Private Person, a Person of Honour, and the like. And so, as the Condition varied, the Person varied also, though the same Man remained. As if an ordinary Person, be first made a Knight, and then a Lord; the Person or Condition is varied, but he is still the same Man that he was before. And he that is this Year, a Lord Mayor, may be, next Year, but an Alderman, or not so much. . . . Hence are those Latin Phrases, frequent in approved Authours; *Personam imponere* (to put a Man into an Office, or confer a Dignity upon him;) *Induere personam* (to take upon him the Office;) *Sustinere personam* (to Bear an Office or Execute an Office;) *Deponere personam* (to Resign the Office, or lay it down;) so, *Agere personam* (to Act a Person,) and many the like . . . . So that there is nothing of Contradiction, nothing of Inconsistence, nothing Absurd or Strange in it, for the same Man to

sustain divers Persons, (either successively, or at the same Time;) or divers Persons to meet in the same Man; according to the true and proper Notion of the word Person. A Man may, at the same time, sustain the Person of a King, and of a Father, if invested with Regal and Paternal Authority; (and these Authorities may be Subordinate one to another;) and he may accordingly Act sometime as a King, and sometime as a Father. (pp. 59-60)

From Wallis's point of view, the fact that in everyday contexts the Latin *persona* was used primarily, if not exclusively, to refer to offices held, took away "the very foundation of their Objection; Which proceeds upon this Mistake, as if Three Persons (in a proper sense) must needs imply Three Men" (p. 60). What was not yet clear, however, was how exactly the appeal to the everyday conception and use of *persona* resolved the problem of the principle of individuation. If anything, it seemed to resolve the problem by so redefining the term used to individuate Father, Son, and Holy Spirit that no real distinctions remained. Surely Wallis would now provide some other term by which Father, Son, and Holy Spirit could be individuated without making them to be three gods.

Unfortunately, Wallis would provide no such term. Instead, he concluded his argument with a series of questions:

> Now if Three Persons (in the proper sense of the word Person) may be One Man; what hinders but that Three Divine Persons (in a sense Metaphorical) may be One God? What hinders but that the same God, considered as the Maker and Sovereign of all the World, may be God the Creator, or God the Father; and the same God considered, as to the special care of Mankind, as the Authour of our Redemption, be God the Redeemer, or God the Son; and the same God, as working effectually on the Hearts of his Elect, be God the Sanctifier, or God the Holy Ghost? And what hinders but that the same God, distinguished according to these three Considerations, may fitly be said to be Three Persons? Or (if the word Person do not please) Three Somewhats that are but One God? (p. 61)

Wallis's questions were met promptly by Stephen Nye, whose response to Wallis was no less devastating than South's had been to Sherlock. Near the outset of his *Considerations on the Explications of the Doctrine of the Trinity,* Nye summarizes Wallis's argument:

All Men know, that the Difference between the Unitarians and their Opponents, the Trinitarians, is (in a few words) this, Whether there be more than one *Divine* Person, or more than one Person, who is the true and most high God? The Unitarians say there can be but one Divine Person; because, not to mention the Scripture-Proofs of it, a *Divine Person* being as much to say a *Divinity,* or a God . . . . But, saith Dr. Wallis, "Here's a reasoning why 'tis grounded on this silly Mistake, that a *Divine* Person is as much as to say a *Divinity,* or a God; when indeed a *Divine* Person is only a *Mode,* a Respect, or Relation of God to his Creatures. He beareth to his Creatures these three Relations, Modes, or Respects, that he is their *Creator,* their *Redeemer,* and their *Sanctifier:* this is *what* we mean, and *all* we mean, when we say God is *three Persons . . . .* See here, one Man sustains (or is) three *Persons,* an Advocate, an Accuser, and a Judg, without being three Men: Why should it be thought incredible, or harsh, to say with the Church, three Divine Persons are but one God? (pp. 7-8; italics in original)[41]

After summarizing Wallis's position, Nye observes that "a very surprising thing hath happened," namely, the Socinians, "in their *Observations on the Letters of Dr. Wallis,* profess that they are of his Mind; they even say that in Honour of him they are content to be called *Wallisians.*" Nye then quickly adds: "This is very odd; for it follows that either the Socinians are the true *Orthodox,* and their Opposers *Tritheists;* or else, that *this good Doctor is a Socinian, and knows it not*" (p. 8; italics in original). What Nye was getting at, of course, was that, if Sherlock's solution to the problem of the principle of individuation had resulted in tritheism, then Wallis's solution amounted to Unitarianism. Indeed, says Nye, Wallis's solution replaces the "Trinity of the Catholick Church" with a "disguised Sabellianism or Socinianism."

According to Nye, there were at least three problems with Wallis's proposal. The first problem had to do with Wallis's conception and use of "person." In arguing that the three divine persons are "but three Relations, Capacities, or Respects of God to his Creatures," Wallis had opened the way for as many divine persons as God has relationships or capacities. "But then," Nye wittily points out, "because God hath also

41. Stephen Nye, *Considerations on the Explications of the Doctrine of the Trinity, by Dr. Wallis, Dr. Sherlock, Dr. S——th, Dr. Cudworth, and Mr. Hooker* (London, 1693).

the Capacity or Relation of a *Judg*, and of a *Provider*, and many more; we must not say that God is only *three* Persons, he is *five* at the least, besides I know not how many more" (pp. 8-9; italics in original).

The second problem was even more devastating. On the basis of Wallis's proposal, it seemed that the second person of the Trinity did not exist from eternity. Thus Nye observes:

> Furthermore, this new-fangled Socinian or Sabellian has introduced a Trinity of Divine Persons that were but of *yesterday.* The Churches Trinity are all of them from all Eternity; *Co-eternal,* saith the Athanasian Creed; *before all Worlds,* saith the Nicene Creed; but Dr. Wallis has three Divine Persons, the first of them begins with the Creation, and the second is no older than the *Crucifixion* or our Saviour; for God was not a *Creator* before he created anything; nor a *Redeemer,* till those words spoken by Our Saviour on the Cross, *It is finished,* i.e., The great Work of Redemption is accomplished. (p. 9; italics in original)

Finally, Nye asks Wallis to explain how, on the basis of Wallis's concept of person, three divine persons could beget one another from eternity. "How," asks Nye, "did *Creation* it self beget *Redemption,* and from all Eternity, that is before either of them were?" Of course, Nye was pointing out that, in Wallis's solution, the entire range of terms developed by the early church fathers for the purpose of individuating the Son from the Father no longer made sense. Far from successfully individuating the three persons of the Trinity, Wallis, it seemed, had systematically annihilated any real distinctions between them.

From Nye's perspective, Wallis had done no more than secure the unity of God, which was the very thing that the Socinians and Unitarians believed. Wallis's conception and use of "person," however strong its etymological basis, seemed to Nye to eliminate the distinctions among the persons altogether. To be sure, the offices or roles were distinguishable, but they did not constitute any *real distinctions* in God. Thus Nye was correct in accusing Wallis of Sabellianism.

Despite the apparent problems with his proposal, Wallis had succeeded in two things. First, he had called attention to the logic, if not the exact language, of the economic Trinity. For one brief moment in the Trinitarian controversy, someone had actually bothered to point out that the Trinity has as much to do with the Christian God's relationship to creation and to humans as it did with the eternal relationships among the three divine persons. Second, Wallis had called attention to the shift that had taken place in the conception and use of the word "person" after Boethius. In doing so, he managed to point the entire debate in a new direction. In Wallis's analysis, the problem was that "person" had been conflated with "substance," or what he liked to call "essence." For Edward Stillingfleet, this insight would be the key to salvaging the Trinity.

CHAPTER 5

Locke's Legacy

All our notions of the doctrine of the Trinity depend on the right understanding [of] the distinction between nature and person.

Edward Stillingfleet

For, to my thinking, I never met with any thing more unintelligible about that subject, nor that is more remote from clear and distinct apprehensions of nature and person.

John Locke, on Stillingfleet's
distinction between nature and person

Unlike William Sherlock and John Wallis, each of whom met the Unitarian challenge head-on, Edward Stillingfleet did his best to stay out of the controversy over the Trinity for the first half of the 1690s. Stillingfleet's only contribution to the debate before 1696 came in 1691, when he published a sermon he had preached at St. Laurence-Jewry entitled *The Mysteries of the Christian faith asserted and vindicated.*[1] Even then, Stillingfleet did not attempt to put the matter to rest by resolving the problem of the principle of individuation. Rather, Stillingfleet was content to reassert what he took to be the sure grounds for belief in the Trinity:

---

1. Edward Stillingfleet, *The Mysteries of the Christian faith asserted and vindicated* (London, 1691).

And truly no Men (by their own Authority) can pretend to a Right to impose on others any Mysteries of Faith, or any such things which are above their Capacity to understand. But that is not our Case; for we all profess to believe and receive Christianity as a Divine Revelation; and God (we say) may require from us the belief of what we may not be able to comprehend, especially if it relates to himself, or such things which are consequent upon the Union of the Divine and Humane Nature. Therefore our business is to consider, whether any such things be contained in that Revelation which we all own; and if they be, we are bound to believe them, although we are not able to comprehend them.[2]

Yet, even though it did not attempt to resolve the problem of the principle of individuation, Stillingfleet's sermon did not escape criticism from the Unitarians. Stephen Nye attacked Stillingfleet's effort to safeguard the Trinity by designating it among those things clearly but incomprehensibly given in divine revelation. In doing so, Nye insisted that Stillingfleet had misunderstood the Unitarian position.

He utterly mistakes, in Thinking, that we deny the articles of the New Christianity, or Athanasian Religion, because they are Mysteries, or because we do not comprehend them; we deny 'em, because we do comprehend them; we have a clear and distinct Perception, that they are not Mysteries, but Contradictions, Impossibilities, and pure Nonsense. We have our Reason in vain, and all Science and Certainty would be destroyed; if we could not distinguish, between Mysteries and Contradictions; which are (by all confessed to be) Impossibilites. But . . . some have learned to call their Non-Sense, the Deep Things of God; and their Contradictions, Mysteries of Religion.[3]

It was this passage in Nye's pamphlet of 1694 that Stillingfleet would eventually cite as providing the occasion for his writing and publishing A Discourse in Vindication of the Doctrine of the Trinity.[4] How-

2. Stillingfleet, Works, 6 vols. (London, 1707-1710), 1:453.
3. Stephen Nye, Considerations on the Explications of the Doctrine of the Trinity, by Dr. Wallis, Dr. Sherlock, Dr. S——th, Dr. Cudworth, and Mr. Hooker (London, 1693), p. 1.
4. The full title is A Discourse in Vindication of the Doctrine of the Trinity: With an Answer to the Late Socinian Objections Against it from Scripture, Antiquity and Reason. And a Preface concerning the different Explications of the Trinity, and the Tendency of the present Socinian Con-

ever, at least three years passed before Stillingfleet finally responded to Nye's provocations, thus giving the impression that he was deeply reluctant to enter the controversy. In the preface to *Vindication,* Stillingfleet goes out of his way to explain his prolonged silence:

> I am so little a Friend to any such Heats and Differences among our selves especially when we are so violently attacked by our common Adversaries, that were there no other reason, I should for the sake of that alone forbear making us of new Explications; but there is another too obvious, which is, the mighty advantage they have taken from hence to represent our Doctrine as uncertain, as well as unintelligible. For as soon as our Unitarians began to appear with that Briskness and Boldness that have done now for several years, some of our Divines thought themselves obliged to write in Defense of the Doctrine of the Trinity.[5]

Stillingfleet continues:

> Thence came several Answers to them, and in several Methods, as the Persons thought most subservient to the same end; but whatever their intentions were [i.e., the Divines], our Adversaries were too much pleased to conceal the Satisfaction which they took in it. For soon after, we had the several Explications set forth and compared with each other; and all managed so, as to make the Cause to suffer by the disagreement of the Advocates for it.[6]

As Furly had pointed out, it did not say much for the intelligibility of the Trinity that some of the most astute and learned divines of the

---

troversy (London, 1697), as reprinted in *The Philosophy of Edward Stillingfleet Including His Replies to John Locke,* 5 vols., ed. G. A. J. Rogers (Bristol, UK: Thoemmes Press, 2000), 4:i-ii. John C. Higgins-Biddle observes that, "although dated 1697," Stillingfleet's *Vindication* "was advertised in the *London Gazette,* 3234 (5-9 Nov. 1696)." See John Locke, *The Reasonableness of Christianity as Delivered in the Scriptures,* Introduction, Notes, Critical Apparatus, and Transcriptions of Related Manuscripts edited by John C. Higgins-Biddle (Oxford: Clarendon Press, 1999), p. xlvii, n. 1.

5. Edward Stillingfleet, *Philosophy of Edward Stillingfleet,* 4:iv.

6. *Philosophy of Edward Stillingfleet,* 4:iv. Stillingfleet is clearly referring to Stephen Nye's earlier pamphlet, *Considerations on the Explications of the Doctrine of the Trinity.* Stillingfleet goes on to identify Nye's typology of trinities, including the Ciceronian, Cartesian, Platonic, and Aristotelian trinities.

Church of England could not agree with one another concerning how best to understand it. Stephen Nye had gone so far as to argue that some forty different versions of the "orthodox" doctrine of the Trinity had emerged. Moreover, Nye had observed that, while some argued for the Trinity by developing a generic concept of substance, others appealed to a numerical concept. Similarly, while some envisioned a Trinity of beings, others argued for a Trinity of properties, or of modes of subsistence, or of relationships to creatures, or of operations.[7] Thus Stillingfleet lamented that, when the Unitarians set these various explications alongside one another, the cause was made "to suffer by the disagreement of the Advocates for it."

It would seem that Stillingfleet had remained on the sidelines for fear that, if he added to the number of explications already offered, he would only further strengthen the impression that the Trinitarians could not agree among themselves concerning something purportedly derived from clear and intelligible propositions in Scripture. Like most Protestant theologians in seventeenth-century England, Stillingfleet was well aware of the Catholic criticism that the Protestant rule of faith led to widespread disagreement over doctrine. He was also aware that, on pain of contradicting the rule of faith, widespread disagreement over the doctrine of the Trinity could mean only one thing: that the Trinity was not among the things necessary to be believed for salvation.

Two things are clear at this point. First, Stillingfleet was concerned that the growing number of attempts to defend the doctrine of the Trinity had actually made the situation worse. Second, it was for this reason that he had refused publicly to respond for three years after his sermon of 1691 had been the subject of Unitarian ridicule. For someone renowned for responding immediately to his critics, the decision to stay out of the debate could not have been an easy one.[8] Given these two facts, it seems unlikely that Nye's pamphlet of 1694 prompted Stillingfleet to break his silence. One suspects that something or someone else forced Stillingfleet to enter the fray.

7. Stephen Nye, *Letter of Resolution concerning the Doctrines of the Trinity and Incarnation* (London, 1695), p. 9.

8. For an excellent review of Stillingfleet's various responses to Catholic criticism of the Protestant rule of faith, see Robert Todd Carroll, *The Common-Sense Philosophy of Bishop Edward Stillingfleet 1635-1699* (Martinus Nijhoff: The Hague, 1975), pp. 50-56.

The Occasion for Stillingfleet's *Vindication*

After declaring that Nye's challenge in 1694 was the "occasion" for the work, Stillingfleet summarized the charges that had come out in a more recent work by Nye, one entitled *A Discourse concerning the Real and Nominal Trinitarians*.[9] On the one hand, says Stillingfleet, the Unitarians argued that the real Trinitarians were guilty of tritheism; on the other, they claimed that the nominal Trinitarians were really Sabellians, which is "the same with Unitarians." Stillingfleet concludes: "And they confidently affirm that all that speak out in this matter, must be driven either to Sabellianism or Tritheism. If they are Nominal Trinitarians, they fall into the former, if Real, into the latter."[10]

In response to this more recent Unitarian work, Stillingfleet declared that the only way to avoid the charges of tritheism and Sabellianism was vigilantly to maintain the distinction between *substance* and *personality*, which was a distinction Wallis had sought to recover. Indeed, it was in coming to Wallis's defense in his preface to *Vindication* that Stillingfleet first emphasized the importance of maintaining the distinction between "one substance" and "three persons," the latter being understood as substance existing under three different modes of subsisting.[11] However, by the end of *Vindication,* Stillingfleet would go so far as to declare that the Trinity was utterly dependent on maintaining the distinction between substance and personality. "All our Notions of the Doctrine of the Trinity," he says, "depend on the right understanding" of "the Distinction between Nature and Person."[12]

Stillingfleet's remark about the dependence of all intelligible notions of the Trinity on the distinction between substance and personal-

9. Stephen Nye, *A Discourse concerning the Real and Nominal Trinitarians* (London, 1695). For an extended response to this pamphlet, see William Sherlock, *The Distinction Between the Real and Nominal Trinitarians, Considered* (London, 1697).

10. *Philosophy of Edward Stillingfleet,* 4:vii.

11. *Philosophy of Edward Stillingfleet,* 4:xiii-xix. For Stillingfleet's familiarity with and defense of Wallis's argument, see M. A. Stewart, "Stillingfleet and the Way of Ideas," in *English Philosophy in the Age of Locke,* ed. M. A. Stewart (Oxford: Clarendon Press, 2000), p. 277.

12. Stillingfleet, *Vindication,* p. 252. With regard to this passage, William S. Babcock notes that, by "nature," we should understand Stillingfleet to mean "substance." See William S. Babcock, "A Changing of the Christian God," *Interpretation* 45, no. 2 (1991): 143.

ity is the clue that reveals what or who prompted him finally to join the debate over the Trinity. As things turned out, it was not any of Nye's publications, but rather John Toland's *Christianity Not Mysterious* (1696), that agitated the aging Stillingfleet to the point that he felt he had no choice but to respond publicly. Even a cursory reading of the lengthy preface to *Vindication* shows that it was deism that provoked Stillingfleet to publish his response.[13] One can see in the last chapter of *Vindication* why Toland's work was particularly alarming to him.[14] According to Stillingfleet, the Unitarians had not "explained the Nature and Bounds of Reason," but rather sometimes spoke of "clear and distinct Perceptions, sometimes of natural Ideas, sometimes of congenit Notions, etc." (p. 231). By contrast, Toland had given precisely the kind of account of the nature and bounds of reason that Stillingfleet had been on guard against for thirty years.[15] According to Toland,

> Every one experiences in himself a Power, or Faculty of forming various Ideas, or Perceptions of things; of affirming, or denying according as he sees them to agree or disagree, and this is Reason in General. It is not the bare receiving Ideas into the Mind, that is strictly Reason, but the Perception of the Agreement, or Disagreement of our Ideas in a greater or lesser Number; wherein soever this Agreement, or Disagreement may consist. If the Perception be immediate without the Assistance of any other Idea, this is not call'd Reason, but Self-Evidence: but when the mind makes use of intermediate

13. *Philosophy of Edward Stillingfleet,* 4:xlvii–lxii. Carroll says: "The *Vindication of the Doctrine of the Trinity* was initially begun by Stillingfleet as an answer to a number of Socinian tracts that appeared between the years 1691-1696, but Toland's *Christianity not Mysterious* prompted the Bishop of Worcester to add a tenth chapter in reply to Toland" (Carroll, *The Common-Sense Philosophy,* p. 87). While Carroll's remark about the beginnings of the work is correct, Stillingfleet did more than simply "add a tenth chapter." The long preface is primarily concerned with deism, not Socinianism, and he made other adjustments throughout the work to account for deism.

14. John Toland, *Christianity Not Mysterious: or, A treatise shewing, that there is nothing in the gospel contrary to reason, nor above it: and that no Christian doctrine can properly be call'd a mystery* (London, 1696). While Toland's work was not published until 1696, Higgins-Biddle observes that, "as early as May 1694, it was rumoured in London that Toland was at work upon a book which was designed to show that there were no mysteries in Christianity" (Toland, *Christianity Not Mysterious,* p. xxxi).

15. See Chapter 3 of this book.

Idea's to discover that Agreement or Disagreement, this method of Knowledge is properly call'd Reason or Demonstration. And so Reason is defined to be that Faculty of the Soul, which discovers certainty of any thing dubious, or obscure by comparing it with something evidently known. (*Vindication,* pp. 231-32)

Up until this point, Stillingfleet declared that he could "perfectly agree" with Toland. Indeed, his problem was not with the general features of Toland's account of reason, but rather with Toland's further point that all "clear and distinct Ideas" must be derived from either "Sensation or Reflection" (pp. 232-33).[16] It was this restricting of the origin of "clear and distinct Ideas" to "Sensation and Reflection" that Stillingfleet called the "new Way of Reason," on the basis of which "we may talk and dispute about *Substance,* as long as we please" without coming to any certainty (pp. 233-34).

It is easy to see why Stillingfleet was so alarmed by Toland. Stillingfleet held that "our certainty of [the Trinity] in Point of Reason, depends upon our Knowledge of the Nature of Substance, and Person and the Distinction between them." According to Toland, humans could have "no clear Idea" in their minds concerning substance; and if so, then they could not show that the Trinity was intelligible by distinguishing between persons and substance.

Stillingfleet rightly discerned that Toland was dependent for his conception of reason and ideas on Locke's *Essay Concerning Human Understanding.* Thus, with a thinly veiled reference to Locke himself, Stillingfleet registered his concern:

Now this is the Case of Substance; it is not intromitted by the Senses, nor depends upon the Operations of the Mind; and so it cannot be within the compass of our Reason. And therefore I do not wonder, that Gentleman of this new way of reasoning, have almost discarded Substance out of the reasonable part of the World. For they not only tell us, That we can have no Idea of it by Sensation or Reflection; but that nothing is signified by it, only an uncertain Supposition of we

---

16. Carroll captures Toland's position nicely when he says that Toland was "blending together the Cartesian criteria for certainty — clear and distinct ideas — and the Lockean account of the origin of ideas in either sensation or the reflection upon the operations of the mind" (Carroll, *The Common-Sense Philosophy,* p. 89).

know not what . . . . If this be the truth of the Case, we must still talk like Children, and I know not how it can be remedied. For, if we cannot come at a rational Idea of Substance, we can have no Principle of certainty to go upon in this Debate. (pp. 234-35)

Convinced that the new way of learning threatened to undermine the Trinity by making it impossible to distinguish between nature and substance, Stillingfleet set out to defend the Trinity. Just as Sherlock had thought that the Boethian definition of person only required some mild Cartesian modifications, Stillingfleet now reasoned that he could salvage the Trinity by making just one modification to Locke's concept of ideas. According to Stillingfleet, Locke's concept of ideas needed to be altered in such a way as to allow for the idea of substance, a suggestion that sparked a lengthy debate with Locke himself over the nature of ideas in general and the idea of substance in particular.[17]

17. The debate between Stillingfleet and Locke turned out to be lengthy, taking up the better part of a year. Moreover, as Babcock says, the exchange of "letters" between Stillingfleet and Locke was an exchange of "more treatises, in fact, than letters" (Babcock, "A Changing of the Christian God," p. 144). The sequence is as follows. After Stillingfleet challenged Locke's "new way of reason" in *Vindication,* Locke responded with *A Letter to the Right Reverend Edward, Lord Bishop of Worcester, concerning some passages relating to Mr. Locke's Essay Concerning Human Understanding, in a Late Discourse of his Lordship's, in Vindication of the Trinity* (1697). In turn, Stillingfleet published *The Bishop of Worcester's Answer to Mr. Locke's Letter Concerning some Passages Relating to his Essay of Humane Understanding* (London, 1697). Locke responded immediately with *Mr. Locke's Reply to the Right Reverend the Lord Bishop of Worcester's Answer to his Letter, etc.* (London, 1697). Stillingfleet countered with another letter that was entitled *The Bishop of Worcester's Answer to Mr. Locke's Second Letter wherein his Notion of Ideas is Prov'd to be Inconsistent with Itself* (London, 1697), to which Locke replied with *Mr. Locke's Reply to the Right Reverend the Lord Bishop of Worcester's Answer to his Second Letter Wherein, besides other incident Matters, what his Lordship has said concerning Certainty by Reason, Certainty by Ideas, and Certainty by Faith; the Resurrection of the Body; the Immateriality of the Soul; the Inconsistency of Mr. Locke's Notions with the Articles of the Christian Faith, and their Tendency to Scepticism; is examined* (London, 1698). For Locke's "letters," see vol. 4 of *The Works of John Locke,* 10 vols. (London, 1823; reprint, Aalen, Germany: Scientia Verlag, 1963; hereafter *Works*). For Stillingfleet's "letters," see vol. 5 of *The Philosophy of Edward Stillingfleet Including his Replies to John Locke* (Bristol: Thoemmes Press, 2000; hereafter *Replies*).

Stillingfleet and the Way of Ideas: Anatomy of a Debate

Given that Stillingfleet's efforts to vindicate the Trinity depended on his ability to secure the idea of substance within the framework of Locke's new way of reasoning, it will help to say a word or two about the framework itself. Stillingfleet's proposal concerning the nature of ideas in general and the idea of substance in particular, like Sherlock's proposal concerning the concept of "person," was fundamentally Cartesian in orientation. As far as Stillingfleet was concerned, the problem with Locke's view of the nature of ideas was that Locke had rejected Descartes's view of substance. M. A. Stewart says:

> Closer scrutiny of Stillingfleet's attack on Locke's handling of the concept [of ideas] shows what was at issue: Locke derived all his ideas from sensation and reflection, but central to his metaphysics were ideas, e.g., of substance, that appeared to have no such origin. To Stillingfleet these were necessarily intellectual, not experiential; and since that is precisely the sense in which clear and distinct ideas functioned in Cartesian philosophy, it is natural to think that Stillingfleet was reading Locke as sending Cartesian signals on which he consistently failed to deliver, indeed could not deliver within his stated terms of reference.[18]

If the conflict between Stillingfleet and Locke had to do with the difference between Stillingfleet's Cartesian position concerning the clear and distinct nature of ideas and the conception of ideas at the heart of Locke's new way of reason, then we need to come to grips with Locke's concept of ideas.[19] A good place to begin in that endeavor is with Locke's conception of language.[20] Once we have a handle on Locke's view of language, we can work our way backwards to his concept of ideas.

18. Stewart, "Stillingfleet and the Way of Ideas," p. 256.

19. For an introduction to Locke's theory of ideas, see Vere Chappell, "Locke's Theory of Ideas," in *The Cambridge Companion to Locke*, ed. Vere Chappell (New York: Cambridge University Press, 1994), pp. 26-55. For a particularly helpful but concise summary of Locke's theory of ideas and theory of language, see William S. Babcock, "A Changing of the Christian God." Because Babcock wrote his summary with the controversy between Locke and Stillingfleet in mind, I refer to it frequently in what follows.

20. For a helpful introduction to Locke's theory of language, see Paul Guyer, "Locke's Philosophy of Language," in *The Cambridge Companion to Locke*, pp. 115-45.

For Locke, words carry no inherent meaning; rather, they are simply articulate sound until they are made by convention the linguistic counters for particular ideas. Therefore, for Locke, the meaning of words was completely a matter of the ideas for which they stand. This, of course, raises the question of where the ideas themselves come from. On this issue, Locke was abundantly clear: there are no innate ideas in the mind. The mind does not come stocked with ideas. Indeed, Locke was so determined to rid the world of innate ideas that he spent the entire first book of the *Essay* arguing against them. According to Locke, all ideas are derived from one of two sources, namely, sensation and reflection. It was this feature of Locke's epistemology that had set Stillingfleet off when he encountered it in Toland.

As far as Stillingfleet was concerned, the crucial issue had to do with the primary purpose for which Locke had developed his theory of ideas in the first place. Locke was not attempting simply to offer a strictly neutral account of the formation of ideas. On the contrary, Locke's theory of ideas was meant "to disqualify the Aristotelian discourse of the schools" and to make possible "another form of discourse about the workings of things (the form associated, for instance, with the chemistry of Robert Boyle or the physics of Isaac Newton)." In particular, Locke's analysis of our complex ideas of substances was designed "to expose . . . as virtually empty of content and therefore devoid of explanatory power" the scholastic notion of substance, since it was precisely this latter notion of substance that stood in the way of "the investigation of things in terms of their chemical composition or their atomic structure." Babcock captures the precise way that Locke's theory of ideas undermined the scholastic notion of substance:

> Locke begins by observing that we find certain combinations of simple ideas (e.g., of color, shape, and size) that "go constantly together." Just because these ideas go constantly together, we presume that they belong to one thing and call them by one name (e.g., horse) as if they constituted a single simple idea. In fact, however, they represent "a complication of many *ideas* together," and we construct the idea of a *substratum,* or substance for them only because we cannot imagine "how these simple ideas can subsist by themselves." Beyond this bare supposition of an underlying something, however, our ideas of substance cannot go. Thus, our "notion of pure substance in

general" is only the idea of "we know not what" supporting those qualities in things that produce the various constant sets of simple ideas in us; and our "ideas of particular sorts of substances" are no more than specific constellations of simple ideas taken together with "the confused *idea* of *something* to which they belong." In short, we have no clear and distinct idea either of substance in general or of any particular sort of substance; and the confused idea that we do have of substance does little more than to delineate a blank which can then be filled in by other means.[21]

Now that we have Locke's position on substance clearly in view, we are ready to consider Stillingfleet's counterproposal. For Stillingfleet, Locke's view of ideas was largely acceptable. It simply needed to be sufficiently modified to accommodate the idea of substance. From Stillingfleet's perspective, the easiest way to do this was to grant Locke's point that the idea of substance did not derive from either sensation or reflection. Rather, as Descartes had argued, the idea of substance was innate. Thus Stillingfleet declares in *Vindication*:

> I do not say, that we can have a clear Idea of Substance, either by Sensation or Reflection; but from hence I argue, that this is a very insufficient Distribution of the Ideas necessary to Reason. For besides these, there must be some general Ideas, which the mind doth form, not by mere comparing these Ideas it has from Sense and Reflection; but by forming distinct general Notions, of things from particular Ideas. And among these general Notions, or rational Ideas, Sub-

---

21. Babcock, "A Changing of the Christian God," p. 138. Babcock cites Locke, *Essay*, 2.23.1-2. While Babcock provides an excellent summary of Locke's lengthy argument concerning the idea of substance in Book II, Locke expresses his position on substance most clearly and succinctly in Book I: "I confess, there is another *Idea*, which would be of general use for Mankind to have, as it is of general talk as if they had it; and that is the *Idea of Substance*, which we neither have, nor can have, by *Sensation or Reflection*. If Nature took care to provide us any *Ideas*, we might well expect it should be such, as by our own Faculties we cannot produce to our selves: But we see on the contrary, that since by those ways, whereby other *Ideas* are brought into our Minds, this is not, we have no such *clear Idea* at all, and therefore signify nothing by the word *Substance*, but only an uncertain supposition of we know not what; (*i.e.*, of something whereof we have no particular distinct positive) *Idea*, which we take to be the *substratum*, or support, of those *Ideas* we do know" (1.4.18; italics in original). For Locke's account of how the two syllables *sub* and *stance* came into use together, see 2.13.19.

stance is one of the first; because we find we can have no true Conceptions of any Modes or Accidents (no matter which) but we must conceive a Substratum, or Subject wherein they are. Since it is Repugnancy to our first Conceptions of things, that Modes or Accidents should subsist by themselves, and therefore the Rational Idea of Substance is one of the first, and most natural Ideas in our minds. (p. 236)

Locke was clearly not arguing that modes or accidents subsist by themselves. Locke even agreed that we "construct the idea of a substratum, or substance . . . because we cannot imagine 'how these simple ideas can subsist by themselves.'" Nor was Stillingfleet unaware of this aspect of Locke's theory. After quoting these very words from Locke's *Essay*, Stillingfleet asks:

And is this all indeed, that is to be said for the being of Substance, that we accustom our Selves to suppose a Substratum? Is that Custom grounded upon true Reason or not? If not, then Accidents or Modes, must subsist of themselves, and these Simple Ideas need no Tortoise to support them: For Figures and Colours, etc., would do well enough of themselves, but for some Fancies men have accustomed themselves to. If it be grounded on plain and evident Reason, then we must allow an Idea of Substance, which comes not in by Sensation of Reflection; and so we may be certain of some things which we have not by those Ideas. (pp. 236-37)

Among Stillingfleet's many worries was the possibility that Locke's position would engender too much skepticism. In other words, Stillingfleet feared that Locke had removed too much. He argued that we need "an intellectual supplement, a reason which both interprets and corrects the senses, and knows how to distinguish evidence from what it is evidence for."[22]

The truth is that Locke's position on the idea of substance was more agnostic than antagonistic. For Locke, the issue was strictly an epistemological one. Due to the limits of human understanding, humans simply cannot know the real essences of things. To be sure, people have general ideas that have to do with types of things, for example,

22. Stewart, "Stillingfleet and the Way of Ideas," p. 278.

the idea of a flower, but these ideas are brought about because of the limits of language. From Locke's standpoint, no language could possibly "sustain a vocabulary so large as to include a separate word for each idea we have of each separate thing." Consequently, humans developed general terms that represent general ideas constructed by subtracting from particular ideas the "specifics of time, of place, and the like, that make them ideas of particular things." Babcock observes:

> The result, however, is not an idea of some new thing (a substance, or essence, supposedly present in the particulars) but rather an idea of sort or kind according to which we classify together things that show relevant similarities to each other (horses, animals, human beings, etc.). Accordingly, these ideas are ideas only of what Locke calls the "nominal," and not the "real," essence of things. They do not tell us what constitutes a thing or makes it what it is; they only pick out those similarities among various sets of particulars on the basis of which we call them by a common term.[23]

At this point it is worth repeating that Locke's opposition to the idea of substance was in keeping with his wider epistemological concerns. There is simply no evidence that Locke had Socinian motivations for opposing the idea of substance. John Marshall agrees:

> The thrust of the argument about substance . . . [was] probably animated by Locke's assessment of the limits of men's understandings, hostility to discussion of the nature of God, and focus on the con-

23. Babcock, "A Changing of the Christian God," p. 139. For Locke's distinction between "real" and "nominal" essences, Babcock cites Locke, *Essay*, 3.3.1-20. However, Locke expressed his position on general ideas most succinctly and clearly in an earlier passage in the *Essay*: "The use of words then being to stand as outward marks of our internal *ideas*, and those *ideas* being taken from particular things, if every particular *idea* that we take in should have a distinct name, names must be endless. To prevent this, the mind makes the particular *ideas* received from particular objects to become general; which is done by considering them as they are in the mind such appearances, separate from all other existences, and the circumstances of real existence, as time, place, or any other concomitant *ideas*. This is called ABSTRACTION, whereby *ideas* taken from particular beings become general representatives of all of the same kind; and their names, general names, applicable to whatever exists conformable to such abstract *ideas*" (2.11.9; italics and capitalization in original). For a helpful discussion of Locke's concept of "general ideas," see Chappell, "Locke's Theory of Ideas," pp. 38-49.

ventionality of language, as any straightforward reading of the *Essay* would suggest, but not invested with Socinian purpose.[24]

Locke himself tried to direct Stillingfleet's attention to the epistemological context within which he had developed his position on substance and within which he thought it should be understood. Moreover, as Marshall notes, Locke went so far as to point out that "the obscurity of the idea of substance limited Unitarians' argument that the Trinity could be said to be simply impossible because they understood the nature of God, as much as it restricted trinitarians' explanations of the Trinity."[25] Unfortunately, Stillingfleet was tone-deaf to Locke's response. As far as Stillingfleet was concerned, Locke's motivations were beside the point. The issue was more basic than that: from Stillingfleet's point of view — and despite Locke's protestations to the contrary — Locke had eliminated the language needed to secure the Trinity.

Clear and Distinct Apprehensions of *Nature* and *Person*

For Stillingfleet, as we have seen, the doctrine of the Trinity depended on the ability to distinguish between substance, essence, or nature on the one hand, and personality on the other. Thus it should come as no surprise that, when Stillingfleet set out to vindicate the doctrine of the Trinity against the charges that it was contrary to reason, he did so by developing and using an argument concerning how best to understand this distinction. After declaring that "the Nature of things properly belongs to our Reason, and not meer Ideas," Stillingfleet indicated more precisely what he meant by nature: "Nature," he says, "may be consider'd two ways." Concerning the first way, he claims in *Vindication*:

> As it is in distinct Individuals, as the Nature of a Man is equally in Peter, James, and John; and this is the common Nature with a particular Subsistence proper to each of them. For the Nature of man, as

24. John Marshall, "Locke, Socinianism, 'Socinianism', Unitarianism," in *English Philosophy in the Age of Locke*, ed. M. A. Stewart (Oxford: Clarendon Press, 2000), p. 157.
    25. Stillingfleet's citations are from Locke, *Essay*, 3.3.6-19.

in Peter, is distinct from that same Nature, as it is in James and John; otherwise, they would be but one Person, as well as have the same Nature. And this Distinction of Persons in them is discerned both by our Senses, as to their different Accidents; and by our Reason, because they have a separate Existence; not coming into it at once and in the same manner. (p. 253)

As for the second way of understanding the meaning of "nature," Stillingfleet observes:

Nature may be consider'd Abstractly, without respect to individual Persons, and then it makes an entire Notion of it self. For however, the same Nature may be in different Individuals, yet the Nature in it self remains one and the same: which appears from this evident Reason; that otherwise every Individual must make a different kind. (pp. 253-54)

Stillingfleet next shows how these two common ways of understanding "nature" fare in Locke's new way of reasoning: "Let us now see, how far these things can come from our simple Ideas, by Reflection and Sensation" (p. 254). Citing numerous passages from Locke's *Essay*, Stillingfleet argues that, if persons ascribe to Locke's theory of ideas, then "there is a Real Essence, which is the Foundation of Powers and Properties," and "we may know these Powers and Properties, although we are ignorant of the Real Essence" (p. 255). On the basis of this argument concerning what was knowable in Locke's "new way of Reason," Stillingfleet infers:

That from those true and adequate Ideas, which we have of the Modes and Properties of Things, we have sufficient certainty of the Real Essence of them: For these Ideas are allow'd to be true; and either by them we may judge of the truth of things; or we can make no Judgment at all of any thing without our selves. If our Ideas be only of the Effects we feel of the Powers of things without us; yet our Reason must be satisfied, that there could be no such Powers, unless there were some real Beings which had them. So that either we may be certain by those Effects of the real Being of Things; or it is not possible, as we are framed, to have any certainty at all of any things without our selves. (pp. 255-56)

The options, as far as Stillingfleet was concerned, were clear. Either we allow for certainty concerning the essence or nature of things, or we will be driven to radical skepticism. From where he stood, Stillingfleet could see no reason not to allow for certainty concerning substance. Thus he asks: "But if we can know so much, as that there are certain Beings in the World, endued with such distinct Powers and Properties, what is it we complain of the want of, in order to our Certainty of Things?" (p. 256). To be sure, says Stillingfleet, we may not be able to "comprehend the internal Frame, or Constitution of things, nor in what manner they do flow from the Substance," but by them "we certainly know that there are such Essences, and that they are distinguished from each other by their Powers and Properties" (p. 257).

Stillingfleet could not have been clearer about what he took to be at stake. As Robert Todd Carroll puts it, "Locke's description of the idea of substance as an 'I know not what' whose source is custom," made the idea only "*psychologically* necessary"; but for Stillingfleet "the idea had to be rationally grounded and *rationally* necessary." Otherwise, "its validity would be questionable and a gulf would thereby be opened between the ideas and the things, between thought and reality — a gulf which might in principle be uncrossable." Carroll adds that, "if the custom which Locke spoke of were not 'grounded upon true Reason,' then accidents and modes might be subsisting by themselves for all we know."[26]

Stillingfleet was not trying to overturn Locke's theories. Rather, he wanted "only to modify them in order to clear a space for just that notion of substance which Locke had taken such pains to undo." Thus, in an effort to "clear a space" for the notion of substance, Stillingfleet proposed "to rejoin the separated ideas of the 'real' and of the 'nomi-

---

26. Carroll, *The Common-Sense Philosophy*, p. 92. In what would prove to be a prophetic remark, Stillingfleet would go so far as to argue that Locke had given "no satisfactory Account, as to the Existence of the plainest Objects of Sense." Stillingfleet says: "For you say, 'The Certainty lies in perceiving the Connexion between Ideas'; and here you grant, 'That Reason cannot perceive the Connexion between the Objects and the Ideas,' how then should we possibly attain any Certainty in the way of Ideas? So that your self gives up the way of 'Certainty by Ideas'" (Stillingfleet, *Replies,* p. 131). For an analysis of how Stillingfleet's criticisms anticipate Hume's attack on Locke, see Richard Popkin, "The Philosophy of Bishop Stillingfleet," *Journal of the History of Philosophy* 10, no. 3 (1971): 303-19.

nal' essences of things in order to claim that we can, in fact, know the substance that makes a thing 'to be what it is.' "[27] In a crucial passage in *Vindication,* Stillingfleet exclaims:

> The Essences of things as they are knowable by us, have a Reality in them: For they are founded on the natural Constitution of Things. And however the abstract Ideas are the work of the mind; yet they are not meer Creatures of the Mind . . . . [T]here must be a Real Essence in every individual of the same kind; for that alone is it, which makes it to be what it is. Peter, and James, and John, are all true and real Men; but what is it which makes them so? Is it the attributing a general Name to them? No certainly, but that the true and Real Essence of a Man is in every one of them. And we must be as certain of this, as we are that they are Men. . . . That the general Idea is not made from the simple Ideas by the meer Act of the Mind abstracting from Circumstances, but from Reason and Consideration of the true Nature of Things. For, when we see so many Individuals, that have the same Powers and Properties, we thence infer, that there must be something common to all, which makes them of one kind: and if the difference of Kinds be real, that which makes them of one kind and not of another, must not be a Nominal, but Real Essence. (pp. 257-59)

Having set forth his position on "nature," or "essence," Stillingfleet turned his attention to the other crucial category in the distinction that he was trying desperately to maintain, namely, "the Idea of a Person": "For, although the common Nature in mankind be the same, yet we see a difference in several Individuals from one another: So that Peter and James, and John are all of the same kind; yet Peter is not James, and James is not John." He then asks: "But what is this Distinction founded upon?" In what would prove to be a fatal mistake, he suggests that the distinctions between persons are not finally founded on "external" differences, that is, on differences of "Features, distance of Place, etc." On the contrary, he says, suppose that "there were no such external difference; yet there is a difference between them, as several Individuals in the same common Nature." What, then, is that difference? Stillingfleet confidently declares:

27. Babcock, "A Changing of the Christian God," p. 143.

And here lies the true Idea of a Person, which arises from that manner of Subsistence which is in one Individual, and is not Communicable to another. An Individual, intelligent Substance, is rather supposed to the making of a Person, than the proper Definition of it; for a Person relates to something which doth distinguish it from another Intelligent Substance in the same Nature; and therefore the Foundation of it lies in the peculiar manner of Subsistence, which agrees to one, and to none else of the Kind and this is it which is called Personality. (pp. 259-60)

Stillingfleet acknowledged the potential objection that, "if the meer Intelligent Substance makes a Person, then there cannot be the Union of two Natures, but there must be two Persons." In order to prevent this unwanted consequence, he modified his definition of Person: "Therefore, a Person is a compleat Intelligent Substance, with a peculiar manner of Subsistence" (p. 261). With this definition of "person" in hand, he was finally ready to show the distinction between substance and personality according to which, as he had repeatedly claimed, the Trinity was a clear and intelligible doctrine necessary to be believed for salvation. He concludes:

But when we speak of Finite Substances and Persons, we are certain that distinct Persons do imply distinct Substances, because they have a distinct and separate Existence; but this will not hold in an infinite Substance, where necessary Existence doth belong to the Idea of it. And although the Argument from the Idea of God, may not be sufficient of it self to prove his Being; yet it will hold as to the excluding any thing from him, which is inconsistent with necessary Existence; therefore, if we suppose a Distinction of Persons in the same Divine Nature, it must be in a way agreeable to the infinite Perfections of it. And no objection can be taken from the Idea of God, to overthrow a Trinity of Co-existing Persons in the same Divine Essence. For necessary Existence doth imply a Co-existence of the Divine Persons; and the Unity of Divine Essence, that there cannot be such a difference of individual Substances, as there is among mankind. (pp. 261-62)

Stillingfleet clearly thought he could maintain that, while in the human case, difference of person implied difference of substance, in the divine case, necessary existence and infinite perfection excluded difference of substance without denying distinction of person. Moreover, he thought that he had "supplied the 'clear and distinct apprehensions of *Nature* and *Person*' that would sustain the doctrine of the Trinity without resorting to the tenuous innovations of a Sherlock and without elevating Trinitarian talk to the misty realms of the unintelligible."[28] Indeed, Stillingfleet thought that he had done all of this merely by modifying Locke's theory of ideas. Predictably, Locke thought otherwise. When William Molyneux suggested that the snipes of "a Man of Great Name" in the Church of England might reflect a wider clerical conspiracy against Locke, the latter replied:

> What [Stillingfleet] says, is, as you observe, not of that moment much to need an answer; but the slye design of it I think necessary to oppose; for I cannot allow any one's great name a right to use me ill. All fair contenders for the opinions they have, I like mightily; but there are so few that have opinions, or at least seem, by their way of defending them, to be really persuaded of the opinions they profess, that I am apt to think there is in the world a great deal more scepticism, or at least want of concern for truth, than is imagin'd.[29]

The irony at the close of Locke's remarks concerning Stillingfleet is hard to miss. After all, it was Stillingfleet who had suggested that Locke's position on the idea of substance could too easily lead to skepticism. But if Locke resorted to irony in his private correspondence with Molyneux, he took a more direct approach in his published response to Stillingfleet:

> But now . . . I am showing that his lordship's way, without ideas, does as little (I will not say less) furnish us with clear and distinct apprehensions concerning nature and person, as my Essay does. . . . Indeed . . . if failing of clear and distinct apprehensions, concerning nature and person, render any book obnoxious to one that vindicates the Trinity, and gives him sufficient cause to write against it, as opposite to that doctrine: I know no book of more dangerous consequence to that article of faith, nor more necessary to be writ against by a de-

28. Babcock, "A Changing of the Christian God," p. 144 (italics in original).
29. Quoted in Stewart, "Stillingfleet and the Way of Ideas," p. 255.

fender of that article, that that part of his lordship's Vindication
which we are now upon. For, to my thinking, I never met with any
thing more unintelligible about that subject, nor that is more remote from clear and distinct apprehensions of nature and person.
For what more effectual method could there be to confound the notions of nature and person, instead of clearing their distinctions,
than to discourse of them, without first defining them? Is this a way
to give clear and distinct apprehensions of two words, upon right
understanding of which, all our notions of the doctrine of the Trinity depend; and without which, we must talk unintelligibly about
that point? (*Works,* 4:163-64)

Concerning Stillingfleet's supposedly "clear and distinct apprehension of nature," Locke simply observed that Stillingfleet never really explained "what nature is, nor what he means by it." Locke also
points out that, for Stillingfleet, "the nature of a man in Peter, and the
nature of a man in James, and the nature of a man in John, is the common nature." Yet, Locke continues, "[t]hat the nature of man in Peter is
the nature of a man, if Peter be supposed to be a man, I certainly know,
let the nature of man be what it will, of which I yet know nothing"
(4:165-66). Locke drives home his point:

But if Peter be not supposed to be the name of a man, but the name
of a horse, all that knowledge vanishes, and I know nothing. But let
Peter be ever so much *a man,* and let it be impossible to give that
name to a horse, yet I cannot understand these words, that the common nature *of man* is in Peter; for whatsoever is in Peter, exists in Peter; and whatsoever exists in Peter, is particular: but the common nature of man, is the general nature of man, or else I understand not
what is meant by common nature. And it confounds my understanding, to make a general a particular. (4:166)

Next, Locke paused to consider Stillingfleet's efforts to qualify his
conception of nature by appeal to the notion of subsistence:

But to help me conceive this matter, I am told, "it is the common nature with a particular subsistence proper to Peter." But this helps not
my understanding in the case: for, first, I do not understand what
subsistence is, if it signifie anything different from existence; and if

it be the same with existence, then it is so far from loosening the knot, that it leaves it just as it was, only covered with the obscure and less known term, subsistence. For the difficulty to me is, to conceive an universal nature, or universal any thing, to exist; which would be, in my mind, to make an universal a particular: which, to me, is impossible. (4:166)

Far from providing a clear idea of substance, Stillingfleet had, from Locke's point of view, simply piled up puzzles that "defied all attempts to unravel them." Moreover, Stillingfleet had "failed to see that the general ideas that we use to classify things together are not themselves the ideas of things."[30] Indeed, Locke concludes his remarks on Stillingfleet's concept of nature by making this very point. Concerning the true meaning of "that vulgar way of speaking of the same common nature, being in several individuals," Locke says, it can be "this, and no more, that every particular individual man or horse, etc., has such a nature or constitution, as agrees and is conformable to that idea, which that general name stands for" (*Works*, 4:175).

Locke next turned his attention to Stillingfleet's supposedly "clear and distinct apprehension of person." On this front, Locke's remarks are equally, if not more, devastating than his remarks on Stillingfleet's concept of nature. "Person being a dissyllable," said Locke, "that in itself signifies nothing; what is meant by the true idea of it . . . I do not understand." After a short discourse explaining why the term "person" as it is "commonly used in the English tongue," could not signify what Stillingfleet said it did, Locke concludes:

But that which more certainly and for ever will hinder me from finding the true signification of person . . . is, that they require me to do what I find is impossible for me to do, i.e., find a difference between two individuals, as several individuals in the same common nature, without any difference. For if I never found any other difference, I should never find two individuals. For first, we find some difference, and by that we find they are two or several individuals; but in this way we are bid to find two individuals without any difference: but that, I find, is too subtle and sublime for my capacity. But when by any difference of time, or place, or any thing else, I have once found

30. Babcock, "A Changing of the Christian God," p. 144.

them to be two, or several, I cannot for ever after consider them but as several. They being once, by some difference, found to be two, it is unavoidable for me, from thenceforth, to consider them as two. But to find several where I find no difference; or, as his lordship is pleased to call it, external difference at all; is, I confess, too hard for me. (4:177)

The problem was plain to see. Without external difference, there remained no way to tell one manner of subsistence from another. Thus Stillingfleet's notion of person simply evaporated for lack of content. As far as Locke was concerned, Stillingfleet had failed to provide clear and distinct apprehensions of nature and person.

If Stillingfleet's definitions appeared to Locke to be devoid of content, it was because the latter was assessing them in light of his distinction between real and nominal essences and ultimately in light of his principle that all of our ideas are derived either from sensation or reflection. But this was Stillingfleet's problem, because these distinctions had, by 1697, attained the status of self-evidence. Babcock captures this point most felicitously:

If Locke came off better in the debate (and he did), it was not because he showed that the Trinity was fatally caught in contradiction but because he succeeded in making Stillingfleet's very style of talk look silly. Such an outcome was only possible, however, because another style of talk was already in place, already functioning as the dominant language of learned discourse and, in fact, already entangling Stillingfleet himself.[31]

Excluding the Trinity from the List of Essential Doctrines

As the rule of faith in English Protestant theology, Scripture was a time bomb waiting to go off. Indeed, it was only a matter of time before substantial disagreement over particular Christian doctrines would arise. When disagreements did arise, proponents of the doctrines being called into question had only two options if they wanted to maintain both their commitment to Scripture as the rule of faith and their com-

31. Babcock, "A Changing of the Christian God," p. 145.

mitment to the doctrines themselves. First, they could prove that the doctrines were contained in or derived from clear and intelligible propositions in Scripture and therefore necessary to be believed for salvation. Second, they could concede that the doctrines were not contained in clear and intelligible propositions and thus not among the things necessary to be believed for salvation. This was the situation in which Stillingfleet and the others had found themselves.

The deep issue that few, if any, noticed was the particular way in which Scripture had been made to function as the rule of faith in English Christianity, and had resulted in a massive transformation in the conception of doctrine in general and the doctrine of the Trinity in particular. Rather than providing the name for God by which humans could respond in worship, praise, and thanksgiving for their salvation, the doctrine of the Trinity was now viewed as a proposition or network of propositions about the eternal nature and being of God that was to be accepted or rejected on the basis of the reigning theory of intelligibility. As J. G. A. Pocock puts it, Christ was now primarily "a being about whom one formed opinions, rather than a being who existed and was present to one and with whom one held communion, in whom one lived and moved and had one's being."[32]

When Socinians, Unitarians, and deists rejected the Trinity as unintelligible, they did so against the backdrop of the "dominant language of learned discourse," namely, the new way of reasoning given systematic expression in Locke's *Essay.* The core of their positions was simply that, according to the reigning theory of intelligibility, the Trinity was unintelligible and hence not to be believed. All three of these groups subscribed to a version of the Protestant rule of faith. The primary difference among them was that the Socinians and Unitarians allowed for mysteries of faith that were not contrary to reason, whatever those might have been, while the deists rejected mysteries altogether.

In response to charges of unintelligibility, Sherlock, Wallis, and now Stillingfleet had attempted to prove that the Trinity was among the clear and intelligible propositions contained in or derived from Scripture. For their part, Sherlock and Wallis sought to supply clear

32. J. G. A. Pocock, "Within the Margins: The Definitions of Orthodoxy," in *The Margins of Orthodoxy: Heterodox Writing and Cultural Response, 1660-1750,* ed. Roger D. Lund (Cambridge, UK: Cambridge University Press, 1995), pp. 46-47.

and intelligible notions of a "Trinity in Unity" by solving the problem of the principle of individuation. Unfortunately, many had concluded that their efforts to do so had resulted in tritheism and Unitarianism respectively.

For his part, Stillingfleet focused more on substance than on the definition of "person": he attempted to modify the reigning theory of intelligibility in such a way as to enable him to distinguish substance from personality. By the late 1690s, however, Locke's theory of ideas was so deeply ensconced in "the dominant language of learned discourse" that Stillingfleet's modifications made the Trinity appear even more unintelligible than it might have otherwise. Moreover, in providing yet one more "clear and intelligible" account of the Trinity, Stillingfleet's initial fears came to fruition. He had contributed to the total number of proposals for how to understand the Trinity, thereby strengthening the appearance of widespread disagreement about the doctrine among Protestants.

In the aftermath of the three failed attempts to prove that the Trinity was among the clear and intelligible propositions contained in or derived from Scripture, a third option emerged on the theological landscape of English Protestantism. A small but growing number of people began to concede that the Trinity appeared to be unintelligible or even contradictory according to the reigning theory of intelligibility. Rather than rejecting the Trinity, however, these people simply concluded that the Trinity was not necessary to be believed for salvation, a position John Marshall has aptly named "irenic trinitarianism."[33] Among the early proponents of irenic Trinitarianism was the Dutch theologian Philip van Limborch, who was a close personal friend of John Locke. After declaring that he believed in the Trinity, van Limborch hastened to add, "Yet we dare not say 'tis necessary to be believed in order to Salvation."[34]

If van Limborch was one of the first advocates of irenic Trinitarianism, then it was Locke himself who, in *The Reasonableness of Christianity*, embraced this option explicitly on the grounds of the Protestant rule of faith. Moreover, while he excluded the Trinity from the doc-

---

33. Marshall, "Locke, Socinianism," p. 117.

34. Philip van Limborch, *A Compleat System, or Body of Divinity*, 2 vols. (London: 1702), 1:103ff; 2:497-500, quoted in Marshall, "Locke, Socinianism," p. 138.

trine of essential doctrines, Locke began more forthrightly to articulate a different vision of God. In doing so, he simply made explicit the vision of God that had tacitly accompanied the Protestant rule of faith all along.

Whether or not John Locke developed the theory of intelligibility in the *Essay* deliberately to undermine the Trinity is a matter that has been hotly debated by Locke specialists for years. Similarly, there has been considerable disagreement among scholars as to whether or not Locke personally disbelieved the Trinity.[35] For example, concerning Locke's intentions in the *Essay,* John Marshall claims: "Locke's stress upon the limits of the idea of substance in the *Essay* was almost certainly neither Socinian in intent nor directly Socinian in effect."[36]

Babcock, however, is doubtful:

> From the outset, Locke protested that Stillingfleet had drawn him into a controversy to which he did not belong. He insisted — perhaps disingenuously — that nothing in his *Essay on Human Understanding* had any bearing on the question of the Trinity; and he professed — again, perhaps disingenuously, for he words the statement carefully — that he was ready to retract "any thing in my book, that contained or implied any opposition in it to any thing revealed in holy writ concerning the Trinity or any other doctrine contained in the Bible."[37]

With regard to the more general question about whether Locke personally disbelieved the Trinity, Gerard Reedy remarks, "It is indeed a point on which his writings offer maximum resistance to certifying our inferences concerning his personal beliefs."[38] While Reedy's remark is undoubtedly true, it reflects a general tendency among scholars to consider these matters from the standpoint of Socinianism and deism. In other words, Locke specialists have framed the issues concerning Locke

---

35. For a review of the various positions that scholars have taken on this issue, see John Marshall, "Locke, Socinianism," pp. 114-15.

36. John Marshall, *John Locke: Resistance, Religion and Responsibility* (New York: Cambridge University Press, 1994), p. 347.

37. Babcock, "A Changing of the Christian God," p. 144; Locke, *Essay,* 4:96.

38. Gerard Reedy, *The Bible and Reason: Anglicans and Scripture in Late Seventeenth Century England* (Philadelphia: The University of Pennsylvania Press, 1985), p. 138.

in terms of whether or not the many charges of Socinianism and deism leveled against him were true. In short, the preoccupying question has been and continues to be, Was Locke a Socinian or a deist?

As a result of the scholarly preoccupation with Locke's relationship with either Socinianism or deism, a standard picture of Locke's theology has emerged: Locke is routinely presented as either a crypto-Socinian or a crypto-deist, and his relationship with mainstream English Protestant theology in the seventeenth century is often obscured or overlooked altogether. At best, Locke is depicted as a marginally orthodox Protestant theologian.[39]

That Locke was committed to Scripture as the rule of faith is evident on every page of the *Reasonableness*. Nor does one have to look very far to find the appeal to Scripture as the rule of faith. Locke makes clear his allegiance to Scripture as the only rule in theology in the first line of the work: "The little Satisfaction and Consistency that is to be found in most of the Systems of Divinity I have met with, made me betake my self to the sole Reading of the Scripture (to which they all appeal) for understanding the Christian Religion."[40]

More than merely indicating his own commitment to Scripture as the rule of faith, Locke's opening statement in the *Reasonableness* also reflects his awareness of the ubiquity of the appeal to Scripture among seventeenth-century English Protestant theologians. Locke also suggests that, in his view, theologians had failed adequately to apply the rule of faith in the development of their "Systems of Divinity." Thus *Reasonableness* can be read as Locke's own effort to apply the English Protestant rule of faith more consistently and thoroughly than his theological predecessors had done in order to establish the true nature and content of the "Christian Religion."

Locke wasted no time demonstrating his orthodoxy concerning the way beliefs are to be derived from Scripture. At the outset of the work, he made it a matter of principle that Scripture was to be understood

---

39. See G. A. J. Rogers, "John Locke: Conservative Radical," in *Margins of Orthodoxy: Heterodox Writing and Cultural Response, 1660-1750*, ed. Roger D. Lund (Cambridge, UK: Cambridge University Press, 1995), pp. 97-118.

40. John Locke, *The Reasonableness of Christianity as delivered in the Scriptures*, edited with an Introduction, Notes, Critical Apparatus and Transcriptions of Related Manuscripts by John C. Higgins-Biddle (Oxford: Clarendon Press, 1999), p. 3.

. . . in the plain direct meaning of the words and phrases, such as they may be supposed to have had in the mouths of the Speakers, who used them according to the Language of that Time and the Country wherein they lived, without such learned, artificial, and forced senses of them, as are sought out, and put upon them in most of the Systems of Divinity, according to the Notions, that each one had been bred up in. (p. 6)

Locke conceded that Scripture was to be interpreted according to the plain sense of it, suggesting that the Law was among the most clear and intelligible of the various components of Scripture. He also noted that not all passages in Scripture are clear.

The other parts of Divine Revelation are Objects of Faith, and are so to be received. They are Truths whereof no one can be rejected; none that is once known to be such, may or ought to be disbelieved. For to acknowledge any Proposition to be of Divine Revelation and Author- ity, and yet to deny or disbelieve it, is to offend against this Funda- mental Article and Ground of Faith, that God is true. But yet a great many of the Truths revealed in the Gospel, every one does, and must confess, a man may be ignorant of; nay, disbelieve, without danger to his Salvation: As is evident in those, who allowing the Authority, dif- fer in the Interpretation and meaning of several Texts of Scripture, not thought Fundamental. (p. 168)

In his appeal to a doctrine of essential doctrines, Locke belonged to the mainstream of English Protestant theology in seventeenth-century England.[41] Like Chillingworth and Stillingfleet, he maintained that there were "Fundamental Articles of Faith" that God had given in Scripture, of which "an explicit belief" was "required of all those to whom the Gospel of Jesus Christ is preached, and Salvation through his Name proposed." Yet, in Locke's generally skeptical point of view, the doctrine of essential doctrines was not simply a list of the things necessary to be believed. It was equally, if not more, a means of cutting

---

41. By "mainstream" I mean those clergy and theologians who represented the Church of England from Laud to Stillingfleet and Tillotson. Thus I am interpreting the Latitudinarian line, broadly conceived, as mainstream. Clearly, I do not have in mind clergy and theologians associated with the Commonwealth.

down or thinning out what was necessary to be believed.[42] Thus Locke declares: "Though all divine Revelation requires the obedience of Faith; yet every truth of inspired Scriptures is not one of those, that by the Law of Faith is required to be explicitly believed to Justification." In a lengthy but crucial passage in *Reasonableness,* Locke makes clear the importance of the doctrine of essential doctrine for both purposes:

> Those are fundamentals; which 'tis not enough not to disbelieve: Every one is required actually to assent to them. But any other Proposition contained in the Scripture, which God has not thus made a necessary part of the Law of Faith, (without an actual assent to which he will not allow any one to be a Believer) a Man may be ignorant of, without hazarding his Salvation by a defect in his Faith. He believes all that God has made necessary for him to believe, and assent to: And as for the rest of the Divine Truths, there is nothing more required of him, but that he receive all the parts of Divine Revelation, with a docility and disposition prepared to imbrace, and assent to all Truths coming from God. . . . Where he, upon fair endeavours, understands it not; How can he avoid being ignorant? And where he cannot put several Texts, and make them consist together; What Remedy? He must either interpret one by the other, or suspend his Opinion. He that thinks that more is, or can be required, of poor frail Man in matters of Faith, will do well to consider what absurdities he will run into. (pp. 168-69)

As is clear in this passage, Locke knew only too well that the English Protestant rule of faith could be applied either minimally or maximally. Generally speaking, Locke's theological predecessors applied the rule of faith maximally, assuming that the Thirty-Nine Articles of Religion or the Nicene Creed were contained in or derived from clear and intelligible propositions in Scripture. By contrast, Locke argued that the Protestant rule of faith secured only formally and provisionally what the rule of faith in the early church and the Thirty-Nine Articles of Religion in the Church of England secured materially. In his *Second Vindication of the Reasonableness of Christianity,*

42. Locke's skepticism was a philosophical disposition that he applied across the spectrum of learning. He was equally skeptical about the limits of knowledge in natural philosophy and religion.

he declares: "The Scripture was direct and plain, that 'twas Faith that justified; The next Question, then, was what Faith that was that justified; What it was which, if a Man believed, it should be imputed to him for Righteousness?"[43]

Calling attention to the fact that people could not assume what was contained in or derived from clear and intelligible propositions in Scripture did not make Locke a Socinian or a deist. It simply meant that Locke understood and embraced fully the implications of making Scripture the rule of faith. Unlike many before him, Locke candidly admitted that the content of the Faith could not be assumed in advance. As in natural philosophy, the solution was not to trust what had been handed down through tradition. Rather, people needed to look for themselves in order to ascertain what was actually contained in Scripture.

The outcome of Locke's quest to discover "what it was, which, if a Man believed, it should be imputed to him for Righteousness" is well-known. Locke concluded that, in order to become Christians, people needed only to believe that God exists and that Jesus was the Messiah. Thus he says: "Whereby it is plain, that the Gospel was writ to induce men into a belief of this Proposition, *that Jesus was the Messiah;* which if they believed, they should *have life.*"[44] Of course, as Pocock rightly observes, Locke "left unanswered the question as to who and what the Messiah was."[45]

Not surprisingly, many divines in the Church of England were alarmed by this assertion, and Locke soon found himself accused of Socinianism.[46] Particularly inflammatory was the complete lack of reference to the Trinity. Thus John Edwards expressed shock that "Jesus' command to baptize in the name of the Father, Son, and Holy Ghost was neglected." At a minimum, says Edwards, "that passage (Matt. 28:19) required all adult proselytes to be taught and believe in the Trin-

---

43. John Locke, *A Second Vindication of the Reasonableness of Christianity, etc.* (London, 1697), preface.

44. Locke, *Reasonableness,* p. 24. A little earlier Locke says: "This was the great Proposition that was then controverted concerning Jesus at *Nazareth,* whether he was the *Messiah* or no; And the assent to that, was that which distinguished Believers from Unbelievers" (Locke, *Reasonableness,* p. 23).

45. Pocock, "Within the Margins," p. 46.

46. For example, see John Edwards, *Socinianism Unmask'd* (London, 1696).

ity."[47] Worse yet, Edwards argues, the "lank faith" presented by Locke in the *Reasonableness of Christianity* was ultimately "no other than the faith of a Turk." According to Edwards, Locke was guilty of "confounding Turky with Christendom."[48]

In fairness to Locke, the mere fact that he did not include the Trinity among the things necessary to be believed for salvation did not necessarily mean he did not personally believe in the Trinity. On the contrary, all that can be said with certainty is that Locke did not think the Trinity was contained in or derived from clear and intelligible propositions in Scripture. On the Protestant rule of faith, this meant that the Trinity could not be counted among the doctrines necessary to be believed *by all Christians* for salvation. In Marshall's terms, the most that can be said is that Locke shared the "irenic trinitarianism" of his close friend Philip van Limborch.

In applying the Protestant rule of faith, Locke had little choice but to exclude the Trinity from the list of doctrines necessary to be believed for salvation. He had at least three reasons for doing so. First, by the time Locke set out to write *Reasonableness,* no one could deny that there was widespread disagreement about the doctrine among those very theologians who argued that the Trinity was contained in clear and intelligible propositions in Scripture. Second, even if Sherlock, South, Wallis, or Stillingfleet could have shown the doctrine of the Trinity to be intelligible by reworking the terms of the doctrine in order to make it fit within Aristotelian, Cartesian, or Lockean frameworks of intelligibility, the very fact that they had to go to such great lengths to do so made it only too clear that the doctrine was not contained in Scripture in such a way that the uneducated or the illiterate could readily understand. Third, it could not be overlooked that the Socinians, Unitarians, and deists were also appealing to the Protestant rule of faith when they insisted the Trinity was not contained in clear and intelligible propositions in Scripture. Therefore, on pain of contradicting the Protestant rule of faith, Locke excluded the Trinity from among the things necessary to be believed for salvation.

47. John Edwards, *Some Thoughts Concerning the Several Causes and Occasions of Atheism* (London, 1695), pp. 105-11.

48. John Edwards, *Socinianism Unmask'd,* pp. 53-54.

Locke's Legacy

In *The Reasonableness of Christianity*, Locke demonstrated that one could be deeply committed to the English Protestant rule of faith while remaining silent on the Trinity. With Locke, the transformation described in Chapter 2 of this book was complete. Scripture and Scripture alone was now the rule of faith in English Protestant theology. Nor was Scripture functioning as *a* rule alongside the Trinitarian rule of faith embodied in the Nicene Creed. Scripture was *the* rule of faith, in the name of which the Trinity was now idling in English Protestant theology.

I am not simply arguing that it is Locke, rather than Schleiermacher, who is to blame for the demise of the Trinity in modern Christian theology. Rather, I speak of Locke's legacy only insofar as Locke brought to systematic expression a range of developments and commitments in theology that had emerged throughout the seventeenth century. Moreover, he did so in the form of a text — *The Reasonableness of Christianity* — that has remained both accessible and influential down through the centuries.[49]

What, then, is Locke's legacy? I suggest that there are at least four dimensions of his legacy. First, Locke helped further to instantiate within English Protestant Christianity a particular conception of Scripture as the rule of faith. According to this conception, Scripture is first and foremost an epistemic criterion by which we can distinguish true from false assertions. It is only secondarily, if at all, a means of grace in and through which we meet and come to know and love the triune God.

Second, according to Locke's conception of Scripture as the rule of faith, Scripture is a network of clear and intelligible propositions given by God for our salvation. In turn, salvation itself is understood epistemologically rather than ontologically. To be saved is to give intellectual assent to clear and intelligible propositions contained in Scripture. Salvation may or may not have to do with invoking the triune God in prayer or with responding to what the triune God has done on behalf of our salvation in worship, love, and praise.

---

49. Incidentally, the same can be said of Locke's *Essay*. Far from an entirely original work in philosophy, the power and influence of the *Essay* stems precisely from the extent to which it gave systematic expression to major intellectual developments in seventeenth-century England.

Third, Locke set in motion a minimalist way of thinking about Christian doctrine that has haunted English Protestant Christianity ever since. Locke's taking that direction was no doubt driven by an advanced form of philosophical skepticism. Nevertheless, such doctrinal minimalism is at best a strange development. After affirming that Scripture is a network of propositions the assent to which is necessary for salvation, Locke claims that very little of real importance is contained clearly and intelligibly therein. As things turn out, only a handful of propositions are really necessary to be believed for salvation. Far from a mysterious encounter the sheer audacity of which evokes wonder, love, and praise, salvation is now well on its way to being a highly mundane affair. In many quarters within English Protestantism to this day, salvation is presented as a matter of making a small adjustment in one's overall network of beliefs by confessing that Jesus is Lord, whatever that might mean. There is often no explicit mention of an expectation that one will encounter the triune God in worship, in baptism, in the Eucharist, in prayer, and the like. Rather, salvation is largely, if not exclusively, a matter of adding on a few beliefs.

Finally, Locke's legacy is especially strong in and around the doctrine of the Trinity. Having adopted Scripture as the rule of faith and having conceived of salvation largely in terms of assent to intelligible propositions contained therein, many English Protestant Christians follow Locke's example, passing over the Trinity in silence. If pushed to talk about the Trinity, they will quickly concede that the Trinity is an irresoluble puzzle. It is the kind of thing that numbs the mind when one thinks about it for too long. Indeed, some will go so far as to say that the Trinity may or may not be essential to Christianity. They know that they are supposed to believe it, but they do not have a clue what it means. Functionally, they are irenic Trinitarians.

By the time Locke wrote *The Reasonableness of Christianity,* making Scripture the rule of faith had resulted in an almost complete loss of the ability to think of the Trinity as anything other than a network of propositions about the eternal being of God. To put it another way, the doctrine of the Trinity now had to do almost exclusively with the immanent Trinity; the economic Trinity was nowhere in sight. People were even less inclined to think of the Trinity in its most primitive sense as the proper personal name for God.

Fortunately, like so many things, there are two sides to the story.

While English Protestant theologians struggled to show that the Trinity was contained in clear and intelligible propositions in Scripture, the Trinity went right on functioning as the name for God in Christian worship. This was to be expected because the Trinity has always been intimately connected to the worshiping life of the church. Nor is it surprising, amid the English Revival, that Charles Wesley would compose hundreds of hymns and prayers to the Trinity. After all, whatever else the English Revival might have been about, it was at least about assisting Christians in coming to know and to love God fully, a task for which the Trinity has always been indispensable.

CHAPTER SIX

Wesley's Hymns and Prayers

*If anything is wanting, it is the application, lest it should ap-
pear to be a mere speculative doctrine, which has no influence
on our hearts and lives; but this is abundantly supplied by my
brothers Hymns.*

John Wesley on the Trinity,
in a letter to Mary Bishop, 17 April 1776

In the preceding chapters I have shown that theological reflection on
the Trinity in late seventeenth-century England was primarily about
demonstrating that the Trinity was contained in clear and intelligible
propositions and thus worthy of intellectual assent. I have also shown
that the various arguments for the clarity and intelligibility of the
Trinity were individually unsuccessful and collectively responsible for
the elimination of the Trinity from the canon of doctrines necessary to
be believed for salvation. Along the way, I suggested that one very important consequence of approaching the Trinity as a network of clear
and intelligible propositions was a loss of emphasis on the Trinity as
the proper personal name for God and thus a loss of emphasis on the
economic Trinity in English Protestant theological reflection.

The loss of emphasis on the economic Trinity in English Protestant
theology was and is a natural result of the relocation of Trinitarian discourse from the ecclesial activities of invocation, praise, and thanksgiving to the rational activity of assent, that is, from doxology and ontology to epistemology. When Trinitarian discourse was closely tied to

the ecclesial activities of invocation, praise, and worship, the saving activities of the economic Trinity *(ad extra)* were always at the forefront of the church's thinking. Consequently, the theological task was to assist in the invocation, worship, and praise of the God that the church encountered initially in the coming of Jesus Christ and of the Holy Spirit and presently in her worshiping life. Thus theologians such as Basil of Caesarea were often concerned with regulating the use of the triune name for God in the church's baptismal and liturgical rites.

By contrast, when Trinitarian discourse became primarily a matter of intellectual or rational assent to clear and intelligible propositions presumably contained in Scripture, English Protestant theologians focused exclusively on the immanent Trinity *(ad intra)* without any reference to the saving activities of the economic Trinity. The goal of Trinitarian theology in England during the late seventeenth and early eighteenth centuries was to show that the propositions purportedly describing the eternal relationships within the Godhead (the relationships among the three divine persons) were clear, intelligible, and rational quite apart from the church's encounter with the saving activities of God in baptism, the Eucharist, worship, and the like. Consequently, Trinitarian discourse had increasingly little, if anything, to do with the Christian life, that is, with people coming to know and love God.

The temptation at this stage is to make grand statements about the fate of the Trinity in modern English Protestant theology. Indeed, it is hard to resist claiming that the Trinity was lost to Western theology in late seventeenth-century England, a full hundred years before Schleiermacher's notorious appendix. To do so, however, would be to prejudice the matter in a way that only reveals half of the truth. As I suggested at the end of the preceding chapter, there is another side to the story.

My thesis at this point is twofold. First, as the proper personal name for God, the natural home for Trinitarian discourse is invocation and praise, that is, in the catechetical and worshiping life of the church. In this realm, Trinitarian discourse is primarily a matter of the church's response to the saving activities of God in Jesus Christ and in the Holy Spirit, and to the ongoing presence of the triune God in her worship. Second, if Trinitarian discourse belongs first and foremost to the work of invocation, praise, and thanksgiving, then the obituary notices for the Trinity are premature, especially if we do not pay close attention to the worshiping life of the church in modern English Protestant Christianity. It is one thing to say that the Trinity was lost or demoted within English Protestant theology; it is another thing altogether to suggest that the Trinity was lost to English Protestant Christianity.

What is at stake here is overcoming a deep tendency in the historiography of modern theology. Until recently, the history of modern theology has focused almost exclusively on the large philosophically oriented works of the great speculative theologians of the modern period. It has paid little, if any, attention to the vision and understanding of God embedded in and mediated by the worshiping life of the church during the modern period, that is, in sermons and hymns, prayers and liturgies, sacred images and sacraments. Fortunately, historical theologians have begun to consider catechetical and liturgical materials and practices as sources of theology in the modern period.[1] In doing so, they have discovered that the story of modern theology is not always as bleak as it is routinely made out to be.

The Trinity as the proper personal name for God continued to function in English Protestant worship long after the Trinitarian controversies of the late seventeenth century had died down. Moreover, in catechetical and liturgical settings, the saving activities of the economic Trinity were rarely, if ever, lost from sight. One example of this, of course, is the liturgical rites contained in *The Book of Common Prayer.* However, what is most fascinating is that Charles Wesley, a half-century after the Trinitarian controversy, set about producing an entire collection of hymns and prayers to the Trinity. In those hymns and prayers the Trinity is clearly functioning as the proper personal name for God whereby the church offers her praise and thanksgiving for the saving activities of the Father, Son, and Holy Spirit on her behalf.

The Revival of the Economic Trinity

Often overlooked as a source of theology, Charles Wesley's prayers and hymns restore Trinitarian discourse to its original function in the life

---

1. For example, see Dawn DeVries, *Jesus Christ in the Preaching of Calvin and Schleiermacher* (Louisville: Westminster John Knox Press, 2002); see also Teresa Berger, *Theology in Hymns? A Study of the Relationship of Doxology and Theology According to* A Collection of Hymns for the People Called Methodists (Nashville: Kingswood Books, 1995).

of the church, namely, invoking, praising, and giving thanks to God.[2] Contrary to the dominant trend in late seventeenth- and early eighteenth-century England, Wesley was more concerned with the purpose of Christian doctrine than with its proof. Nor was this fact lost on those who were most familiar with his hymns. For example, in a letter to Mary Bishop concerning the doctrine of the Trinity, John Wesley, Charles's more famous brother, observes: "If anything is wanting, it is the application, lest [the Trinity] should appear to be a mere speculative doctrine, which has no influence on our hearts and lives; but this is abundantly supplied by my brothers *Hymns*."[3]

Similarly, consider the following statement from the advertisement for Charles Wesley's *Hymns on the Trinity:*

And he has never lost sight of the experimental and practical bearings of that doctrine. Mr. Jones has an excellent paragraph at the conclusion of his argument, warning his readers that a sound belief without a holy life will not profit them. But our poet . . . makes experience the connecting link between knowledge and practice, and devotes an entire section of his work to "Hymns and Prayers to the Trinity," in which the doctrine is presented in most intimate connection with his own spiritual interests, and those of his readers. Such a mode of treating it is the best answer to those who represent it as a mere metaphysical speculation devoid of practical interest.[4]

Whereas many of his English Protestant theological predecessors and contemporaries had been preoccupied with showing that the doc-

---

2. For the most comprehensive introduction to the life and work of Charles Wesley, see Kenneth G. C. Newport and Ted A. Campbell, eds., *Charles Wesley: Life, Literature and Legacy* (London: Epworth Press, 2007). For a new biography of Charles Wesley, see John R. Tyson, *Assist Me to Proclaim: The Life and Hymns of Charles Wesley* (Grand Rapids: Eerdmans, 2007). For a wide sampling of Charles Wesley's works, see John Tyson, ed., *Charles Wesley: A Reader* (Oxford: Oxford University Press, 1989).

3. John Wesley, *Letters of John Wesley*, 8 vols., ed. John Telford (London: The Epworth Press, 1931), 6:213.

4. George Osborn, *The Poetical Works of John and Charles Wesley*, 13 vols. (London: Wesleyan-Methodist Conference Office, 1870), 7:203-4. "Mr. Jones" refers to William Jones, whose 1756 treatise *The Catholic Doctrine of the Trinity, proved by above an hundred short and clear arguments, expressed in terms of the Holy Scripture* was the inspiration and pattern for Charles Wesley's 1767 *Hymns on the Trinity*.

trine of the immanent Trinity was contained in clear and intelligible propositions, Charles Wesley was concerned primarily with fostering the proper response to the saving activities of the economic Trinity. More specifically, while speculative theologians were trying unsuccessfully to demonstrate the intelligibility of the immanent Trinity, Wesley was gradually recovering the crucial place of the economic Trinity through extended reflection on the work of the Holy Spirit in bringing people to God. Thus there is a deep difference between Wesley's approach to theology and the prevailing approach to theology in post-Restoration England. Whereas Wesley's predecessors and contemporaries were primarily concerned with epistemological questions, he was primarily concerned with ontological and doxological matters, for example, with the church's encounter with God in the incarnation, in the coming of the Holy Spirit to dwell in us at our baptism, and with the church's proper response in thanksgiving and praise.

When scholars have sought to get at Wesley's understanding of the Trinity, they have turned primarily, if not exclusively, to two sources: the 1746 collection of hymns entitled *Gloria Patri, &c., or Hymns to the Trinity,* and the 1767 collection that is simply entitled *Hymns on the Trinity.*[5] Since he is best known for his hymns, this tendency in scholarship is understandable. But an exclusive reliance on Wesley's hymns obscures a crucial component in his overall development as a Trinitarian theologian, namely, the marked increase in his interest in the presence and work of the Holy Spirit beginning in 1738-1739. The best place to look for this development is in his sermons.[6]

Wesley's interest in the Holy Spirit underwent two important transitions in his sermons.[7] First, there was a transition from an early

5. For example, see Laura A. Bartels, "Hymns of the Status Quo: Charles Wesley on the Trinity," *Methodist History* 41, no. 2 (Jan. 2003): 25-32; see also Barry E. Bryant, "Trinity and Hymnody: The Doctrine of the Trinity in the Hymns of Charles Wesley," *Wesleyan Theological Journal* (Fall 1990): 64-73. For more information on Charles's sources for these hymn collections, see Wilma J. Quantrille, "Introduction," in Charles Wesley, *Hymns on the Trinity,* ed. S. T. Kimbrough, Jr. (Madison, NJ: The Charles Wesley Society, 1988), pp. vii-xiii (hereafter *HT*).

6. Fortunately, a critical edition of Wesley's sermons has recently been made available. See Kenneth G. C. Newport, ed., *The Sermons of Charles Wesley: A Critical Edition, with Introduction and Notes* (Oxford: Oxford University Press, 2001 [hereafter *SCW*, cited with relevant sermon number and page number]).

7. For more on Charles Wesley's doctrine of the Holy Spirit, see Jason E. Vickers,

binitarian period, in which there are no clear references to the Holy Spirit, to an initial period of interest in and reflection on the work of the Holy Spirit (1738-1739). During this period, however, Wesley did not integrate his emerging doctrine of the Holy Spirit into a wider Trinitarian framework in any meaningful way. Second, there is a transition from the period of initial interest in the Holy Spirit to a period in which his sermons are virtually saturated with talk of the Holy Spirit (1740-1742). During this period Wesley integrated his reflections on the Holy Spirit into a robust theology of the economic Trinity.

In the sermons before 1738 (Sermons 1-3), one looks in vain for clear references to the Holy Spirit. This is especially startling in light of the fact that these sermons are largely about the pursuit of holiness or Christian perfection and the need for singleness of focus. For example, in the second undisputed sermon, Wesley declares: "We say then that a state of voluntary imperfection, a half *course* of piety, a life divided between God and the world, is a state which God has nowhere promised to accept nor yet assured us of a reward for it."[8] Similarly, in the third undisputed sermon, he reflects on the way Christian virtues stem from the graces of humility, faith, hope, and love. Yet his theological outlook was binitarian: references to the work of the Holy Spirit are noticeably absent.

The first clear references to the Holy Spirit occur in the sermons preached during the 1738-1739 period, or what is commonly viewed as the period of Wesley's evangelical conversion.[9] There is some evidence that his interest in the presence and work of the Holy Spirit first emerged sometime after his evangelical conversion, since all three candidates for the so-called "conversion hymn" are binitarian in content.[10]

"Charles Wesley's Doctrine of the Holy Spirit: A Vital Resource for the Renewal of Methodism Today," *Asbury Journal* 61, no. 1 (Spring 2006): 47-60.

8. *SCW,* Serm. 2, p. 116. According to Newport, Wesley preached this sermon at least four times in 1736. I have limited this research to what Newport identifies as the "undisputed sermons," i.e., to those sermons about which there are no doubts that Charles Wesley was the author.

9. For Wesley's evangelical conversion, see Arnold Dallimore, *A Heart Set Free: The Life of Charles Wesley* (Westchester, IL: Crossway Books, 1988), and T. Crichton Mitchell, *Charles Wesley: Man with the Dancing Heart* (Kansas City: Beacon Press, 1994).

10. For the three "conversion hymns," see *Charles Wesley: A Reader,* pp. 101-4. See also Dallimore, *A Heart Set Free,* pp. 61-63; Mitchell, *Charles Wesley,* pp. 70-71.

However, where the conversion hymns are silent, the serm period are not. In the fourth undisputed sermon — a serm preached at least twenty-one times between 1738 and 1739 — Wesley picts the Spirit at work convicting people of sin and ultimately rescuing them from sin. Moreover, he refers to the activity of the Spirit in fulfilling the promises of Scripture to a soul "thus disposed for Christ," giving special attention to the activity of comforting and bringing assurance of salvation.[11]

Despite this initial interest in the activity of the Holy Spirit in the fourth undisputed sermon, Wesley had not yet fully integrated the activity of the Holy Spirit into his theology. This is true of the sixth and seventh undisputed sermons as well. While he emphasized that the Spirit convicts people of sin and frees them from it, he did not connect the work of the Spirit with Christ or with the Father in any significant way. However, the real flowering of Wesley's Trinitarian theology was just around the corner.

Beginning with the seventh undisputed sermon, Wesley deliberately integrates his reflections on the presence and work of the Holy Spirit into a wider doctrine of the economic Trinity. Once again, he begins by noting the Spirit's work in convicting individuals of and rescuing them from sin. He then reflects on the Spirit's role in divine revelation:

> So our Lord assures us no man can come unto the Son except the Father draw him. No man cometh to the Father, but by the Son. They only believe, to whom it is given to know the mind of Christ. Eye hath not seen, nor ear heard, neither have entered into the heart of man, the things which God hath prepared for them that love him. But God hath revealed them unto us by his Spirit, for the Spirit searcheth all things, yea, the deep things of God. For what man knoweth the things of a man but the spirit of man which is in him? Even so the things of God knoweth no man but the Spirit of God. But the natural man receiveth not the things of the Spirit of God, for they are foolishness unto him; neither can he know them because they are spiritually discerned. God hath hid these things from the wise and prudent, and revealed them unto babes. No man knoweth

11. *SCW*, Serm. 4, p. 145. It is worth noting that the source for Wesley's understanding of the Holy Spirit in this sermon is John Norris's *Practical Discourses on Several Divine Subjects* (1690).

ither knoweth any man the Father save the
ever the Son will reveal him. (*SCW,* p. 201)

beginning to move in the direction of a ro-
omic Trinity. Thus the Spirit makes known to
in turn reveals the Father. Unlike many of his
English Protestant predecessors, Wesley increas-
role of the Spirit and not the role of unaided or
natural discerning divine revelation. Indeed, he virtually excluded the possibility of identifying or comprehending divine revelation by reason alone:

> These and numberless other Scriptures demonstrate the impossibil-
> ity of believing God hath given us the spirit of revelation. We can
> never know the things of God till he hath revealed them by his
> Spirit, till we have received the Son of God that we should know the
> things which are freely given us of God. For this cause Jesus is called
> the author of our faith, because we receive in one and the same mo-
> ment, power to believe and the Holy Ghost, who is therefore called
> the Spirit of faith. And a true faith we cannot have till God gives us
> the Holy Ghost purifying our hearts by faith. (*SCW,* p. 202)

Wesley also attributed the shedding abroad of God's love in believers' hearts to the presence and work of the Holy Spirit. By extension, he
developed a doctrine of divine empowerment by the Spirit, saying that
the Spirit enables all believers to keep Christ's commandments in love by
delivering them "not only from the guilt of sin but also from the power
of sin" (*SCW,* p. 202). Here one can see Wesley hard at work filling out his
understanding of the work of the Spirit. But it was his next move that
was most crucial. Having emphasized the Spirit's role in conviction, pardon, divine revelation, and divine empowerment, Wesley expanded his
understanding of the presence and work of the Spirit in a decidedly Trinitarian direction by developing a doctrine of divine indwelling. For Wesley, the end or purpose of divine indwelling was nothing less than the
hallmark of the patristic doctrine of the economic Trinity, namely, that
humans might become "partakers of the divine nature" (2 Pet. 1:4):

> This is the greatest and most glorious privilege of the true believer:
> whosoever shall confess that Jesus is the Son of God, God dwelleth

in him and he in God: and hereby knoweth he that God abideth in him, by the Spirit which he hath given him. He that believeth hath the witness in himself, even the Spirit of God bearing witness with his Spirit that he is a child of God. Christ is formed in his heart by faith. He is one with Christ and Christ with him. He is a real partaker of the divine nature. Truly his fellowship is with the Father and the Son. The Father and the Son are come unto him and make their abode with him, and his very body is the temple of the Holy Ghost. (*SCW*, p. 203)[12]

On the heels of the Trinitarian controversy, Charles Wesley was at work recovering the heart of the fourth-century fathers' approach to theology and their understanding of the Trinity. Thus he increasingly placed the emphasis squarely on what God has done and is doing to bring about the elevation of human beings to the divine. He concludes the seventh undisputed sermon by repeating the major themes that he had been developing with the following Trinitarian benediction:

Now to God the Father, who first loved us and made us accepted in the Beloved; to the Son who loved us and washed us from our sins in his own blood, to God the Holy Ghost who sheddeth abroad the love of God in our hearts, be all praise and all glory in time and in eternity. (*SCW*, p. 210)

If any doubts remained concerning the centrality of the doctrine of divine indwelling in his theology, Wesley put them to rest once and for all in the eighth undisputed sermon, a sermon he preached in 1742 at the University of Oxford. In this sermon he works backwards from our becoming partakers of the divine nature to the doctrine of the indwelling of the Holy Spirit via a series of powerful rhetorical questions:

Are thou "partaker of the divine nature"? Knowest thou not that Christ is in thee, except thou be reprobate? Knowest thou that "God dwelleth in thee, and thou in God, by his Spirit which he hath given thee"? Knowest thou not that "thy body is the temple of the Holy Ghost, which thou hast of God"? Hast thou the "witness in thyself",

12. Wesley here paraphrases the following Scripture texts: 1 John 4:15; 3:24; 4:13; 5:10; Gal. 4:19; 2 Pet. 1:4; 1 John 1:3; John 14:23; 1 Cor. 6:19.

"the earnest of thine inheritance"? Are thou "sealed by that Spirit of promise unto the day of redemption"? Hast thou "received the Holy Ghost"? Or dost thou start at the question, not knowing whether there be any Holy Ghost? (*SCW,* p. 218)[13]

Following this flurry of rhetorical questions, Wesley declares that humans' reception of the Holy Spirit and their partaking of the divine nature are both the criterion of Christian identity and the marker of "true religion."

> Yet on the authority of God's Word and our own Church I must re-peat the question, "Hast thou received the Holy Ghost?" If thou hast not thou art not yet a Christian; for a Christian is a man that is "anointed with the Holy Ghost and with power." Thou art yet made a partaker of pure religion and undefiled. Dost thou know what reli-gion is? That it is a participation in the divine nature, the life of God in the soul of man: Christ in thee, the "hope of glory"; "Christ formed in thy heart," happiness and holiness; heaven begun on earth; a "kingdom of God within thee," "not meat and drink," no outward thing, "but righteousness, and peace, and joy in the Holy Ghost." (*SCW,* p. 218)[14]

Finally, Wesley reiterates that he regarded the indwelling of the Spirit as the criterion of Christian identity: "He is a Christian who hath received the Spirit of Christ. He is not a Christian who hath not received him" (*SCW,* p. 221). He then concludes by labeling those who deny the indwelling of the Holy Spirit as "Antichrist" and by repeating for a third time that the divine indwelling is "the criterion of a real Christian."

> He is Antichrist whoever denies the inspiration of the Holy Ghost, or that the indwelling Spirit of God is the common privilege of all be-lievers, the blessing of the gospel, the unspeakable gift, the universal promise, the criterion of a real Christian. (*SCW,* p. 222)

---

13. Wesley here paraphrases the following Scripture texts: 2 Pet. 1:4; 2 Cor. 13:5; 1 John 3:24; 4:12-13; 5:10; 1 Cor. 6:19; Eph. 1:13-14; 4:30; Acts 19:2.

14. Scripture paraphrases include: Acts 10:38; James 1:27; 2 Pet. 1:4; Col. 1:27; Gal. 4:19; Luke 17:21; Rom. 14:17; Phil. 4:7; 1 Pet. 1:8.

This is a good time to step back and take stock of the terrain we have covered so far. In the seventh and eighth undisputed sermons, Wesley develops the doctrine of the Holy Spirit into a robust doctrine of the economic Trinity. This stands in stark contrast to the dominant orientation of Trinitarian theology in England during the late seventeenth and early eighteenth centuries. The overriding concern of many of Charles Wesley's predecessors and contemporaries was to show that the doctrine of the immanent Trinity (often without any reference to the economic Trinity) consisted of clear and intelligible propositions, that is, propositions compatible with and confirmable by various accounts of reason and rationality. By contrast, Wesley's understanding of and approach to the Trinity is very similar to the understanding of an approach that prevailed in the fourth century. For example, in a statement that parallels much of what Wesley says about the Trinity in the seventh undisputed sermon, Basil of Caesarea says:

> "No one knows the Father except the Son, and no one can say 'Jesus is Lord' except in the Holy Spirit." Notice that it does not say *through* the Spirit but *in* the Spirit. . . . [The Spirit] reveals the glory of the Only-Begotten in Himself, and He gives true worshippers the knowledge of God in Himself. The way to divine knowledge ascends from one Spirit through the one Son to the one Father. Likewise, natural goodness, inherent holiness and royal dignity reaches from the Father through the Only-Begotten to the Spirit.[15]

It might be tempting at this point to think that there is not that great a difference between Wesley's and Basil's understanding of the Trinity, on the one hand, and the understanding of many late seventeenth- and early eighteenth-century English Protestant theologians, on the other. After all, Wesley and Basil both speak of the Spirit bringing about knowledge of God. Presumably, such knowledge has propositional content and thus is either intelligible or unintelligible; it is either compatible or incompatible with human reason.

However, despite those initial appearances, the knowledge of which Charles and Basil spoke is a vastly different kind of knowledge than that sought by the English Protestant theologians of the late seven-

---

15. St. Basil the Great, *On the Holy Spirit*, trans. David Anderson (Crestwood, NY: St. Vladimir's, 1997), p. 74 (italics in original).

teenth and early eighteenth centuries. One way to capture this difference is to say that, for Wesley and Basil alike, humans come to know God "personally," and their natures are healed and restored, even transformed, by coming to know God personally, so that they became "partakers of the divine nature." Both Wesley and Basil were concerned with ontology rather than epistemology. Everything here hinges on taking the coming of God in the incarnation and in the presence and work of the Holy Spirit in revelation and in divine indwelling with absolute seriousness. As Basil puts it, "[The Spirit] does not reveal [knowledge] to them from outside sources, but leads them to knowledge personally. . . ."[16]

Finally, I must point out that the robust doctrine of the economic Trinity in Charles's sermons is mirrored in some of Wesley's hymns from the same period. In 1740, for example, he penned the following hymn inviting the Holy Spirit to dwell in human beings:

> I want the spirit of power within,
>   Of love, and of a healthful mind:
> Of power to conquer inbred sin,
>   Of love to thee and all mankind,
> Of health, that pain and death defies,
>   Most vig'rous when the body dies.
>
> When shall I hear the inward voice
>   Which only faithful souls can hear?
> Pardon and peace, and heavenly joys
>   Attend the promised Comforter.
> O come, and righteousness divine,
>   And Christ, and all with Christ is mine!
>
> O that the Comforter would come!
>   Nor visit as a transient guest,
> But fix in me his constant home
>   And take possession of my breast;
> And fix in me his loved abode,
>   The temple of indwelling God!

16. St. Basil the Great, *On the Holy Spirit*, p. 74.

Come, Holy Ghost, my heart inspire!
   Attest that I am born again!
Come, and baptize me with fire,
   Nor let thy former gifts be vain.
I cannot rest in sins forgiven;
   Where is the earnest of my heaven?

Where the indubitable seal
   That ascertains the kingdom mine?
The powerful stamp I long to feel,
   The signature of love divine!
O shed it in my heart abroad,
   Fullness of love — of heaven — of God![17]

The Economic and Immanent Trinity in Charles Wesley's Hymns

In the previous section I suggested that Wesley's understanding of the Trinity emerges out of his theological reflections on the presence and work of the Holy Spirit. I maintained that his doctrine of the Trinity is primarily, if not exclusively, concerned with the divine economy, that is, with the Holy Spirit's coming to dwell in humans so that they might become "partakers of the divine nature," and not with demonstrating that a doctrine of the immanent Trinity was compatible with or confirmable by unaided human reason. This does not mean that Wesley did not have anything to say about the immanent Trinity. On the contrary, he went on to reflect on the doctrine of the immanent Trinity as well. But what makes Wesley's reflections on the immanent Trinity stand out is that they presuppose at every turn what he has already said regarding the economic Trinity. Even when he was reflecting on the immanent Trinity, his outlook was primarily ontological and not epistemological or speculative. Wesley simply refused to separate the ✗ immanent Trinity from the economic Trinity.

The first thing to observe about Charles Wesley's doctrine of the immanent Trinity is that, while his doctrine of the economic Trinity

17. Hymn 365 in *The Works of John Wesley*, 7 vols. (Nashville: Abingdon, 1983), 7:534-35.

can be seen in both sermons and hymns, his reflections on the immanent Trinity are largely, if not entirely, located in hymns. By locating his
reflections on the immanent Trinity in hymns, Wesley brilliantly extended — whether by intention, intuition, or otherwise — the logic of
early patristic arguments concerning the full divinity of the second and
third persons of the Trinity. The reader will here recall that a major
premise in patristic Trinitarian reasoning and argumentation is that
the church worshiped, sang hymns to, and offered prayers to the Son
and to the Spirit *(lex orandi, lex credendi)*. Such activities, they observed,
only made sense if the Son and the Spirit were fully divine. Otherwise,
they were guilty of idolatry.

In some respects, the hymn setting of Wesley's reflections on the
immanent Trinity did more than simply extend the logic of patristic
Trinitarian reasoning; it embodied it. The effect of the hymn setting
was to situate theological reflection on the immanent Trinity in doxology. Given the nature of late seventeenth- and early eighteenth-century
approaches to the Trinity, this was truly extraordinary. Rather than
submitting the propositional contents related to the immanent Trinity
to human reason, the doxological context invited people to submit
themselves in praise and thanksgiving to the triune God. With regard
to the content of the hymns themselves, three aspects are especially important. First, whether Wesley was reflecting on the divinity of Christ,
the divinity of the Spirit, the plurality of persons, or the unity of the
Trinity, he never lost sight of the economic Trinity.[18] This is also true of
the additional section, entitled "Hymns and Prayers to the Trinity."[19]
One can call this the *soteriological* aspect of the hymns. It is also the aspect that reveals the persistent ontological orientation of Charles Wesley's theology. The following are examples of this aspect of the hymns
taken from each of the four major sections.

In Hymn VIII, Wesley emphasizes Christ's role in the saving economy of God:

> The voice of God the Father sounds
>   Salvation to our sinful race:

18. The four main sections of *Hymns on the Trinity* are derived directly from William
Jones's *The Catholic Doctrine of the Trinity*.

19. This section is not found in Jones's work; therefore, many feel that it is most
representative of Charles Wesley's personal reflections on the Trinity.

His grace above our sin abounds,
   His glory shines in Jesus' face,
And by the Person of the Son
The Father makes Salvation known.

Saved by the Son, the Lord our God,
   Jehovah's Fellow we proclaim,
Who washes us in his own blood,
   To us declares his Father's name
His nature pure, his love imparts,
With all his fullness to our hearts. (*HT,* p. 8)[20]

In Hymn LXII, Wesley highlights the Spirit's role in the divine economy:

The Holy Ghost in part we know,
   For with us He resides,
Our whole of good to Him we owe
   Whom by his grace he guides:
He doth our virtuous thoughts inspire,
   The evil he averts,
And every seed of good desire
   He planted in our hearts.

He, whom the world cannot receive,
   But fight against his power,
Will come, we steadfastly believe,
   In his appointed hour:
He now the future grace reveals,
   Bespeaks his mean abode;
And in us when the Spirit dwells,
   We all are filled with God. (*HT,* pp. 41-42)[21]

---

20. Other hymns on the divinity of Christ that accentuate Christ's role in the divine economy include III, XII, XIII, XXXII, XXXIII, XXXV, L, LIV, and LV.

21. Other hymns on the divinity of the Holy Spirit that accentuate the Spirit's role in the divine economy include LVIII, LXI, LXIII, LXV, LXVII, LXVIII, LXXX, LXXXIII, and LXXXVI.

Turning to "The Plurality and Trinity of Persons," Wesley refers specifically to the "economy of grace" in Hymn CII:

Jehovah is but One
  Eternal God and true:
The Father sent the Son,
  His Spirit sent him too,
The everlasting Spirit filled,
And Jesus our Salvation sealed.

  Senders and Sent we praise,
    With equal thanks approve
  The economy of grace.
    The Triune God of love,
And humbly prostrated before
The One thrice holy God, adore! (*HT,* p. 66)[22]

When Wesley turned to "The Trinity in Unity," that is, to the topic that was at the center of the Trinitarian controversy, he juxtaposed his ontological orientation (first stanza) with the epistemological orientation of rationalist theologians (second stanza). Thus Hymn CXXIV says:

By the Father, and the Son,
  And blessed Spirit made,
God in Persons Three we own,
  And hang upon his aid:

  Reason asks, how can it be?
But who by simple faith embrace,
  We shall know the mystery,
    And see Him face to face. (*HT,* pp. 79-80)[23]

In Hymn CXXIX, Wesley returned to that most crucial component of the saving economy, namely, the indwelling by which people have knowledge of God and by which humans are made divine.

22. Other hymns on the plurality of persons that emphasize the divine economy include XCI, XCV, XCVIII, CI, CV, CVI, and CVII.

23. For the divine economy in the section "The Trinity in Unity," see Hymns CX, CXVI, CXVII, CXXXIV, and CXXXV.

The Father, Son, and Spirit dwell
   By faith in all his saints below,
And then in love unspeakable
   The glorious Trinity we know
Created after God to shine,
Filled with the Plentitude Divine. (*HT,* p. 82)

Finally, in "Hymns and Prayers to the Trinity," Wesley gives thanks for "[t]hy divine economy" in Hymn L:

Triune God of pardoning love,
   Thy divine economy
All our thankful hearts approve,
   Thee adore in Persons Three;
Each our canceled sin reveals,
   Each confirms the babes forgiven,
Each the heirs of glory seals,
   Each conducts our souls to heaven. (*HT,* p. 130)

A second aspect of the hymns that is especially important is the way in which Wesley captured the element of mystery or ineffability that is appropriate to divine transcendence. One might call this the *apophatic* aspect of the hymns. It is also an *eschatological* aspect of the hymns, because Wesley often contrasted the limited knowledge of God that Christians have now with the knowledge that they will have when they behold God in the fullness of God's glory. Here are a few examples of this aspect of *The Hymns on the Trinity.*
From Hymn LXXI:

The things invisible, Divine,
   Searched out by none but God can be:
Too short man's or angel's line
   To sound the depths of Deity:
The Spirit which in our God doth dwell,
Which is our God, alone can tell.

None of a different nature can
   A far superior nature know:
Incomprehensible to man

Is God, unless Himself he show,
Unless his heavenly Spirit impart
His light to man's infernal heart. (*HT*, p. 47)

From "Hymns and Prayers to the Trinity," Hymn XIX:

My notions true are notions vain;
By them I cannot grace obtain,
   Or saved from sin arise:
Knowledge acquired by books or creeds
My learned self-righteous pride it feeds;
    'Tis love that edifies.

Furnished with intellectual light,
In vain I speak of Thee aright,
   While unrevealed Thou art:
That only can suffice for me,
The whole mysterious Trinity
    Inhabiting my heart. (*HT*, pp. 102-3)

Finally, from "Hymns and Prayers to the Trinity," Hymn XL:

He hath to us made known
   The awful mystery,
The Trinity in One,
   And Unity in Three,
And taught the ransom'd sons of men
What angels never could explain.

Beyond our utmost thought,
   And reason's proudest flight,
We comprehend Him not,
   Nor grasp the Infinite,
But worship in the Mystic Three
One God to all eternity. (*HT*, p. 124)

A third and final aspect worth noting is that, throughout *Hymns on the Trinity*, Wesley summons his readers to praise, adoration, thanksgiving, and love for God. One can call this the *doxological* aspect of the hymns. Of course, this is precisely what one would expect. On the one hand, Wesley calls people to praise or adore God because of what God has done in Christ and in the Holy Spirit to restore them to communion with God. Thus the soteriological aspect evokes doxology. On the other hand, Wesley urges people to praise and adore the Trinity in mystery. Thus even the *apophatic,* or eschatological, dimension is intended to evoke praise and thanksgiving. Naturally, the hymns are doxological throughout; indeed, one might say that they are theology in the form of direct address to God. A good example is found in Hymn CIX:

> Hail holy, holy, holy Lord,
>   Whom One in Three we know,
> By all thy heavenly host ador'd,
>   By all thy church below!
> One undivided Trinity
>   With triumph we proclaim:
> The universe is full of Thee,
>   And speaks thy glorious name.
>
> Thee, holy Father, we confess,
>   Thee, holy Son adore,
> Thee, Spirit of true holiness,
>   We worship evermore:
> Thine incommunicable right,
>   Almighty God, receive,
> Which angel-quires and saints in light
>   And saints embodied give.
>
> Three Persons equally Divine
>   We magnify and love:
> And both the quires erelong shall join
>   To sing the praise above:
> Hail holy, holy, holy Lord,
>   (Our heavenly song shall be)
> Supreme, Essential One ador'd
>   In co-eternal Three. (*HT,* pp. 69-70)

The Trinity in Modern Theology and Worship

Summarizing the dominant approach to theology in England during the late seventeenth and early eighteenth centuries, Mark Pattison quips: "Christianity appeared made for nothing else but to be 'proved'; what use to make of it when it was proved was not much thought about."[24] While this certainly applies to the way many English Protestants approached theology during that time and well beyond it, it applies in a special way to the doctrine of the Trinity. Indeed, were one to attempt to summarize much Trinitarian discourse in the modern period, one could do worse than paraphrase Pattison: the Trinity appeared made for nothing else but to be proved; how it relates to our life with God and with one another was not much thought about.

I have suggested that two things are chiefly responsible for this development in modern theology. First, there was a gradual and subtle shift in the doctrine of divine revelation from the Holy Spirit to reason. While this shift had a great deal to do with the interpretation of Scripture, it also reflected and furthered a much deeper shift already underway from ontology to epistemology. Second, moving in a parallel direction, there was a tendency to reflect on the doctrine of the immanent Trinity in isolation from the divine economy.

In contrast, Charles Wesley maintained an ontological orientation in his approach to theology. For him, the principle aim of theology was to reflect on the church's encounter with God, beginning with the revealing and convicting activities of the Holy Spirit and continuing all the way to the Spirit's making us "partakers of the divine nature." Further, Wesley's ontological orientation expressed itself materially in his doctrine of the Trinity. Put simply, his ontological orientation did not allow him to think about the immanent Trinity apart from the economic Trinity. Thus, even in those sections of the *Hymns on the Trinity* that have to do with the immanent Trinity, Wesley persistently redirects the reader's attention to the divine economy.

In the late twentieth and early twenty-first centuries, theologians from many traditions have been struggling to overcome the modern

24. Mark Pattison, "Tendencies of Religious Thought in England, 1688-1750," *Essays,* 2 vols. (Oxford: Clarendon Press, 1889), 2:48.

preoccupation with epistemology and speculative metaphysics.[25] Some theologians are even beginning to move in a decidedly ontological direction.[26] At the same time, many theologians are hard at work emphasizing the indispensability of the economic Trinity for reflection on the immanent Trinity. The work of Karl Barth, Karl Rahner, and Catherine LaCugna has been extremely important in the movement in this direction.[27] Generally speaking, these developments are often foregrounded by a depiction of the Trinity's story in modern theology in terms of almost total loss. In the modern period, so the story goes, the Trinity was relegated to a mere appendix to theology.

Amid the well-rehearsed stories of the loss of the Trinity in modern theology (and especially in modern Protestant theology), there is a new development on the horizon. As I suggested near the beginning of this chapter, a few theologians and historians of doctrine have begun to call into question the narrative of total loss.[28] This development is fueled largely by one simple idea: that one can find the Trinity in modern theology if one looks in the right places.

It is true that Charles Wesley did not write a major work in systematic theology or even a technical treatise on the Trinity. But that does not mean that he did not help revive Trinitarian doctrine and piety in English Protestant theology. On the contrary, by engaging in theological reflection almost entirely in sermons and hymns, Charles may have done more to preserve the Trinity than he could have by writing the technical kinds of treatises on the Trinity that were so common in his day. Indeed, Charles Wesley's contribution to modern theology may lie precisely in that he reminds us that theology's true home is in worship and prayer, its true task the work of praise and thanksgiving to God.

---

25. Within the Methodist tradition, see Geoffrey Wainwright, *Doxology: The Praise of God in Worship, Doctrine and Life* (Oxford: Oxford University Press, 1984).

26. An early example of this can be seen in the work of Yves Congar and other Catholic *ressourcement* theologians. Examples in the Eastern Orthodox tradition are prevalent, but the work of Alexander Schmemann and Vladimir Lossky is exemplary in this respect.

27. For a mostly reliable introduction to the work of Barth, Rahner, and LaCugna (among others) on the Trinity, see Stanley Grenz, *Rediscovering the Triune God: The Trinity in Contemporary Theology* (Minneapolis: Augsburg Fortress, 2004).

28. For example, see Amy Plantinga Pauw, *The Supreme Harmony of All: The Trinitarian Theology of Jonathan Edwards* (Grand Rapids: Eerdmans, 2002).

CHAPTER 7

The Work of Trinitarian Theology Today

My purpose in this book has been twofold. On the one hand, I have intended to help fill in a crucial gap in the history of the doctrine of the Trinity. Theologians have for too long blamed Schleiermacher for the loss of interest in the Trinity in much of modern Protestant theology. The time has come for theologians to attend to the focused work of developing a more sophisticated account of what happened to the Trinity and why. The preceding narrative constitutes only one chapter in such an account.

On the other hand, I have meant this book to be not merely a contribution to the history of theology and doctrine. Rather, my purpose is to call attention to the devastating effects that at least one version of *sola Scriptura* has had for Trinitarian theology, effects I believe are still very much with us today. In much English Protestant theology, the combining of *sola Scriptura* with a rationalist hermeneutics and a canon of essential doctrine has shifted the emphasis in Trinitarian theology from invocation to assent, that is, from reflection on the use of the divine name in the full range of the church's catechetical and liturgical activities to reflection on the rationality or intelligibility of a network of propositions and assertions regarding the divine nature *ad intra* (the immanent Trinity). Thus I will conclude this study by making several observations about the reinvigoration of Trinitarian theology today.

In many Protestant circles today, one can see the lingering effects of *sola Scriptura* on perceptions of the Trinity. Apart from the wider catechetical, liturgical, and sacramental life of the church, it is all too easy to perceive the Trinity as a network of propositions about the inner being of God, which, like any other network of propositions, must be evaluated for rationality and intelligibility. What is lost here is the native sense that, whatever else the Trinity is, it is first and foremost the proper personal name for the Christian God, which, when filled out with identifying descriptions of what the Father, Son, and Holy Spirit have done for us and for our salvation, enables Christians to encounter, to know, and to love their God in prayer, baptism, worship, and the like.

As Roderick Leupp once quipped, people tend to see the Trinity as "a riddle wrapped up inside a puzzle and buried in an enigma."[1] There is little, if any, sense that the Trinity is "a practical doctrine with radical consequences for Christian life," as Catherine LaCugna has so memorably expressed it.[2] When asked to "explain" the Trinity, many Protestant clergy and laypeople grope around for analogies that purportedly can explain how one thing can take three forms, or consist of three ingredients, and so on. Unfortunately, these analogies are intended to illustrate the life shared by the three divine persons with each other from eternity; they rarely say anything about the life shared by the three divine persons *with us*. It is no wonder, then, that many Protestants see no vital connection between the Trinity and the Christian life. Given the emphasis in Protestant Evangelicalism on a personal relationship with God, this is an extremely ironic and sad development.

What is desperately needed in many quarters today is a recovery of emphasis on the Trinity as the proper personal name for God. Such a recovery would do two things at once. First, it would help refocus the church's understanding of the Trinity in an ontological rather than an epistemological or speculative metaphysical direction. In other words, a recovery of emphasis on the Trinity as the proper personal name for God would assist the church in its proper task, namely, informing people through evangelism and catechesis about the saving activities of God in the coming of Christ and the coming of the Holy Spirit, as well as helping to facilitate the human encounter with the triune God in worship, prayer, and praise through the hard work of initiation and

---

1. Roderick Leupp, *Knowing the Name of God: A Trinitarian Tapestry of Grace, Faith and Community* (Downers Grove, IL: InterVarsity Press, 1996), p. 16.

2. Catherine Mowry LaCugna, *God for Us: The Trinity and Christian Life* (New York: Harper Collins, 1991), p. 1.

Christian formation. Instead of conceiving of the Trinity as a network of propositions to be "explained," such a move will help clergy think of the Trinity as divine persons to be *introduced.*

Second, recovering the Trinity as the proper personal name for God will help to reorient Christian worship itself. In many quarters Christian worship has fallen on hard times. Rather than occasioning communion with the triune God through invocation and other forms of direct address, much Protestant worship has devolved into various forms of self-help and therapy in which talking about ourselves replaces talking to and listening to God. Talking to — and even listening to — God requires, among other things, having the right personal name for God.

All of the above is headed in a positive direction. On the negative side, the Trinitarian controversy in late seventeenth-century England should serve as a warning regarding all future attempts to provide intelligible accounts of the immanent Trinity, for example, by solving the problem of individuation with regard to the three divine persons. The immanent Trinity may very well remain shrouded in mystery, not only in this life but even in the life to come. The real problem with attempts to explain the immanent Trinity is that such attempts distract attention from the knowledge that matters most, namely, personal as opposed to speculative or metaphysical knowledge. Thus it is entirely possible that one could come up with a compelling solution to the problem of the principle of individuation and not yet possess personal knowledge of the triune God.

Personal knowledge of God was the only knowledge that finally mattered in early Christianity. Indeed, early Christian theologians had little time for or interest in purely speculative knowledge of God. Their primary concern was with fostering and facilitating people's personal encounter with the living God. Thus, regarding Christians' knowledge of the triune God, Basil of Caesarea says: "[The Spirit] does not reveal [knowledge] to them from outside sources, but *leads them to knowledge personally.*"[3]

What is at stake here? To put it simply, knowledge of the triune God is first and foremost a gift of the Holy Spirit; moreover, it occurs in the Holy Spirit and by the Holy Spirit. Thus Basil continues:

3. St. Basil the Great, *On the Holy Spirit,* trans. David Anderson (Crestwood, NY: St. Vladimir's, 1997), p. 74 (italics in original).

If we are illumined by divine power, and fix our eyes on the beauty of the image of the invisible God, and through the image are led up to the indescribable beauty of its source, it is because we have been inseparably joined to the Spirit of knowledge. . . . "No one knows the Father except the Son, and no one can say 'Jesus is Lord' except in the Holy Spirit." Notice that it does not say through the Spirit but in the Spirit. . . . [The Spirit] reveals the glory of the Only-Begotten in Himself, and He gives true worshippers the knowledge of God in Himself. The way to divine knowledge ascends from one Spirit through the one Son to the one Father. Likewise, natural goodness, inherent holiness and royal dignity reaches from the Father through the Only-Begotten to the Spirit.[4]

What Basil's remarks should make clear is that knowledge of the triune God is not only personal in nature, but it is also inherently transformative. Coming to know and love the triune God is not like coming to know the Periodic Table or the mechanics of internal combustion. When the Holy Spirit enables people to invoke the name of Jesus Christ in prayer and in worship, they embark on a journey to holiness and sanctification. All of this clearly presupposes the ongoing presence and work of the Holy Spirit in the worshiping life of the people of God. To be a Trinitarian theologian in this setting is not to set one's mind to the tough task of solving the problem of the principle of individuation. On the contrary, to be a Trinitarian theologian is to be a midwife of the Holy Spirit, actively participating in the birthing of new Christians in and through baptism. It is this image that I most want to leave with my readers.

Trinitarian theology conceived along these lines is hard work. But it is not hard work because it involves finding a calculus to explain the eternal relationships that constitute the immanent Trinity from everlasting to everlasting. Rather, it is hard work because it involves immersion in the life of the church and a great deal of sensitivity and discernment with regard to the presence and work of the Holy Spirit in evangelism, catechesis, initiation, and formation. Coming to know God personally is more like developing a capacity for art or music than it is like learning the alphabet: it involves the patient work of learning

4. St. Basil the Great, *On the Holy Spirit,* p. 74 (italics in original).

skills, developing proper dispositions (e.g., humility), as well as learning a new vocabulary. To be a Trinitarian theologian is first and foremost to be available to the Holy Spirit for this work.

In the early stages of this work, a Trinitarian theologian's chief responsibility is to assist the Holy Spirit in introducing people to the triune name for God and in sharing the good news both of the historic events of the incarnation and Pentecost. Happily, the good news does not end there. Rather, the Trinitarian theologian is keen to inform her listeners of the ongoing presence and work of the Holy Spirit and Jesus Christ in the worshiping life of the people of God.

A critical stage in the work of Trinitarian theology according to this understanding comes in the work of catechesis and initiation. As with evangelism, this work is ultimately the work of the Holy Spirit. The task of the Trinitarian theologian is simply to come alongside the Holy Spirit, to facilitate and foster the requisite knowledge and skills needed for encountering the triune God in the worshiping life of the church. Throughout the work of evangelism, catechesis, and initiation, no skill will be more important than prayer. Indeed, teaching people how to pray is of the very essence of Trinitarian theology.

The astute reader can surely extend the logic from here. The Trinitarian theologian as midwife of the Holy Spirit will assist Christians in coming to encounter Jesus Christ in baptism and the Eucharist, in joining with Christ in obedience and surrender to God the Father. The end of Trinitarian theology as such will not be to explain God but to worship God, to give thanks and praise to God, to surrender one's will and one's life to God in obedience, and ultimately to become like God.

Finally, the work of Trinitarian theology in the contexts of evangelism, catechesis, and worship will invariably give rise to questions about the immanent Trinity. This is entirely natural and appropriate. For one thing, we do not simply observe the interactions of the Father, Son, and Holy Spirit with us in the saving actions of the triune God on our behalf; we also witness interaction among the three divine persons themselves. Thus it is natural to reflect on the nature and manner of the relationships among Father, Son, and Holy Spirit, including the begetting of the Son, the sending of the Spirit, and the like.

When such questions arise, the Trinitarian theologian as midwife of the Holy Spirit can offer the following threefold response. First, she can point out that the interactions we observe among the three divine persons are a function of the triune God's saving actions on our behalf (the economic Trinity). She can suggest that, while these interactions give us a glimpse of the truth about the nature and manner of the relationships among the three divine persons from eternity (the immanent Trinity), we should be slow to claim too much here. Surely there are things about the nature and manner of the eternal relationships among the three divine persons that are not disclosed in and by the saving activities of the triune God on our behalf.[5] On the one hand, we believe and confess that what we can observe about the relationships among the three divine persons in their mutual work of creating, redeeming, and sanctifying is grounded in and reflects the true nature of God from eternity. On the other hand, divine transcendence and otherness requires us to confess that we may not know all there is to know about the precise nature of the divine relationships from eternity. Therefore, all positive assertions about the immanent Trinity must be located within the wider sphere of apophatic discourse required by divine transcendence.

Second, the Trinitarian theologian can, with Chrysostom, encourage initiates to remain focused on that birth that we have seen and heard and not to become overly distracted by what we have not seen or heard, namely, the manner of the eternal generation of the Son from the Father, the manner of the Spirit's procession, and so on. The theologian can and will work to assist beginners in balancing their desire for the knowledge of God with intellectual humility and appreciation for divine transcendence and mystery. To that end, she will need to help people in the waning days of the modern age to understand that darkness is not necessarily an evil to be overcome; that what is withheld may be as much a gift to humans as what is revealed; that a lack of total, comprehensive knowledge is not simply okay but is a crucial check against violence and a liberating source of freedom and joy.

Third, when moving from the transfiguring light of the divine

---

5. For a helpful discussion of the extent to which what is observed of the nature and manner of relationships among the three divine persons in the divine economy can simply be transferred to the immanent Trinity, see Fred Sanders, "The Trinity," in *The Oxford Handbook of Systematic Theology*, ed. John Webster, Kathryn Tanner, and Iain Torrance (Oxford: Oxford University Press, 2007), pp. 35-53. See also Bruce D. Marshall, "The Trinity," in *The Blackwell Companion to Modern Theology*, ed. Gareth Jones (Oxford: Blackwell, 2004), pp. 183-203.

economy to the darkness of the immanent Trinity, the theologian can help people who are maturing spiritually and theologically to stop groping around for analogies long enough to close their eyes and to pray, "Holy, Holy, Holy." In doing so, she can help them see that contemplating what is unknown is not altogether unlike contemplating what is known. She can show them that, when approached rightly, theological reflection on the immanent Trinity really is like theological reflection on the economic Trinity. Both end in doxology.

Bibliography

Abraham, William J. *Canon and Criterion in Christian Theology: From the Fathers to Feminism*. Oxford: Clarendon Press, 1999.

————. "Cumulative Case Arguments." In *The Rationality of Religious Belief: Essays in Honor of Basil Mitchell*, edited by William J. Abraham and Steven Holtzer. New York: Oxford University Press, 1987.

Abraham, William J., Jason E. Vickers, and Natalie B. Van Kirk, eds. *Canonical Theism: A Proposal for Theology and the Church*. Grand Rapids: Eerdmans, 2008.

Ashton, Margaret. *England's Iconoclasts: Laws Against Images*. Oxford: Clarendon Press, 1988.

Atkinson, Nigel. *Richard Hooker and the Authority of Scripture, Tradition and Reason: Reformed Theologian of the Church of England*. Carlisle: Paternoster Press, 1997.

Austin, J. L. *How to Do Things with Words*. Cambridge: Harvard University Press, 1962.

Babcock, William S. "A Changing of the Christian God." *Interpretation* 45 (1991).

————. "The Commerce Between the Mind and Things." In *The Unbounded Community: Papers in Christian Ecumenism in Honor of Jaroslav Pelikan*, edited by William Caferro and Duncan G. Fisher. New York and London: Garland Publishing, 1996.

Bartels, Laura A. "Hymns of the Status Quo: Charles Wesley on the Trinity." *Methodist History* 41, no. 2 (Jan. 2003).

Basil the Great. *On the Holy Spirit*, translated by David Anderson. Crestwood, NY: St. Vladimir's, 1997.

Beiser, Frederick. *The Sovereignty of Reason: The Defense of Rationality in the Early English Enlightenment*. Princeton: Princeton University Press, 1996.

Berger, Teresa. *Theology in Hymns? A Study of the Relationship of Doxology and Theology According to* A Collection of Hymns for the People Called Methodists. Nashville: Kingswood Books, 1995.

Berlin, Isaiah. *The Roots of Romanticism.* Princeton: Princeton University Press, 1999.

Bettenson, Henry, ed., *Documents of the Christian Church.* New York: Oxford University Press, 1947.

Birch, Thomas. "Life of Mr. William Chillingworth." In *Works of William Chillingworth, M.A.,* 10th ed. London, 1762.

Boethius. *Boethius: The Theological Tractates, The Consolation of Philosophy,* translated by H. F. Stewart, E. K. Rand, and S. J. Tester. Revised edition, Loeb Classical Library. Cambridge, MA: Harvard University Press, 1973.

Bray, Gerald. *Documents of the English Reformation.* Minneapolis: Fortress Press, 1994.

Bredvold, Louis I. *The Intellectual Milieu of John Dryden.* Ann Arbor: University of Michigan Press, 1934.

Burthogge, Richard. *An Essay upon Reason, and the nature of spirits.* London, 1694.

Byrne, Peter. *Natural Religion and the Nature of Religion: The Legacy of Deism.* New York: Routledge, 1989.

Calvin, John. *Calvin: Institutes of the Christian Religion.* Edited by John T. McNeill and translated by Ford Lewis Battles. 2 vols. Philadelphia: Westminster Press, 1960.

———. "On the Necessity of Reforming the Church." In *Calvin: Theological Treatises,* translated by J. K. S. Reid. Philadelphia: Westminster Press, 1954.

Carroll, Robert Todd. *The Common-Sense Philosophy of Religion of Bishop Edward Stillingfleet, 1635-1699.* The Hague: Martinus Nijhoff, 1975.

Cassirer, Ernst. *The Platonic Renaissance in England,* translated by James P. Pettigrove. London: Nelson, 1953.

Chappell, Vere. "Locke's Theory of Ideas." *The Cambridge Companion to Locke,* ed. Vere Chappell. New York: Cambridge University Press, 1994.

Charry, Ellen T. "Augustine of Hippo: Father of Christian Psychology." *Anglican Theological Review* 88, no. 4 (2006).

———. *By the Renewing of Your Minds: The Pastoral Function of Christian Doctrine.* Oxford: Clarendon Press, 1997.

Cheynell, Francis. *Mr. Chillingworth's novissima, or the Sicknesse, Heresy, Death, and Buriall of William Chillingworth, (in his own Phrase) Clerk of Oxford, and in the conceit of his Fellow Soldiers the Queen's Arch-Engineer and Grand Intelligencer. Set forth in a letter to his eminent and learned Friends; a Relation of his Apprehension at Arundell; a Discovery of his Errours in a brief Catechism; and a short Oration at the Burial of his heretical Book.* London, 1644.

———. *The Divine Triunity of the Father, Son and Holy Spirit.* London, 1650.

Chillingworth,William. *The Religion of Protestants: A Safe Way to Salvation.* London, 1638.

Chrysostom, John. *St. John Chrysostom: Baptismal Instructions,* translated by Paul W. Harkins. New York: Paulist Press, 1963.

Cosin, John. *The history of popish transubstantiation to which is premised and opposed the catholic doctrin of Holy Scripture, the ancient fathers and the reformed churches about the sacred elements, and presence of Christ in the blessed sacrament of the Eucharist.* London, 1679.

Cragg, Gerald R. *Freedom and Authority: A Study of English Thought in the Early Seventeenth Century.* Philadelphia: Westminster Press, 1975.

————. *From Puritanism to the Age of Reason: A Study of Changes in Religious Thought within the Church of England 1660 to 1700.* London: Cambridge University Press, 1950.

Cressy, Hugh. *Exomologesis.* Paris, 1647.

————. *Fanaticism Fanatically Imputed to the Catholic Church.* London, 1672.

Cudworth, Ralph. *The True Intellectual System of the Universe.* London, 1678.

Cyril of Jerusalem, "The Catechetical Lectures." In *Nicene and Post-Nicene Fathers,* 2nd series, edited by Philip Schaff. New York: Christian Publishing, 1893.

Dallimore, Arnold A. *A Heart Set Free: The Life of Charles Wesley.* Westchester, IL: Crossway Books, 1988.

Descartes, René. *Philosophical Writings,* translated by J. Cottingham et al., 3 vols. Cambridge, UK: Cambridge University Press, 1984-91.

DeVries, Dawn. *Jesus Christ in the Preaching of Calvin and Schleiermacher.* Louisville: Westminster John Knox Press, 2002.

A Dialogue Between a New Catholic Convert and a Protestant Shewing the Doctrine of Transubstantiation to be as Reasonable to be Believ'd as the Great Mystery of the Trinity by all Good Catholicks. London, 1686.

Dixon, Philip. *Nice and Hot Disputes: The Doctrine of the Trinity in the Seventeenth Century.* London: T&T Clark, 2003.

Dreyden, John. *Defense of the Papers Written by the Late King . . . and Duchess of York.* London, 1686.

Duffy, Eamon. *The Stripping of the Altars: Traditional Religion in England 1400-1580.* New Haven: Yale University Press, 1992.

Edwards, John. *Socinianism Unmask'd.* London, 1696.

————. *Some Thoughts Concerning the Several Causes and Occasions of Atheism.* London, 1695.

Feine, Paul. *Die Gestalt des apostolischen Glaubensbekenntnisses in der Zeit des N.T.* Leipzig, 1925.

Fuhrmann, Paul T. *An Introduction to the Great Creeds of the Church.* Philadelphia: Westminster Press, 1960.

Gavrilyuk, Paul. *The Suffering of the Impassable God: The Dialectics of Patristic Thought.* Oxford: Oxford University Press, 2005.

George, Edward Augustus. *Seventeenth Century Men of Latitude: Forerunners of the New Theology.* London: T. Fisher Unwin, 1908.

Gerrish, Brian. "To the Unknown God: Luther and Calvin on the Hiddenness of God." *Journal of Religion* 53 (1973).

Gracia, J. J. E. *Introduction to the Problem of Individuation in the Early Middle Ages.* Washington, DC: The Catholic University of America Press, 1984.

———, ed. *Individuation in Scholasticism: The Later Middle Ages and the Counter Reformation (1160-1650).* Albany: State University of New York Press, 1994.

Gray, Madeleine. *The Protestant Reformation: Beliefs and Practices.* Brighton, UK: Sussex Academic Press, 2003.

Green, Ian. *The Christian's ABC.* Oxford: Oxford University Press, 1996.

Gregory of Nyssa. "Address on Religious Instruction." In *Christology of the Later Fathers,* edited by Edward Hardy. Philadelphia: Westminster, 1954.

Gregory of Nyssa. *An Answer to Ablabius: That We Should Not Think of Saying There Are Three Gods in Christology of the Later Fathers,* edited by Edward R. Hardy. Philadelphia: Westminster, 1954.

Grenz, Stanley. *Rediscovering the Trine God: The Trinity in Contemporary Theology.* Minneapolis: Fortress Press, 2004.

Guyer, Paul. "Locke's Philosophy of Language." In *The Cambridge Companion to Locke,* edited by Vere Chappell. New York: Cambridge University Press, 1994.

Harnack, Adolf von. *Outlines of the History of Dogma.* Boston: Beacon Press, 1957.

Harrison, Peter. *The Bible, Protestantism, and the Rise of Natural Science.* New York: Cambridge University Press, 1998.

———. *'Religion' and the Religions in the English Enlightenment.* New York: Cambridge University Press, 1990.

Hogg, James. *The Private Memoirs and Confessions of a Justified Sinner.* New York: Oxford University Press, 1969.

Hooker, Richard. *The Lawes of Ecclesiastical Polity, eight books.* London, 1604.

Hopkins, Keith. *A World Full of Gods: The Strange Triumph of Christianity.* New York: Plume, 2001.

Hume, David. *An Enquiry Concerning Human Understanding,* edited by L. A. Selby-Bigge and P. H. Nidditch. Oxford: Clarendon Press, 1975.

Hutchinson, William. *A rational discourse concerning transubstantiation in a letter to a person of honor from a Master of Arts of the University of Cambridge.* London, 1676.

Hyde, Edward. *Animadversions upon a Book Entitled Fanaticism fanatically imputed to the Catholic Church by Dr. Stillingfleet.* London, 1674.

Irenaeus. *Adversus haereses.* In *Creeds and Confessions of Faith in the Christian Tradi-*

tions, edited by Jaroslav Pelikan and Valerie Hotchkiss, 3 vols. New Haven: Yale University Press, 2003.

Jenson, Robert. *The Triune Identity: God According to the Gospel.* Philadelphia: Fortress Press, 1982.

―――. *Systematic Theology, Volume 1: The Triune God.* Oxford: Oxford University Press, 1997.

John of Damascus. *On the Divine Images: Three Apologies Against Those Who Attack the Divine Images,* translated by David Anderson. Crestwood: St. Vladimir's, 1997.

von Karlstadt, Andreas. "On the Abolition of Images." In *European Reformations Sourcebook,* edited by Cater Lindberg. Oxford: Blackwell Publishers, 2000.

Katz, David. *God's Last Words: Reading the English Bible from the Reformation to Fundamentalism.* New Haven: Yale University Press, 2004.

Kelly, J. N. D. *Early Christian Creeds.* New York: Harper Collins, 1978.

―――. *Early Christian Doctrines.* New York: Harper Collins, 1958.

Khomiakov, Alexei. *Ultimate Questions,* edited by Alexander Schmemann. Crestwood, NY: St. Vladimir's, 1975.

Kripke, Saul. "Naming and Necessity." In *Semantics of Natural Language,* edited by Donald Davidson and Gilbert Harman. Dordrecht: D. Reidel Publishing Company, 1972.

LaCugna, Catherine Mowry. *God for Us: The Trinity and the Christian Life.* San Francisco: HarperSanFrancisco, 2001.

―――. "The Trinitarian Mystery of God." In *Systematic Theology: Roman Catholic Perspectives,* edited by Francis Schüssler Fiorenza and John P. Galvin. Volume 1. Minneapolis: Fortress Press, 1991.

Lash, Nicholas. "Considering the Trinity." *Modern Theology* 2 (1986).

Laud, William. *A Relation of the Conference between William Laud and Mr. Fisher the Jesuit.* London: Macmillan and Co., 1901.

Lehmberg, Stanford E. *The Reformation of Cathedrals: Cathedrals in English Society, 1485-1603.* Princeton: Princeton University Press, 1988.

Leslie, Charles. *The charge of Socinianism against Dr. Tillotson Considered.* Edinburgh, 1695.

Leupp, Roderick. *Knowing the Name of God: A Trinitarian Tapestry of Grace, Faith and Community.* Downers Grove, IL: InterVarsity Press, 1996.

Limborch, Philip van. *A Compleat System, or Body of Divinity,* 2 vols. London, 1702.

Locke, John. *An Essay Concerning Human Understanding,* edited by Peter H. Nidditch. Oxford: Clarendon Press, 1975.

―――. *Essays on the Laws of Nature,* edited by W. von Leyden. Oxford: Clarendon Press, 1988.

―――. *The Reasonableness of Christianity: As Delivered in the Scriptures,* edited

with an introduction, notes, critical apparatus, and transcriptions of related manuscripts by John C. Higgins-Biddle. Oxford: Clarendon Press,
1999.

———. "Second Reply to the Bishop of Worchester." *The Words of John Locke*, 10
vols. London 1823. Reprint, Aalen: Scientia Verlag, 1963.

———. *A Second Vindication of the Reasonableness of Christianity, etc.* London,
1697.

Lockyer, Roger. *The Early Stuarts.* London: Longman, 1989.

Luther, Martin. "On the Councils and the Churches." In *Selected Writings of
Martin Luther, 1539-1546,* edited by Theodore G. Tappert. Philadelphia: Fortress, 1967.

———. *Sermons of Martin Luther,* edited by John Nicholas Lenker. Grand
Rapids: Baker Book House, 1988.

———. *Werke.* Weimar: H. Bohlau, 1883.

———. *What Luther Says: An Anthology.* Vol. 1, translated by Ewald M. Plass. St.
Louis: Concordia, 1959.

Marshall, Bruce D. "The Trinity." In *The Blackwell Companion to Modern Theology,* edited by Gareth Jones. Oxford: Blackwell, 2004.

Marshall, John. *John Locke: Resistance, Religion and Responsibility.* New York: Cambridge University Press, 1994.

———. "Locke, Socinianism, 'Socinianism,' Unitarianism." In *English Philosophy in the Age of Locke,* edited by M. A. Stewart. Oxford: Clarendon Press,
2000.

McLachlan, H. John. *Socinianism in Seventeenth-Century England.* London: Oxford University Press, 1951.

McLachlan, Herbert. *The Religious Opinions of Milton, Locke, and Newton.* New
York: Russell and Russell, 1972.

Mitchell, T. Crichton. *Charles Wesley: Man with the Dancing Heart.* Kansas City:
Beacon Hill Press, 1994.

Moorman, J. R. H. *A History of the Church of England.* London: A & C Black, 1986.

More, Henry. *An Antidote Against Atheisme.* London, 1653.

———. *A Brief Discourse of the Real Presence of the body and blood of Christ in the
Celebration of the Holy Eucharist.* London, 1686.

Newport, Kenneth G. C., and Ted A. Campbell, eds. *Charles Wesley: Life, Literature and Legacy.* London: Epworth Press, 2007.

———, ed. *The Sermons of Charles Wesley: A Critical Edition, with Introduction and
Notes.* Oxford: Oxford University Press, 2001.

Norris, John. *Practical Discourses on Several Divine Subjects.* London, 1690.

Nye, Stephen. *Considerations on the explications of the doctrine of the Trinity.* London, 1694.

———. *Considerations on the Explications of the doctrine of the Trinity, by Dr. Wallis,*

Dr. Sherlock, Dr. S———h, Dr. Cudworth, and Mr. Hooker; as also on the account given by those that say, the Trinity is an unconceivable and inexplicable Mystery. London, 1693.

———. *A Discourse concerning the Real and Nominal Trinitarians.* London 1695.

———. *Letter of Resolution concerning the Doctrines of the Trinity and Incarnation.* London 1695.

Olson, Roger E., and Christopher A. Hall. *The Trinity.* Grand Rapids: Eerdmans, 2002.

Orr, Robert. *Reason and Authority: The Thought of William Chillingworth.* Oxford: Clarendon Press, 1967.

Osborn, George. *The Poetical Works of John and Charles Wesley,* 13 vols. London: Wesleyan-Methodist Conference Office, 1870.

Pattison, Mark. "Tendencies of Religious Thought in England, 1688-1750." In *Essays.* 2 vols. Oxford: Clarendon Press, 1889.

Pauw, Amy Plantinga. *The Supreme Harmony of All: The Trinitarian Theology of Jonathan Edwards.* Grand Rapids: Eerdmans, 2002.

Pelikan, Jaroslav. *The Emergence of the Catholic Tradition.* Volume 1 of *The Christian Tradition: A History of the Development of Doctrine.* Chicago: University of Chicago Press, 1971.

———. *Credo: Historical and Theological Guide to Creeds and Confessions of Faith in the Christian Tradition.* New Haven: Yale University Press, 2003.

Phillips, John. *The Reformation of Images: Destruction of Art in England, 1535-1660.* Berkeley: University of California Press, 1973.

Placher, William. *The Domestication of Transcendence: How Modern Thinking about God Went Wrong.* Louisville: Westminster Press, 1996.

Plantinga, Alvin. *Warranted Christian Belief.* New York: Oxford University Press, 2000.

Pocock, J. G. A. "Within the Margins: The Definitions of Orthodoxy." In *The Margins of Orthodoxy: Heterodox Writing and Cultural Response, 1660-1750,* edited by Roger D. Lund. Cambridge, UK: Cambridge University Press, 1995.

Popkin, Richard H. *The History of Scepticism from Erasmus to Spinoza.* Berkeley: University of California Press, 1979.

———. "The Philosophy of the Royal Society of England." In *The Columbia History of Western Philosophy,* edited by Richard H. Popkin. New York: Columbia University Press, 1999.

Porter, H. C. *Reformation and Reaction in Tudor Cambridge.* Cambridge: Cambridge University Press, 1958.

Potter, Christopher. *Want of Charity justly Charged.* London, 1633.

Popkin, Richard. "The Philosophy of Bishop Stillingfleet." *Journal of the History of Philosophy* 10, no. 3 (1971).

The Protestants Plea for a Socinian: Justifying His Doctrine from being opposite to Scrip-

ture or Church-Authority; And Him from being Guilty of Heresie, or Schism. In five Conferences. London, 1686.

Quantrille, Wilma J. "Introduction." In *Charles Wesley, Hymns on the Trinity,* edited by S. T. Kimbrough, Jr. Madison, NJ: The Charles Wesley Society, 1988.

The Racovian Catechism, translated by Thomas Rees. Lexington: The American Theological Library Association, 1962.

Redwood, John. *Reason, Ridicule, and Religion: The Age of Enlightenment in England 1660-1750.* London: Thames and Hudson, 1976.

Reedy, Gerard. *The Bible and Reason: Anglicans and Scripture in Late Seventeenth Century England.* Philadelphia: University of Pennsylvania Press, 1985.

———. *Robert South: An Introduction to His Life and Sermons.* New York: Cambridge University Press, 1992.

Rogers, G. A. J., ed. *The Philosophy of Edward Stillingfleet Including His Replies to John Locke,* 5 vols. Bristol, UK: Thoemmes Press, 2000.

———. "John Locke: Conservative Radical." In *Margins of Orthodoxy: Heterodox Writing and Cultural Response, 1660-1750,* edited by Roger D. Lund. New York: Cambridge University Press, 1995.

Sanders, Fred. "The Trinity." In *The Oxford Handbook of Systematic Theology,* edited by John Webster, Kathryn Tanner, and Ian Torrance. Oxford: Oxford University Press, 2007.

Seeberg, A. *Der Katechismus der Urchristenheit.* Leipzig, 1903.

Sergeant, John. *Sure Footing in Christianity, or Rational Discourses on the Rule of Faith.* London, 1665.

Shapiro, Barbara. *Probability and Certainty in Seventeenth Century England: A Study of the Relationships between Natural Science, Religion, History, Law, and Literature.* Princeton: Princeton University Press, 1983.

Sherlock, William. *An Answer to a Late Dialogue Between a New Catholick Convert and a Protestant, To Prove the Mystery of the Trinity to be as absurd a Doctrine as Transubstantiation.* By way of short Notes on the said Dialogue. London, 1687.

———. *A Defence of Dr. Sherlock's Notion of a Trinity in Unity.* London, 1694.

———. *The Distinction Between the Real and Nominal Trinitarians, Considered.* London, 1697.

———. *A Vindication of the Doctrine of the Holy and Ever Blessed Trinity, and the Incarnation of the Son of God, Occasioned by the Brief Notes on the Creed of St. Athanasius, and the Brief History of the Unitarians, or Socinians; and containing an Answer to both.* London, 1690.

Simon, Irene. *Three Restoration Divines: Barrow, South, Tillotson.* Paris: Les Belles Lettres, 1967.

Simon, Richard. *A Critical history of the Old Testament,* translated by H. Dickinson. London, 1682.

Soskice, Janet Martin. *Metaphor and Religious Language.* Oxford: Oxford University Press, 1985.

South, Robert. *Animadversions upon Dr. Sherlock's book.* London, 1693.

———. *Tritheism charged upon Dr. Sherlock's new notion of the Trinity.* London, 1695.

Southgate, Beverley C. "'Beating Down Skepticism': The Solid Philosophy of John Sergeant, 1623-1707." In *English Philosophy in the Age of Locke,* edited by M. A. Stewart. Oxford: Clarendon Press, 2000.

Spurr, John. *The Restoration Church of England.* London: Yale University Press, 1991.

Stegmann, Joachim. *Brevis Disquisitio.* Amsterdam, 1633.

Steinmetz, David. *Calvin in Context.* New York: Oxford University Press, 1995.

Stewart, M. A. "Stillingfleet and the Way of Ideas." In *English Philosophy in the Age of Locke,* edited by M. A. Stewart. Oxford: Clarendon Press, 2000.

Stillingfleet, Edward. *An Answer to Some Papers Lately Printed, Concerning the Authority of the Catholick Church in Matters of Faith, and the Reformation of the Church of England.* London, 1686.

———. *A Discourse in Vindication of the Doctrine of the Trinity.* London 1697.

———. *Discourse on Idolatry.* London, 1671.

———. *The Doctrine of the Trinity and Transubstantiation Compared, as to Scripture, Reason, and Tradition. In a New Dialogue between a Protestant and a Papist. The First Part. Wherein an Answer is given to the late Proofs of the Antiquity of Transubstantiation, in the Books called Consenses Veterum, and Nubes Testium, etc.* London, 1686.

———. *The Doctrine of the Trinity and Transubstantiation Compared, as to Scripture, Reason, and Tradition. In a New Dialogue between a Protestant and a Papist. The Second Part. Wherein the Doctrine of the Trinity is shewed to be agreeable to Scripture and Reason, and Transubstantiation repugnant to both.* London, 1687.

———. *Irenicium: A Weapon-Salve for the Churches Wounds: or the Divine Right of Particular Forms of Church Government, Discussed and examined according to the Principles of the Law of Nature, the positive Laws of God, the Practice of the Apostles, and the Primitive Church, and the Judgment of Reformed Divines. Whereby a Foundation is laid for the Church's Peace, and the Accommodation of our present Differences.* London, 1659.

———. *The Mysteries of the Christian Faith asserted and Vindicated in a Sermon Preached at S. Laurence Jewry in London.* London, 1691.

———. *Origines Sacrae, or a Rational Account of the Grounds of Christian Faith, as the Truth and Divine Authority of the Scripture, and the Matters therein contained.* London, 1662.

———. *A Rational Account of the Grounds of the Protestant Religion.* London, 1664.

———. *A Reply to Mr. Serjeant's Third Appendix.* London, 1665.

———. *A Second Discourse, in Vindication of the Protestant Grounds of Faith.* London, 1673.

———. *Works.* 6 vols. London, 1707-10.

Stump, Eleonore. "Revelation and Biblical Exegesis: Augustine, Aquinas, and Swinburne." In *Reason and the Christian Religion: Essays in Honour of Richard Swinburne,* edited by Alan G. Padgett. Oxford: Clarendon Press, 1994.

Tappert, Theodore G., ed., *Selected Writings of Martin Luther, 1539-1546.* Philadelphia: Fortress Press, 1967.

Taylor, Jeremy. *The real presence and spirituall of Christ in the blessed sacrament proved against the doctrine of transubstantiation.* London, 1653.

Tenison, Thomas. *The Difference Betwixt the Protestant and Socinian Methods: In Answer to a Book Written by a Romanist, and Intituled The Protestants Plea for a Socinian.* London, 1687.

Tertullian, *De praescriptione haereticorum.* In *Creeds and Confessions of Faith in the Christian Traditions,* edited by Jaroslav Pelikan and Valerie Hotchkiss, 3 vols. New Haven: Yale University Press, 2003.

Thiel, Udo. "Individuation." In *The Cambridge History of Seventeenth Century Philosophy,* edited by D. Garber and M. R. Ayers, 2 vols. Cambridge: Cambridge University Press, 1998.

———. "Personal Identity." In *The Cambridge History of Seventeenth Century Philosophy,* edited by D. Garber and M. R. Ayers, 2 vols. Cambridge: Cambridge University Press 1998.

———. "The Trinity and Human Personal Identity." In *English Philosophy in the Age of Locke,* edited by M. A. Stewart. Oxford: Clarendon Press, 2000.

Tillotson, John. *A Discourse Against Transubstantiation.* London, 1684.

———. *The Rule of Faith: Or an Answer to the Treatise of Mr. I. S. Entituled, Sure-footing, etc.* London, 1666.

———. *A Sermon Concerning the Unity of the Divine Nature and the Blessed Trinity.* London, 1693.

Tolland, John. *Christianity Not Mysterious.* London, 1696.

Trevor-Roper, Hugh. *Archbishop Laud, 1573-1645.* London: Macmillan, 1988.

———. *Catholics, Anglicans, and Puritans: Seventeenth Century Essays.* Chicago: University of Chicago Press, 1988.

Tulloch, John. *Rational Theology and Christian Philosophy.* Reprint of 1823 edition. Germany: Georg Olms Verlagsbuchhandlung, 1966.

Twelftree, Graham H. *In the Name of Jesus: Exorcism among Early Christians.* Grand Rapids: Baker Academic, 2007.

Tyacke, Nicholas. *Anti-Calvinists: The Rise of English Arminianism c. 1590-1640.* Oxford: Oxford University Press, 1987.

Tyson, John R. *Assist Me to Proclaim: The Life and Hymns of Charles Wesley.* Grand Rapids: Eerdmans, 2007.

———. *Charles Wesley: A Reader.* Oxford: Oxford University Press, 1989.

Verón, François. *The Rule of Catholick Faith: Sever'd from the Opinions of the Schools, Mistakes of the Ignorant, and Abuses of the Vulgar.* Paris, 1660.

Vickers, Jason E. "Charles Wesley's Doctrine of the Holy Spirit: A Vital Resource for the Renewal of Methodism Today." *Asbury Journal* 61, no. 1 (Spring 2006).

Wainwright, Geoffrey. *Doxology: The Praise of God in Worship, Doctrine and Life.* Oxford: Oxford University Press, 1984.

Wallis, John. *An Explication of the Athanasian Creed in a Third Letter Pursuant of Two former, Concerning the Sacred Trinity Together with a Postscript, in Answer to Another Letter.* Cheapside, 1691.

———. *Three Sermons.* Cheapside, 1691.

Watson, J. R. *The English Hymn.* Oxford: Oxford University Press, 1997.

Weaver, Rebecca. "Reading the Signs." *Interpretation* 58, no. 1 (2004).

Wedeking, G. "Locke on Personal Identity and the Trinity Controversy of the 1690s." *Dialogue* 29 (1990).

Wesley, John. *Letters of John Wesley,* 8 vols., edited by John Telford. London: The Epworth Press, 1931.

———. *The Works of John Wesley,* 7 vols. Nashville: Abingdon, 1983.

Westphal, Merold. "Taking St. Paul Seriously: Sin as an Epistemological Category." In *Christian Philosophy,* edited by Thomas Flint. Notre Dame: University of Notre Dame Press, 1990.

Whichcote, Benjamin. *Moral and Religious Aphorisms . . . to which are added Eight Letters which passed between Dr. Whichcote . . . and Dr. Tuckney.* London, 1753.

Wiles, Maurice. *Archetypal Heresy: Arianism through the Centuries.* Oxford: Clarendon Press, 1996.

Wiley, Margaret L. *The Subtle Knot, Creative Scepticism in Seventeenth Century England.* London: George Allen & Unwin Ltd., 1952.

Wilken, Robert Louis. *The Spirit of Early Christian Thought: Seeking the Face of God.* New Haven: Yale University Press, 2003.

Williams, Rowan. *Arius: Heresy and Tradition.* London: Darton, Longman, and Todd, 1987.

Wilson, Matthew. *Charity Mistaken.* London, 1633.

———. *Mercy and Truth, or Charity Maintayned.* London, 1634.

Woodhead, Abraham. *Dr. Stillingfleet's Principles, Giving an Account of the Faith of Protestants by N. O.* Paris, 1671.

———. *The Guide in Controversies of Religion: Reflecting on the Later Writings of Protestants; Particularly Archbishop Laud and Dr. Stillingfleet on this Subject.* N.P., 1666.

Wormald, B. H. G. *Clarendon.* Cambridge: Cambridge University Press, 1951.

Worsley, Edward. *Protestancy without Principles or, Sectaries Unhappy Fall from Infallibility to Fancy.* Antwerp, 1668.

———. *Reason and Religion, or the Certain Rule of Faith, Where the Infallibility of the Roman Catholick Church is Asserted, against Atheists, Heathens, Jews, Turks, and all Sectaries.* Antwerp, 1672.

Young, Frances. "Augustine's Hermeneutics and Postmodern Criticism." *Interpretation* 58, no. 1 (2004).

———. *The Making of the Creeds.* Harrisburg: Trinity Press International, 1991.

Index

Abraham, William J., 90
absolution, 2, 32
Act of Uniformity, 63
Arians, 11, 25n.40, 77-79
Arius (4th c.), 25-26
Arminianism, 42-44, 46, 91
Arminius (Jacob Harmensen), 42
assent (assensus), xv, xviii, 1-2, 2n.2, 28-30, 44-48, 52, 55n.58, 57, 67, 84, 100, 104, 162, 165-66, 169-70, 191
assurance, 42; crisis of, 30, 32-34, 40-41, 91; of faith, 9; of salvation, 41-43, 45, 47-50, 54, 57, 70, 79, 93, 95, 175
Athanasius, 27, 94, 97
atheism, 64, 93, 95, 97
atonement, 63, 84
Augsburg Confession, 31, 52
Augustine, xi, 27, 106
authority, 40, 43, 81, 85, 130, 136, 161; of the Church, 78, 81; ecclesial, 34-35, 43; of Scripture, 58-60, 66, 77, 95, 178

Babcock, William, 26-27, 107-9, 144, 147, 156, 159
Bacon, Francis, 83
baptism, xviii, 3-4, 8, 10-14, 16, 19-23, 28-29, 33, 35, 37-38, 45, 55, 57, 111, 166, 170, 173, 189, 192, 194
baptismal formula, 13, 14, 23, 28
Barth, Karl, x, 170, 189
Basil of Caesarea, 170, 179-80, 193-94
Bishop, Mary, 172
Boethius: definition of "person," 107, 111, 118, 121-22, 126, 128, 133, 142
Boff, Leonardo, x
Book of Common Prayer, 38, 171
Boyle, Robert, 144
Brevis Disquisitio, 58-59
Burthogge, Richard, 116n.23, 120-21
Bury, Arthur, 122; The Naked Gospel, 122

Calvin, John, 31, 35, 40-41, 43, 51-52, 88-91, 93; Deus absconditus, 88, 93
Calvinism, 40n.22, 42, 49, 62-63, 93n.42
Cambridge Platonism, 64, 91-96, 100
canon, 30, 37; of doctrines, 169; of essential doctrine, 103, 191
Carroll, Robert Todd, 150
catechesis, xii, 2-3, 10-13, 16, 20, 22, 28-29, 104, 110, 192, 194-95
Catholic, 34-35, 39, 43, 50, 54, 57, 65; Counter-Reformation, 40, 66; propagandists, 47, 58, 66, 70, 81; theol-

ogy, 47, 53, 57, 60, 66; view of limits
of reason, 86
Chalcedonian, 107
Charles, brother of James II, 71
Charry, Ellen, x
Cheynell, Francis, 50n.49, 57
Chillingworth, William, 48-51, 53-54,
56, 58-60, 62, 64, 74-76, 91, 93, 97,
100, 161; *The Religion of the Protestants,* 49, 51, 74-76, 91, 93, 97, 100
Christ, Jesus: atoning sacrifice of, 32;
coming of, xiv, 4, 22, 186, 192;
divinity of, 123, 182, 183n.20; doctrine of, 52; Gospel of, 161; life,
death, resurrection, 5, 110; mind of,
175; nature of, 84, 107; oneness with
the Father, 74; person of, 26, 107;
real presence of, 32, 61, 87n.31;
saving activities of, xiv, 24, 186;
ubiquity of, 66
Christ Church, Oxford, 112
Chrysostom, John, 13, 19-20, 196
Church of England, 50n.48, 52, 63, 65,
70-71, 138, 153, 161n.41, 162-63
Coakley, Sarah, x
Council of, Constantinople (381), 25,
106; Nicea, 31
Cranmer, Thomas, 38
creed, 6, 11, 22, 37, 51, 56, 103; Apostles', 12, 36n.15, 38, 63; Athanasian,
37, 97, 132; function of, 10; Nicene,
6, 9, 12-13, 19, 28, 31, 38, 132, 162, 165;
Scotch, 84
creeds: baptism and, 9-11; Christian,
90; declaratory, 13, 17; early Christian, 7; interrogatory, 13, 17
criterion: epistemic, 30, 37, 39, 52, 165;
in epistemology, 26; of identity, 11,
20, 22, 178
Cudworth, Ralph, 93, 95, 97; *The True
Intellectual System of the Universe*
(1678), 93-94
Cyril of Jerusalem, 6

deism, 92, 140, 157, 159-60, 163
depravity, doctrine of total, 88-89; inherited, 63
Descartes, René, 112-13, 119, 145
divine economy, 104, 181, 183, 188
doxological activity (doxology), 28, 37,
45, 169, 173, 182, 186-87, 197

Edwards, John, 163-64
election, doctrine of, 41-42
epistemology, xii, 26, 30, 37, 45, 56, 69,
146-48, 165, 169, 173, 181, 183, 188-89,
192
essence, 31, 74, 108, 111-12, 115, 120, 124,
133, 148-49, 150-52
Eucharist, xiii, 2-4, 16, 23, 28, 32-33, 35,
38, 45, 57, 110, 166, 170, 195
Evagrius, xii-xiii, 1
evangelism, 2-3, 192, 194-95
exorcism, xii, 2, 4, 10, 12-13, 22, 28-29,
45, 55; free will, 42, 62

Furly, Benjamin, 121, 137

Gloria Patri, 173
God, being of, xi, 21, 27, 157, 166, 192;
doctrine of, 57; existence of, 64, 93-
97, 99; knowledge of, 40, 85, 88n.33,
90-92, 179, 184-85, 193-94, 196; nature of, 25, 86, 91, 147-48, 157, 167,
196; proper personal name for, xii-
xiii, 14, 16, 23, 25, 29, 157, 166, 169-71,
192-93, 195; transcendence of, 40-41,
185, 196; unity of, 106, 109, 132; vision of, 43, 51, 56, 159, 161, 171
Gray, Madelyn, 41
Great Schism, 34
Great Tew Circle, 49, 62-63
Gregory of Nazianzus, 27
Gregory of Nyssa, 23, 106, 109-10
Gunton, Colin, x

Hales, John, 62
Harrison, Peter, 45, 87n.31, 92

Hippolytus, *Apostolic Tradition,* 14, 19
Holy Spirit, 14, 20-24, 28-29, 43, 57, 89,
    170, 174, 177-80, 193-95; coming of,
    xiv, 4-5, 16, 170, 173, 192, 194; divin-
    ity of, 182; indwelling of, 173, 177-78,
    180, 184; illumination of, 88-89; in-
    ner witness of, 35, 43-45, 88-89; mid-
    wife of the, 195; presence of, xv, 21,
    24, 57, 173, 176, 180, 194-95; saving
    activities of, xix, 2, 19, 170-71, 175,
    188, 195; sending of, 24; work of, xv,
    5, 21, 57, 110, 173-76, 180-81, 194-95
homoiousios, 106
homoousios, 106
Hooker, Richard, 38, 48
Hume, David, 61n.71, 69
Hyde, Anne, 71
hypostases, 106
hypostasis, 106

Iconodules, 35
images, 30, 32-35, 110, 171
incarnation, 24, 29, 45, 61, 84-87, 90,
    100, 105, 110-12, 119, 121, 180, 193, 195
individuation *(principium individua-*
    tion), principle of, 101, 105, 107-10,
    114, 116-17, 119-20, 122, 126-27, 130,
    135-36
initiation, xii, 2-3, 17, 192, 194-95
invocation, 1-3, 15-16, 45, 55, 165, 169-
    70, 191-93
Irenaeus, 5, 11, 19, 21

James II, 71
Jenson, Robert, x
Jewell, William, 38
Johnson, Elizabeth, x
Judaism, 106
justification, 1, 34, 88-89, 162
Justin Martyr, 22

Kelly, J. N. D., 7-12
knowledge, divine, 89, 92, 179; of God,
    40-41, 85, 90-91, 179, 184-86, 194-96;

natural, 82-83, 91-92; of ourselves,
    112-18; saving, xv, 46, 51, 84, 87-88,
    90-91, 108

LaCugna, Catherine Mowry, x, xi, 20,
    24, 189, 192
Lash, Nicholas, xix
Latitudinarian, 80, 91-92, 97
Laud, Archbishop William, 43-47, 51,
    58-60, 64, 72, 75, 91, 93, 97, 100
law, natural, 92, 94
Leupp, Roderick, 192
Limborch, Philip van, "irenic trinitari-
    anism," 158, 164
liturgy, 10, 12-13, 22, 28, 104, 110, 170-71
Locke, John, xvii, 69, 118-19, 142-44,
    147-49, 153-55, 158-66
Luther, Martin, 33-35, 40-43, 51, 87-88

Marshall, Bruce, x
Marshall, John, 62, 94, 147-48, 158-59,
    164
means of grace, xv, 30, 37, 39, 165
Melanchthon, Philip, 52
metaphysics, 20, 24-25, 143, 189, 192
modalism, 25
Moltmann, Jürgen, x
Molyneux, William, 153
Monarchian debate, 25
More, Henry, 93
mystery, 26, 61, 78, 81, 83-84, 97, 184-
    87, 193

names: proper personal, xii, 2-3, 13-18,
    24-25, 192
nature, 148-51, 154, 156
Newbigin, Lesslie, 69
Newman, John Henry, 69
Newton, Isaac, 144
Nye, Stephen, 65, 130-32, 136, 138-40

ontology, xiv, 69, 165, 169, 173, 180-83,
    188, 192
ousia, 106

Pannenberg, Wolfhart, x
Pattison, Mark, xviii, 188
Pelagianism, 35, 41-42
Pelikan, Jaroslav, 11
penance, 32
Pentecost, 4-5, 29, 195
person, xii, xvi, 27, 99-101, 104, 107, 115, 121, 132-33, 143, 152, 155-56; conception of, 126; definition of, 152; English word, 126-27; idea of, 151-52; medieval notion of, 122
persona, 122, 126-30
personae, 106-7
personality, 139, 148, 152, 158
personhood, Cartesian concept of, xvii, 104
Pocock, J. G. A., 157, 163
prayer, xi-xii, xiii, xviii, 1, 4, 10, 28, 55, 104, 192, 194, 195
prayers, 165-66, 171, 182, 189; to the Virgin, 32
preaching, 2, 8-10, 12-13, 22, 28
predestination, doctrine of double, 41-42, 45, 93
principle of selective designation, 17, 19
Puritan Commonwealth, 64

Racovian Catechism, 58-59, 65, 108
Rahner, Karl, x, 189
reason, 44-49, 52, 57-61, 63-66, 69-71, 76-100, 108-9, 116-17, 119-20, 124, 127, 136-38, 140-43, 145-46, 148-51, 157, 176, 179, 181-82, 184, 188
Reedy, Gerard, 48, 159
Reformation, 31, 37, 108; Continental, xiv, 87; English, 37-38; iconoclasts, 35
revelation, 24, 57, 69, 82-86, 91, 96, 100, 108, 136, 161-62, 175-76, 180, 188
Revival, English, 167
Royal Society, 84,
rule of faith, xii, xiv-xvi, 2, 4-7, 9, 11-12, 21-22, 24, 26-30, 32, 36-40, 45, 51-56,

58-59, 62-64, 66, 70-75, 79, 100-101, 111, 123, 132, 138, 156-58, 162-65

Sabellianism, 108, 131-32, 139
Salvation, xiii-xiv, xvii, xviii, xix, 1-3, 19-24, 26-28, 30, 33-36, 41-43, 45, 47-51, 54-57, 63, 67, 70, 72, 74-75, 79, 81, 86, 88-91, 99-103, 111, 122, 126, 138, 152, 157-58, 161, 164, 166, 169, 175, 192
sanctification, 4, 194
Sandius, Christopher, *Bibliotecha Anti-Trinitariorum* (1684), 65
Sargeant, John, 40
Schleiermacher, Friedrich, x, xii, 165, 170-71, 191
Scripture, 6, 30, 34-37, 40, 44, 49-50, 55-56, 64, 73-76, 85, 94, 98, 101, 124, 156-66, 170, 175, 188; authority of, 59-60, 66, 77, 95; conception of, 165; function of, 30, 37, 52; interpretation of, 78, 97-98, 188
self-consciousness, 113-21
Sherlock, William, xvii, 73, 79, 81, 85-91, 96-104, 110, 113-18, 121, 126, 135, 153, 157, 164
sin, 23, 34, 63, 175-76, 180, 183, 185-86; epistemic consequences of, 44, 88, 90
skepticism, 118-19, 121, 146, 150, 153, 166
Socinian, 58-59, 61-63, 65-66, 70-81, 85-86, 100, 108, 111, 123-24, 126-28, 130-32, 147-48, 157, 159-60, 163
Socinianism, 58-66, 70-71, 73, 74-76, 131, 159, 160
sola Scriptura, xi, 34, 57, 77, 191; doctrine of, 88
South, Robert, xvii, 112, 115-18, 120-21, 164
St. John's College, Cambridge, 95
St. Mary's Church, Oxford, 122
Stewart, M. A., 143
Stillingfleet, Edward, xvii, 45, 54, 57, 61-63, 72-73, 79-91, 95-105, 126, 133-57, 161, 164

subordinationism, 25
subsistence, 138, 148, 152, 154, 156
substance, xvii, 133, 138-39, 141, 145, 148, 150, 152-53, 158; idea of, 142, 144-46, 150, 153, 159; scholastic notion of, 144
Swinburne, Richard, 69

Tennant, F. R., 69
Tertullian, 5, 19, 106
Test Act of 1673, 63
Theil, Udo, 111, 119
Thirty-Nine Articles of Religion, 38, 63-65, 84, 162
Tillotson, John, xvii, 48, 51-52, 57, 60, 62-63, 144
Toland, John, *Christianity Not Mysterious* (1696), 140-41
Toleration Act, 65
Torrance, Thomas F., x
transubstantiation, 60-61, 63, 66, 77-79, 81-82, 84, 86, 98
Trelawny, Bishop of Exeter, 122
Trinity, xix, 38, 55, 61, 66-67, 74, 81-85, 90, 92, 95, 99-103, 114, 120-28, 133, 141-42, 148, 152, 158, 164-69; doctrine of, xv, 31, 56-57, 69-74, 81, 84, 91, 97, 100-101, 110, 123, 136-39, 148, 153, 157, 166, 172, 181, 188; economic (ad extra), xi-xii, xvii, 19, 24, 28, 56-57, 101, 104, 126, 132, 166, 169, 170, 173-78, 180-81, 196-97; immanent (ad intra), xi, xv, xvii, 19, 24, 27, 101, 104, 126, 166, 170-71, 179, 181-82, 188, 191, 193, 196-97
tritheism, 120, 131, 139, 158

Unitarianism, xvi-xvii, 65-66, 70, 72-73, 76, 79, 81, 86, 95, 97, 99-105, 122, 128, 131, 135-40, 148, 157
University College, Oxford, 71
University of Oxford, 177
Urs von Balthasar, Hans, x

Volf, Miroslav, x

Wallis, John, xvii, 101, 103-4, 122-33, 135, 139, 157, 164
Wesley, Charles, xix, 167, 171-89
Wesley, John, 169, 172
Westminster Confession, 85
Whichote, Benjamin, 93, 97
Wittgenstein, Ludwig, 15
Woodhead, Abraham, 71
Word of God, 45, 74, 89-90
worship, xii-xiii, xviii, 2, 23, 28, 37, 45, 55, 57, 104, 157, 165-67, 170, 189, 192-95

Young, Frances, 7, 11

Zizioulas, John, x